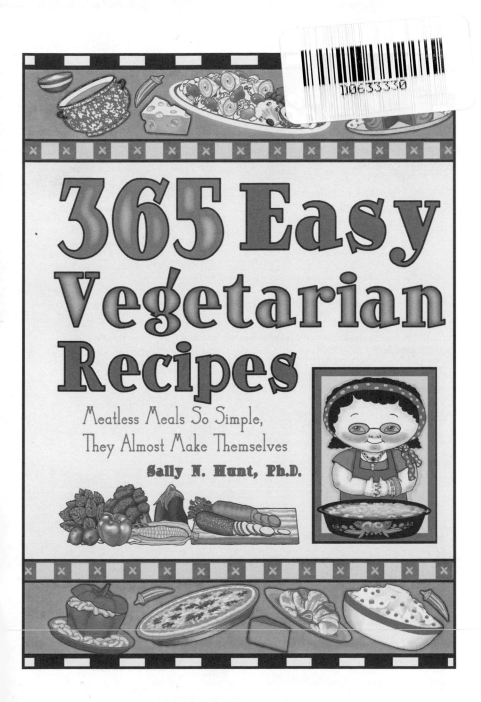

365 Easy

Vegetarian Recipes

Meatless Meals So Simple,
They Almost Make Themselves

Sally N. Hunt, Ph.D.

Cookbook Resources LLC
Highland Village, Texas

365 Easy Vegetarian Recipes
Meatless Meals So Simple, They Almost Make Themselves

1st Printing - November 2007
2nd Printing - September 2008

International Standard Book No. 978-1-931294-74-4

Library of Congress No. 2007935955

Library of Congress Cataloging-in-Publication Data

  Hunt, Sally N.

   365 easy vegetarian recipes : meatless meals so simple, they almost make themselves / Sally N. Hunt.

    p. cm.

   Includes index.

   ISBN 978-1-931294-74-4

   1. Vegetarian cookery. 2. Quick and easy cookery. I. Title. II. Title: Three hundred sixty-five easy vegetarian recipes. III. Title: Three hundred and sixty-five easy vegetarian recipes.

   TX837.H8585 2007

   641.5'636--dc22

                                        2007044601

Cover by Nancy Bohanan
Illustrations by Nancy Murphy Griffith

Edited, Designed and Published in the United States of America
and Manufactured in China by
Cookbook Resources, LLC
541 Doubletree Drive
Highland Village, Texas 75077
Toll free 866-229-2665

www.cookbookresources.com

cookbook
resources LLC
The Ultimate Source for Easy Cookbooks

Introduction

These vegetarian recipes are a great way to enjoy cooking healthy, nutritious meals for your family and friends – while giving them all the flavors they like!

Nutrition facts for each recipe helps you balance your menus while avoiding lots of fat and cholesterol; you'll always know what you're eating. Created by Sally N. Hunt, Ph.D., the recipes include a terrific variety of foods for every meal in the day. (For more about Dr. Hunt, see page 6.)

This book is dedicated to all cooks who love to bring family and friends together around the table – with good food that's good for them!

Contents

Contents

About the Author

Developing *365 Easy Vegetarian Recipes* was an exciting venture for Dr. Hunt. One of her goals is to help readers improve their health through new ways of preparing food. Her varied culinary and educational experiences provided a strong background for exploring the world of vegetarian cooking.

Sally N. Hunt, Ph.D.

Dr. Hunt's early life was spent in West Texas and New Mexico, where the cultures, cuisine and traditions of the Southwest influenced her tastes and interests. Her enthusiasm for cooking and enjoyment of good food comes naturally from a family tradition of "good cooks". Having lived in Louisiana for nearly 30 years, she is also influenced by the flavorful and delicious Cajun and Creole cookery. She now resides in Texas and continues to expand her experiences and her knowledge of the exciting cultures and cuisines of the Southwest.

Breakfast
&
Brunch

Contents

Cantaloupe and Frosted Grapes

Here's a refreshing fruit dessert for those hot summer days.

1 egg white, slightly beaten	
1 pound seedless green or red grapes	455 g
½ cup sugar	100 g
1 medium cantaloupe, cold	

Combine egg white and 2 teaspoons (10 ml) water in small bowl. Break grapes into small clusters and brush egg white over clusters. Sprinkle clusters with sugar and dry on wire rack.

Cut cantaloupe in half and carefully scoop out seeds. Cut each half into 4 wedges and trim off rind. Arrange 1 cantaloupe wedge with grape cluster on dessert plates for each serving.

Serves 8.
Serving size: 1 wedge with grape cluster

TIP: To determine if cantaloupe is ripe, smell the stem end for flavorful aroma. Cantaloupe should be pale yellow with few blemishes and feel heavy for its size.

One Serving

Calories: 116	Sodium: 19 mg
Calories from Fat: 3	Total Carbohydrates: 29 g
Total Fat: 0 g	Dietary Fiber: 1 g
Saturated Fat: 0 g	Sugars: 28 g
Cholesterol: 0 mg	Protein: 1 g

Banana-Berry-Orange Delight

3 firm ripe bananas, peeled, sliced	
Juice of 1 lemon	
1½ cups fresh blackberries or frozen unsweetened blueberries, thawed slightly	220 g
1 cup reduced-fat sour cream	240 g
¼ cup orange juice	60 ml
½ teaspoon grated orange peel	2 ml
2 tablespoons sugar or sugar substitute	25 g

Combine banana slices and lemon juice in bowl. Distribute banana slices and berries evenly into 6 dessert dishes.

Stir sour cream, orange juice, orange peel and sugar in medium bowl. Spoon 2 tablespoons (30 ml) of mixture on top of each serving of fruit.

Serves 6.
Serving size: 1 cup (250 ml)

One Serving
Nutrition facts are based on sugar substitute.

Calories: 148	Sodium: 29 mg
Calories from Fat: 54	Total Carbohydrates: 22 g
Total Fat: 6 g	Dietary Fiber: 3 g
Saturated Fat: 4 g	Sugars: 10 g
Cholesterol: 14 mg	Protein: 4 g

Honey-Citrus-Melon Balls

Have fun serving this in large wine glasses.

¼ cup honey	85 g
1 teaspoon finely grated orange peel	5 ml
1 teaspoon finely grated lime peel	5 ml
½ cup orange juice	125 ml
2 tablespoons lime juice	30 ml
4 cups melon balls (cantaloupe, honeydew)	710 g
Fresh mint sprigs	

Combine honey, orange and lime peels and juices in small bowl. Drizzle honey mixture over melon balls in large bowl. Spoon into wine glasses or dessert dishes.

Cover and refrigerate at least 2 hours. Garnish each serving with mint sprigs.

Serves 4 to 6.
Serving size: ¾ cup (175 ml)

TIP: Use a Microplane® grater available in specialty and department stores for preparing finely grated peels in a jiffy.

One Serving

Calories: 93	Sodium: 37 mg
Calories from Fat: 3	Total Carbohydrates: 24 g
Total Fat: 0 g	Dietary Fiber: 1 g
Saturated Fat: 0 g	Sugars: 12 g
Cholesterol: 0 mg	Protein: 1 g

Peach-Blueberry Bowl

This is a delicious summertime treat.

2 cups peeled, sliced peaches	310 g
½ - 1 cup fresh blueberries	75 - 150 g
¼ cup lemon juice	60 ml
½ cup sugar or sugar substitute	100 g

Combine peaches and blueberries in medium bowl. In separate bowl, stir lemon juice and sugar until sugar dissolves. Pour lemon juice mixture over fruits. Toss gently, cover and refrigerate at least 1 hour. To serve, spoon into 4 dessert dishes.

Serves 4.
Serving size: ¾ cup (175 ml)

TIP: Add other fruits such as pears, apples or bananas.

One Serving
Nutrition facts are based on sugar substitute.

Calories: 138	Sodium: 0 mg
Calories from Fat: 2	Total Carbohydrates: 35 g
Total Fat: 0 g	Dietary Fiber: 2 g
Saturated Fat: 0 g	Sugars: 33 g
Cholesterol: 0 mg	Protein: 1 g

Golden Curried Fruit

This delicious golden fruit dessert brightens any meal.

¼ cup butter	55 g
½ cup packed brown sugar	110 g
2 teaspoons curry powder	10 ml
1 (15 ounce) can sliced peaches in light syrup, drained	425 g
1 (15 ounce) can pineapple chunks in juice, drained	425 g
1 (15 ounce) can apricot halves in extra-light syrup, drained	425 g

Preheat oven to 325° (160° C).

Melt butter in small saucepan over medium heat. Stir in brown sugar and curry powder and heat until sugar dissolves.

Arrange fruit in sprayed 9 x 13-inch (23 x 33 cm) baking dish. Drizzle brown sugar mixture over fruit. Bake uncovered for 50 to 60 minutes.

Serve hot or at room temperature.

Serves 8.
Serving size: ½ cup (125 ml)

TIP: Be sure to check the labels of canned fruits to avoid heavy sweet syrups.

One Serving

Calories: 164	Cholesterol: 8 mg	Dietary Fiber: 2 g
Calories from Fat: 27	Sodium: 10 mg	Sugars: 28 g
Total Fat: 3 g	Total Carbohydrates: 36 g	Protein: 1 g
Saturated Fat: 2 g		

Melon Medley

1 cup small pieces or balls cantaloupe	180 g
1 cup small pieces or balls honeydew melon	180 g
1 cup small pieces or balls watermelon, seeded, drained	155 g
½ cup Citrus Honey Dressing (page 103)	125 ml
Toasted shredded coconut	

Combine melons in bowl. Spoon Citrus Honey Dressing over melons and mix gently.

Refrigerate at least 2 hours before serving. To serve, spoon into 4 dessert dishes and garnish with coconut.

Serves 4.
Serving size: ¾ cup (175 ml)

One Serving

Calories: 81	Sodium: 16 mg
Calories from Fat: 0	Total Carbohydrates: 19 g
Total Fat: 0 g	Dietary Fiber: 3 g
Saturated Fat: 0g	Sugars: 13 g
Cholesterol: 0 mg	Protein: 3 g

Hotsy Totsy Pink Grapefruit

This is great as a warm breakfast fruit for wintry mornings or a satisfying dessert anytime.

2 medium pink grapefruit, halved	
¼ cup butter, melted	60 g
4 teaspoons brown sugar	20 ml
¼ teaspoon ground cinnamon	1 ml

With grapefruit knife or serrated knife, cut around every grapefruit section close to membrane. (Sections should be completely loose from rind.) Place grapefruit halves in shallow baking pan.

Combine butter, brown sugar and cinnamon in small bowl. Drizzle mixture over cut grapefruit halves and let stand at room temperature about 1 hour to marinate fruit.

Broil grapefruit in baking pan 4 inches (10 cm) from broiler until tops brown and juice is bubbling hot.

Serves 4.
Serving size: ½ grapefruit

TIP: For dessert, add ¼ cup (60 ml) orange liqueur to butter mixture.

One Serving

Calories: 171	Sodium: 3 mg
Calories from Fat: 2	Total Carbohydrates: 18 g
Total Fat: 12 g	Dietary Fiber: 2 g
Saturated Fat: 7 g	Sugars: 13 g
Cholesterol: 31 mg	Protein: 1 g

Apple-Orange Yogurt

There are now some 2,500 varieties of apples grown in the United States.

1 large red or golden delicious
    apple with peel
1 large Granny Smith apple
    with peel
1 large navel orange
½ cup dark or golden raisins   80 g
1 (8 ounce) carton reduced-fat
    vanilla yogurt   230 g

Core and chop apples. Peel orange and cut slices into ½-inch (1.2 cm) pieces. Combine apples, orange and raisins in large bowl and stir. Divide into 4 individual servings and spoon one-fourth yogurt on each.

Serves 4.
Serving size: 1 cup (250 ml)

TIP: Mix cut apples with apple juice or citrus juices to prevent discoloration.

One Serving

Calories: 219	Sodium: 41 mg
Calories from Fat: 7	Total Carbohydrates: 38 g
Total Fat: 1 g	Dietary Fiber: 3 g
Saturated Fat: 1 g	Sugars: 30 g
Cholesterol: 3 mg	Protein: 4 g

Breakfast Berry Parfaits

Make breakfast something special with these parfaits.

2 cups sliced strawberries (or
    blueberries, raspberries
    or blackberries)   300 g
2 cups reduced-fat vanilla
    yogurt   455 g
¼ cup toasted nuts (almonds,
    walnuts or pecans)
    or granola   30 g

Layer ¼ cup (40 g) fruit, ¼ cup (60 g) yogurt, ¼ cup (40 g) fruit, ¼ cup (60 g) yogurt and 1 tablespoon (15 ml) nuts in stemmed or parfait glasses.

Serves 4.
Serving size: 1 parfait

TIP: Purchase the berries at peak of season when plentiful and at lowest prices or use frozen berries year-round.

One Serving

Calories: 297	Sodium: 163 mg
Calories from Fat: 160	Total Carbohydrates: 28 g
Total Fat: 18g	Dietary Fiber: 3 g
Saturated Fat: 4g	Sugars: 21 g
Cholesterol: 6 mg	Protein: 11 g

Toasted Muesli

*Muesli is a fun mixture of lots of tasty ingredients
and is usually eaten with milk, yogurt or fruit juice.*

6 cups old-fashioned oats	480 g
2 cups wheat germ	230 g
1 cup packed brown sugar	220 g
6 tablespoons almonds, walnuts or pecans	50 g
3 tablespoons sesame, pumpkin or sunflower seeds	25 g
¼ cup unsweetened frozen coconut, thawed	60 ml
¾ cup dark or light raisins	120 g

Preheat oven to 350° (175° C).

Combine oats, wheat germ and brown sugar in large bowl. Add nuts, seeds and coconut. Spread oat mixture on cookie sheets and bake 20 to 30 minutes.

Stir every 5 minutes to keep muesli from sticking or burning. Cool and add raisins. Store in tightly covered container.

Serves 42.
Serving size: ¼ cup (60 ml)
Makes 10½ cups (2.5 L).

TIP: This recipe will stay fresh for a couple of weeks. If you don't think you can eat it all, just cut the recipe in half.

One Serving

Calories: 110	Cholesterol: 0 mg	Dietary Fiber: 2 g
Calories from Fat: 28	Sodium: 4 mg	Sugars: 7 g
Total Fat: 3 g	Total Carbohydrates: 18 g	Protein: 4 g
Saturated Fat: 1 g		

Mixed Fruit-Nut Granola

*This is a basic granola recipe in which you choose
the fruit and nuts to make your own special snack.*

1½ cups oats	120 g
½ cup coarsely chopped nuts	65 g
¼ cup chopped dried fruit	40 g
2 tablespoons butter	30 g
2 tablespoons light brown sugar	25 g
1 tablespoon honey	15 ml
½ teaspoon ground cinnamon	2 ml

Preheat oven to 350° (175° C).

Spread oats and nuts on baking sheet. Bake for 10 to 15 minutes and shake every 3 or 4 minutes. Cool. Combine dried fruit with oat mixture in large bowl.

Combine butter, brown sugar, honey and cinnamon in 1-quart (1 L) saucepan over medium heat. Cook and stir until butter melts. Drizzle evenly over oat mixture. Cool and store in tightly covered container.

Serves 10.
Serving size: ¼ cup (60 ml)

TIP: Nuts such as walnuts, pecans, cashews or macadamia nuts work well. The same is true for cherries, raisins, cranberries and apricots. You choose your favorites.

One Serving

Calories 169	Cholesterol: 12 mg	Dietary Fiber: 2 g
Calories from Fat: 85	Sodium: 5 mg	Sugars: 7 g
Total Fat: 9 g	Total Carbohydrates: 20 g	Protein: 3 g.
Saturated Fat: 4 g		

Almond-Coconut-Fruit Granola

Great topper for frozen yogurt or ice cream

½ cup packed dark or light brown sugar	110 g
4 cups old-fashioned oats	320 g
½ cup sliced or slivered almonds	90 g
¾ cup flaked coconut	60 g
⅓ cup honey	115 g
¼ cup canola oil	60 ml
1 cup mixed dried fruit	160 g

Preheat oven to 300° (150° C).

Place brown sugar in large bowl, break up any lumps and mix in oats, almonds and coconut.

In separate bowl, combine honey, oil and ¾ teaspoon (4 ml) salt.

Combine oat mixture and honey mixture and pour half into 2 baking pans. Bake for 1 hour 15 minutes and stir every 15 minutes for even browning.

Remove from oven, transfer to large bowl and cool. Stir in fruit and mix well. Store in airtight container.

Serves 10 to 12.
Serving size: ¼ cup (60 ml)

TIP: There are lots of good dried fruits such as raisins, cranberries, mangoes, apricots and cherries, but watch servings and serving sizes.

One Serving

Calories: 305	Cholesterol: 0mg	Dietary Fiber: 3 g
Calories from Fat: 103	Sodium: 78 mg	Sugars: 20 g
Total Fat: 11 g	Total Carbohydrates: 30 g	Protein: 4 g
Saturated Fat: 3 g		

Overnight Irish Oatmeal

In Ireland, oatmeal is served with lots of fresh cream and butter. It's really delicious!

1 cup Irish oatmeal   160 g

Bring 4 cups (1 L) water in 2-quart (2 L) saucepan to a brisk boil. Turn off heat and add oatmeal. Cover saucepan and leave overnight.

The next day, cook oatmeal on low for 9 to 12 minutes and stir occasionally.

Serves 4.
Serving Size: 1 cup (250 ml)

One Serving

Calories: 150	Sodium: 0 mg
Calories from Fat: 20	Total Carbohydrates: 26 g
Total Fat: 2 g	Dietary Fiber: 4 g
Saturated Fat: 0 g	Sugars: 0 g
Cholesterol: 0 mg	Protein: 4 g

Simple Breakfast Grits

This is a great breakfast treat served with sunny-side-up eggs.

1⅓ cups quick grits, white or yellow	**200 g**
1 tablespoon butter	**15 ml**
½ cup shredded sharp cheddar cheese	**60 g**

Bring 5⅓ cups (1.3 L) water in 2-quart (2 L) saucepan to a boil and add ½ teaspoon (2 ml) salt. Use whisk to stir in grits. Return to boiling, reduce heat and cover. Simmer for 5 to 7 minutes and stir occasionally or until thick.

Stir in butter and cheese. Serve hot.

Serves 5 to 6.
Serving size: ¾ cup (175 ml)

TIP: Grits are always on restaurant breakfast menus in the South and served daily in many homes.

One Serving

Calories: 186	Sodium: 59 mg
Calories from Fat: 67	Total Carbohydrates: 26 g
Total Fat: 7 g	Dietary Fiber: 2 g
Saturated Fat: 4 g	Sugars: 0 g
Cholesterol: 20 mg	Protein: 5 g

Creamy Scrambled Eggs

1 cup egg substitute	245 g
2 teaspoons finely chopped green onion	10 ml
1 teaspoon butter	5 ml
2 tablespoons reduced-fat cream cheese	30 g

Combine egg substitute, onion and 2 tablespoons (30 ml) water in bowl. Add ½ teaspoon (2 ml) salt and ⅛ teaspoon (.5 ml) pepper.

Melt butter in non-stick 10-inch (25 cm) skillet over medium-high heat. Pour in egg mixture. With heat-safe spatula, gently stir and turn egg mixture until partially cooked. Add cream cheese and continue to stir and turn until mixture is set but still shiny and moist.

Serves 4.
Serving size: ½ cup (125 ml)

One Serving

Calories: 96	Cholesterol: 11 mg	Dietary Fiber: 0 g
Calories from Fat: 52	Sodium: 156 mg	Sugars: 0 g
Total Fat: 6 g	Total Carbohydrates: 1 g	Protein: 9 g
Saturated Fat: 2 g		

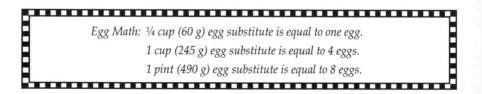

Egg Math: ¼ cup (60 g) egg substitute is equal to one egg.

1 cup (245 g) egg substitute is equal to 4 eggs.

1 pint (490 g) egg substitute is equal to 8 eggs.

Egg Scramble

2 teaspoons olive oil	10 ml
¼ cup finely diced onion	40 g
¼ cup finely diced green or red bell pepper	40 g
3 beaten eggs or ¾ cup egg substitute	185 g
¼ cup chopped fresh tomato, drained	45 g

Heat oil in non-stick 10-inch (25 cm) skillet over medium heat. Add onion and bell pepper; cook and stir until tender, about 4 to 5 minutes.

Lower heat, add eggs, 1 teaspoon (5 ml) salt and ¼ teaspoon (1 ml) pepper. Cook and stir gently until eggs set but are still moist. Stir in tomato.

Serves 2 to 3.
Serving size: 1 cup (250 ml)

One Serving
Nutrition facts are based on egg substitute.

Calories: 82	Sodium: 84 mg
Calories from Fat: 54	Total Carbohydrates: 1 g
Total Fat: 6 g	Dietary Fiber: 0 g
Saturated Fat: 1 g	Sugars: 1 g
Cholesterol: 0 mg	Protein: 6 g

Skillet Eggs and Garden Vegetables

2 tablespoons butter	30 g
1 cup grated zucchini	125 g
½ cup grated carrots	55 g
¼ cup finely chopped onion	40 g
8 beaten eggs or 2 cups egg substitute	490 g
½ cup reduced-fat small curd cottage cheese, well drained	115 g

Melt butter in non-stick 12-inch (32 cm) skillet over medium heat. Add zucchini, carrots and onion. Cook and stir until vegetables are tender, about 4 to 5 minutes.

Reduce heat to medium-low and add eggs. Cook and stir until eggs set but are still moist. Gently stir in cottage cheese, 1 teaspoon (5 ml) salt and ¼ teaspoon (1 ml) pepper. Cook about 2 to 3 minutes.

Serves 6 to 8.
Serving size: 1 cup (250 ml)

One Serving
Nutrition facts are based on egg substitute.

Calories: 94	Sodium: 175 mg
Calories from Fat: 46	Total Carbohydrates: 2 g
Total Fat: 5 g	Dietary Fiber: 0 g
Saturated Fat: 2 g	Sugars: 1 g
Cholesterol: 9 mg	Protein: 10 g

Scrambled Eggs with Tomatoes

Some people like ketchup on eggs. Others prefer the flavor of fresh tomatoes just like this recipe.

1 tablespoon butter	15 ml
1 cup finely chopped onion	160 g
1 garlic clove, minced	
3 roma or pear tomatoes, seeded, diced	
6 beaten eggs or 1½ cups egg substitute	365 g

Melt butter in non-stick 10-inch (25 cm) skillet over medium heat. Add onion and garlic; cook and stir until onion is tender. Add tomatoes and 1 teaspoon (5 ml) salt. Cover and simmer about 10 minutes. Add eggs to skillet and cook and stir until eggs set but are still shiny and moist.

Serves 4.
Serving size: 1 cup (250 ml)

TIP: Roma tomatoes, also called Italian or plum tomatoes, are flavorful, egg-shaped and generally have a firmer flesh than the larger round beefsteak tomatoes.

One Serving
Nutrition facts are based on egg substitute.

Calories: 125	Sodium: 169 mg
Calories from Fat: 54	Total Carbohydrates: 6 g
Total Fat: 6 g	Dietary Fiber: 1 g
Saturated Fat: 3 g	Sugars: 3 g
Cholesterol: 9 mg	Protein: 12 g

Tortilla-Bell Pepper Scramble

Combine crispy tortilla strips, bell pepper and parsley with soft-set eggs for a great entree anytime.

3 beaten eggs or ¾ cup egg substitute	185 g
¼ cup finely diced red bell pepper	40 g
2 tablespoons finely chopped parsley	10 g
2 teaspoons canola oil	10 ml
3 corn tortillas, halved, cut in ½-inch strips	1.2 cm

Combine eggs, bell pepper, parsley, ½ teaspoon (2 ml) salt and ⅛ teaspoon (.5 ml) pepper in medium bowl.

Heat oil in non-stick 10-inch (25 cm) skillet over medium heat. Add tortillas and cook until crispy. Remove from skillet, drain and set aside.

Add egg mixture to skillet; cook and stir until eggs set but are still moist. Garnish eggs with crispy tortilla strips.

Serves 3.
Serving size: 1 cup (250 ml)

One Serving
Nutrition facts are based on egg substitute.

Calories: 148	Sodium: 120 mg
Calories from Fat: 78	Total Carbohydrates: 9 g
Total Fat: 9 g	Dietary Fiber: 1 g
Saturated Fat: 1 g	Sugars: 1 g
Cholesterol: 1 mg	Protein: 8 g

Omelet for One

*A simple satisfying meal
for one hungry person.*

2 eggs or ½ cup egg substitute 125 g
2 teaspoons butter 10 ml

Combine eggs, 2 tablespoons (15 ml) water, ½ teaspoon (2 ml) salt and ⅛ teaspoon (.5 ml) pepper in small bowl. Beat with fork until it blends but is not frothy.

Melt butter in non-stick 8-inch (20 cm) skillet with flared sides over medium-high heat. Add egg mixture and lower heat to medium.

Stir gently until mixture has small pieces of cooked egg in liquid. Stop stirring and cook 1 to 3 minutes longer or until egg mixture sets but is still shiny. Lift and fold omelet with spatula and transfer to warmed plate.

Serves 1.
Serving size: 2 eggs

TIP: Uncooked egg in omelet will continue to cook after you remove it form the skillet, but will stay soft and creamy instead of hard-cooked. Overcooking can toughen the protein in eggs.

One Serving
Nutrition facts are based on egg substitute.

Calories: 172	Sodium: 223 mg
Calories from Fat: 103	Total Carbohydrates: 1 g
Total Fat: 11 g	Dietary Fiber: 0 g
Saturated Fat: 6 g	Sugars: 1 g
Cholesterol: 21 mg	Protein: 15g.

Pizza Omelet

Eggs and mozzarella cheese with the zesty flavor of pizza sauce adds a little surprise in the morning.

2 beaten eggs or ½ cup egg substitute 125 g
2 teaspoons butter 30 g
2 tablespoons tomato-pizza sauce 30 ml
3 tablespoons reduced-fat finely shredded mozzarella cheese 25 g

Combine eggs, 2 tablespoons (30 ml) water, ½ teaspoon (2 ml) salt and ⅛ teaspoon (.5 ml) pepper in small bowl. Beat with fork to combine but do not let mixture become frothy.

Melt butter in non-stick 8-inch (20 cm) skillet with flared sides over medium-high heat. Add egg mixture and lower heat to medium.

Stir gently until mixture has small pieces of cooked egg in liquid. Stop stirring and cook 1 to 3 minutes or until egg mixture sets but is still shiny.

Lift and fold omelet with wide spatula and transfer to warmed plate. Spoon pizza sauce over omelet and sprinkle with cheese.

Serves 2.
Serving size: about ¾ cup (175 ml)

One Serving
Nutrition facts are based on egg substitute.

Calories: 171	Sodium: 242 mg
Calories from Fat: 116	Total Carbohydrates: 1 g
Total Fat: 13 g	Dietary Fiber: 0 g
Saturated Fat: 7 g	Sugars: 0 g
Cholesterol: 33 mg	Protein: 13 g

Onion-Mushroom Omelet

A quick and satisfying brunch or supper dish.

8 beaten eggs or 2 cups egg substitute	490 g
½ cup light plain soymilk	125 ml
2 tablespoons butter	30 g
½ cup chopped fresh mushrooms	40 g
2 sliced green onions	

Stir eggs, soymilk, 1 teaspoon (5 ml) salt and ¼ teaspoon (1 ml) pepper in medium bowl.

Melt butter in non-stick 10-inch (25 cm) skillet with flared sides over medium-high heat. Add mushrooms and onion; cook and stir about 4 to 5 minutes or until mushrooms are tender. Remove and set aside.

Reduce heat to medium and pour in egg mixture. When eggs begin to set, lift edges with spatula to allow uncooked eggs to flow underneath. Continue cooking until eggs set but are still moist.

Spread mushrooms and onions on one side of omelet. Carefully fold omelet in half with wide spatula and slide onto warmed serving dish.

Serves about 6.
Serving size: ¾ cup (175 ml)

TIP: *An omelet pan or a flared-edge skillet makes it easier to fold and remove the cooked omelet.*

One Serving
Nutrition facts are based on egg substitute.

Calories: 115	Cholesterol: 11 mg	Dietary Fiber: 0 g
Calories from Fat: 64	Sodium: 160 mg	Sugars: 1 g
Total Fat: 7 g	Total Carbohydrates: 2 g	Protein: 11 g
Saturated Fat: 3 g		

Red Potato and Chive Omelet

This is a hearty fresh-flavored omelet for two.

2 eggs or ½ cup egg substitute	125 g
2 teaspoons butter	10 ml
¼ cup diced cooked new (red) potatoes with peels	40 g
2 teaspoons fresh minced chives or 1 tablespoon finely chopped green onion tops	10 ml/15 ml

Combine eggs, 1 tablespoon (15 ml) water, ¼ teaspoon (1 ml) salt and ⅛ teaspoon (.5 ml) pepper in small bowl. Beat with fork to combine but do not let mixture become frothy.

Melt butter in non-stick 8-inch (20 cm) skillet with flared sides over medium-high heat. Add potatoes and chives and stir until hot. Reduce heat to medium and add egg mixture.

Cook and stir until egg combines with potatoes and chives. Stop stirring and cook 1 to 3 minutes longer or until egg mixture sets but is still shiny.

Lift and fold omelet with wide spatula and transfer to warmed plate. Egg mixture will continue to cook but will still be soft and creamy.

Serves 2.
Serving size: ¾ cup (175 ml)

One Serving
Nutrition facts are based on egg substitute.

Calories: 101	Cholesterol: 11 mg	Dietary Fiber: 1 g
Calories from Fat: 54	Sodium: 112 mg	Sugars: 0 g
Total Fat: 6 g	Total Carbohydrates: 4 g	Protein: 8 g
Saturated Fat: 3 g		

Cream Cheese-Cinnamon Strata

8 slices cinnamon-raisin bread	
5 ounces reduced-fat cream cheese, cubed, softened	**145 g**
2 teaspoons ground cinnamon	**10 ml**
2 cups egg substitute or 8 eggs	**490 g**
4 cups 2% reduced-fat milk	**1 L**
¼ cup honey or sugar	**85 g/50 g**

Cut bread slices diagonally into 4 triangles. Arrange half bread triangles in sprayed 9 x 13-inch (23 x 33 cm) baking dish.

Beat cream cheese and cinnamon. Spread evenly on bread triangles. Top with remaining bread triangles.

Whisk egg substitute or eggs, milk, honey or sugar and cream cheese mixture in large bowl. Pour over bread. Seal tightly with foil and refrigerate at least 2 hours. Bake within 24 hours.

When ready to bake, preheat oven to 325° (160° C). Bake covered for 30 minutes. Remove foil and bake additional 40 minutes or until knife inserted in center comes out clean. Let stand 10 minutes.

Serves 6.
Serving size: 3-inch (8 cm) square

TIP: *Easy to make and eat, strata dishes are somewhere between baked custards and French toast.*

One Serving
Nutrition facts are based on egg substitute.

Calories: 308	Cholesterol: 21 mg	Dietary Fiber: 2 g
Calories from Fat: 86	Sodium: 387 mg	Sugars: 19 g
Total Fat: 10 g	Total Carbohydrates: 36 g	Protein: 19 g
Saturated Fat: 4 g		

Basic Cheese Strata

A strata is a versatile, layered bread and custard dish that can be savory or sweet.

8 slices firm bread, white or whole wheat	
2½ cups reduced-fat shredded sharp cheddar cheese, divided	285 g
2 cups egg substitute	490 g
4 cups light plain soymilk or fat-free skim milk	1 L
1 teaspoon ground mustard	5 ml
¼ teaspoon ground red pepper	1 ml

Cut bread slices diagonally into 4 triangles. Place half bread triangles in 9 x 13-inch (23 x 33 cm) baking dish. Sprinkle with 2 cups (225 g) cheese and top with remaining bread triangles.

Whisk egg substitute, soymilk, mustard, red pepper, 1 teaspoon (5 ml) salt and ¼ teaspoon (1 ml) pepper in large bowl. Pour over bread. Seal tightly with foil and refrigerate at least 2 hours. Cook within 24 hours.

Preheat oven to 325° (160° C). Bake covered for 30 minutes. Remove foil and bake 40 minutes or until knife inserted in center comes out clean. Top with remaining cheese and bake 5 minutes or until cheese melts. Let stand 10 minutes.

Serves 6.
Serving size: 3-inch (8 cm) square

One Serving

Calories: 325	Cholesterol: 11 mg	Dietary Fiber: 3 g
Calories from Fat: 86	Sodium: 699 mg	Sugars: 4 g
Total Fat: 10 g	Total Carbohydrates: 25 g	Protein: 32 g
Saturated Fat: 3 g		

Artichoke Frittata

In Castroville, California, the artichoke capital of the United States,
Marilyn Monroe was named the first Artichoke Queen in 1948.

1 (14 ounce) can artichoke hearts in water	400 g
1 tablespoon butter	15 ml
1 small onion, halved, sliced	
1 garlic clove, minced	
1 cup egg substitute	245 g
1 cup liquid egg whites	225 g
⅓ cup reduced-fat shredded Swiss cheese	35 g

Drain artichoke hearts and cut into bite-size pieces. Melt butter in ovenproof 10-inch (25 cm) skillet over medium heat. Add artichoke hearts, onion and garlic. Cook and stir until tender.

Combine egg substitute, egg whites, ½ teaspoon (2 ml) salt and ¼ teaspoon (1 ml) pepper in small bowl. Spread artichoke mixture in single layer in skillet and pour in egg mixture. Stir until mixture has small pieces of cooked egg in liquid. Turn heat to low, cover and cook 7 to 10 minutes without stirring.

Top with Swiss cheese and broil 4 inches (10 cm) from broiler 2 to 3 minutes or until eggs set. Cut into wedges to serve.

Serves 4.
Serving size: About 1 cup (250 ml)

One Serving

Calories: 179	Cholesterol: 11 mg	Dietary Fiber: 5 g
Calories from Fat: 50	Sodium: 542 mg	Sugars: 3 g
Total Fat: 6 g	Total Carbohydrates: 13 g	Protein: 20 g
Saturated Fat: 3 g		

Zucchini-Potato Frittata

A frittata is simply an Italian omelet.

1 medium zucchini, thinly sliced	
¾ pound new (red) potatoes with peels, thinly sliced	340 g
1 medium onion, halved, thinly sliced	
6 beaten eggs or 1½ cups egg substitute	365 g
1 cup reduced-fat shredded cheddar or mozzarella cheese	115 g

Preheat oven to 350° (175° C).

Cook zucchini in sprayed 10-inch (25 cm) ovenproof skillet over medium heat about 4 minutes or until tender. Remove zucchini from skillet and keep warm.

Add potatoes and onion to skillet and cook covered over medium heat until potatoes are tender, about 20 minutes. Increase heat and continue cooking until potatoes brown, about 5 minutes. Remove potato mixture from skillet and keep warm.

Combine eggs, zucchini, potato mixture and cheese in medium bowl and pour mixture into skillet. Cook over medium-low heat without stirring until bottom sets, about 10 minutes.

Transfer skillet to oven and bake uncovered until top of egg mixture sets, about 10 minutes. Cut into wedges to serve.

Serves 6.
Serving size: 1 wedge

One Serving
Nutrition facts are based on egg substitute.

Calories: 165	Cholesterol: 21 mg	Dietary Fiber: 2 g
Calories from Fat: 74	Sodium: 235 mg	Sugars: 1 g
Total Fat: 8 g	Total Carbohydrates: 9 g	Protein: 14 g
Saturated Fat: 5 g		

Tomato-Feta Frittata

1½ cups egg substitute	365 g
2 tablespoons chopped green onions	15 g
1 garlic clove, minced	
1 tablespoon butter	15 ml
4 roma tomatoes, halved, seeded, diced	
3 tablespoons crumbled feta cheese	20 g

Preheat oven on broil.

Stir egg substitute, green onions, garlic, ½ teaspoon (2 ml) salt and ¼ teaspoon (1 ml) pepper in medium bowl.

Melt butter in ovenproof 10-inch (25 cm) skillet over medium heat. Pour in egg mixture, lower heat and sprinkle tomatoes and cheese evenly on top. Cook until eggs set.

Broil until top browns. Slide frittata onto serving plate.

Serves 6.
Serving size: ¾ cup (175 ml)

One Serving
Calories: 103	Sodium: 245 mg
Calories from Fat: 58	Total Carbohydrates: 2 g
Total Fat: 6 g	Dietary Fiber: 0 g
Saturated Fat: 4 g	Sugars: 2 g
Cholesterol: 16 mg	Protein: 9 g

Jalapeno-Cheese Squares

1 cup reduced-fat, small curd cottage cheese, drained	225 g
1 (3 ounce) package reduced-fat cream cheese, cubed	85 g
1 cup egg substitute	245 g
½ cup liquid egg whites	115 g
1 cup fat-free half-and-half cream or light plain soymilk	250 ml
1 (6 ounce) package Mexican-style cornbread mix	170 g
3 tablespoons melted butter	45 g
1 cup shredded Monterey Jack cheese with jalapenos	115 g

Preheat oven to 350° (175° C).

Beat cottage cheese and cream cheese until smooth. Add egg substitute, liquid egg whites, half-and-half cream, 1 teaspoon (5 ml) salt and beat about 30 seconds. Add cornbread mix and melted butter and beat about 1 to 2 minutes. Stir in cheese.

Pour into sprayed 9 x 9-inch (23 x 23 cm) baking dish and bake for about 45 minutes or until knife inserted in center comes out clean.

Serves 6.
Serving size: ¾ cup (175 ml)

One Serving
Calories: 308	Sodium: 667 mg
Calories from Fat: 102	Total Carbohydrates: 30 g
Total Fat: 12 g	Dietary Fiber: 1 g
Saturated Fat: 6 g	Sugars: 9 g
Cholesterol: 27 mg	Protein: 20 g

Eggs Florentine

Florentine refers to cooking in the style of Florence, Italy. Traditionally, it refers to eggs or fish served on a bed of spinach covered with cheese sauce.

1 (10 ounce) package chopped spinach, thawed	280 g
1 tablespoon butter	15 ml
1 tablespoon unbleached white flour	15 ml
¾ cup fat-free skim milk	175 ml
4 eggs	

Squeeze spinach between paper towels to completely remove excess moisture.

Melt butter in 1-quart (1 L) saucepan over medium heat. Stir in flour and ¼ teaspoon (1 ml) salt. Cook and stir until it bubbles. Pour in milk, reduce heat and cook until it is thick. Remove from heat and stir in spinach. Transfer spinach mixture to sprayed non-stick 10-inch (25 cm) skillet. Spread spinach evenly in the bottom.

Heat spinach mixture over low heat until hot. Use large spoon and make 4 hollows in spinach. Break each egg into small bowl and slip into hollow. Cover and cook about 5 minutes. With spatula, divide eggs with spinach into 4 servings.

Serves 4.
Serving size: 1 egg with spinach

One Serving

Calories: 64	Cholesterol: 8 mg	Dietary Fiber: 2 g
Calories from Fat: 32	Sodium: 77 mg	Sugars: 3 g
Total Fat: 4 g	Total Carbohydrates: 5 g	Protein: 4 g
Saturated Fat: 2 g		

Ranch-Style Eggs

*Ranch-style eggs are also known as huevos rancheros. This dish
is especially good for brunch and satisfies taste buds any time of day.*

4 eggs	
1 cup Red Chile Sauce (page 238) or mild salsa	250 ml
4 (10 inch) whole wheat or multigrain tortillas	4 (25 cm)
½ cup finely shredded cheddar Jack cheese	60 g
3 tablespoons thinly sliced green onions	20 g

Preheat oven to 325° (160° C).

To prepare sunny-side-up eggs, heat sprayed non-stick 10-inch (25 cm) skillet over medium heat. Carefully add each egg to skillet. Add about 2 tablespoons (30 ml) water. Cover and cook until egg whites set and yolks are still moist. Remove eggs and keep warm.

Heat Red Chile Sauce in 10-inch (25 cm) skillet over medium-high heat until it boils. Reduce heat to low.

Dip tortillas in sauce to soften and transfer to ovenproof serving plates. Spoon one-fourth warmed sauce onto each tortilla and top with egg, 2 tablespoons (30 ml) cheese and 1 teaspoon (5 ml) onions. Place in oven and heat until cheese melts.

Serves 4.
Serving size: 1 tortilla

TIP: If you prefer egg substitute, scramble 1 cup (245 g) egg substitute in non-stick 10-inch (25 cm) skillet and follow directions for layering Red Chile Sauce, cheese and onions.

One Serving

Calories: 367	Cholesterol: 224 mg	Dietary Fiber: 2 g
Calories from Fat: 136	Sodium: 608 mg	Sugars: 2 g
Total Fat: 15 g	Total Carbohydrates: 41 g	Protein: 15 g
Saturated Fat: 6 g		

Creamy Cheese Enchiladas

Traditionally, this enchilada dish is made with sour cream. Calories are saved by using yogurt instead of sour cream. It's amazingly good!

2 cups nonfat plain yogurt	455 g
1 cup chopped green onions, divided	100 g
½ teaspoon ground cumin	2 ml
3 cups reduced-fat shredded Monterey Jack cheese, divided	350 g
2 (10 ounce) cans mild green or red enchilada sauce, divided	2 (280 g)
8 - 10 (7 inch) flour tortillas	8 - 10 (18 cm)

Preheat oven to 350° (175° C).

Combine yogurt, ¾ cup (75 g) green onions, cumin and 1½ cups (170 g) cheese.

Heat 1 can enchilada sauce in 10-inch (25 cm) skillet to a simmer.

Cover cutting board or tray with wax paper. Slide tortillas into warmed enchilada sauce and quickly transfer to wax paper. Pour warm enchilada sauce into sprayed 9 x 13-inch (23 x 33 cm) baking dish. Spoon 2 to 3 tablespoons (30 ml) yogurt filling onto tortilla. Roll and place seam-side down on enchilada sauce.

Pour remaining can enchilada sauce over rolled tortillas and sprinkle remaining cheese on top.

Bake uncovered for about 30 minutes. Garnish with remaining green onions.

Servings 10.
Serving size: 1 enchilada

One Serving

Calories: 318	Cholesterol: 37 mg	Dietary Fiber: 1 g
Calories from Fat: 143	Sodium: 716 mg	Sugars: 9 g
Total Fat: 16 g	Total Carbohydrates: 30 g	Protein: 14 g
Saturated Fat: 8 g		

Green Chile Chilaquiles

2 cups reduced-fat shredded Monterey Jack cheese, divided	230 g
1 cup reduced-fat sour cream	240 g
1 (4 ounce) can chopped green chilies, drained	115 g
1 (19 ounce) can mild green enchilada sauce, divided	540 g
8 - 10 whole wheat or multigrain tortillas, torn in small pieces, divided	

Preheat oven to 350° (175° C).

Stir 1½ cups (170 g) cheese, sour cream and green chilies in medium bowl.

Spread ½ cup (125 ml) enchilada sauce into 9 x 13-inch (23 x 33 cm) baking dish and arrange half tortilla pieces on top of sauce. Spoon half cheese mixture on tortilla pieces and spread with ½ cup (125 ml) enchilada sauce. Make another layer of remaining tortilla pieces, remaining cheese mixture and remaining enchilada sauce. Sprinkle with remaining ½ cup (60 g) cheese.

Bake for 35 minutes.

Serves 8.
Serving size: ¾ cup (175 ml)

TIP: In Mexico, chilaquiles were once known as the "poor man's enchiladas" and are typically made with red chile sauce.

One Serving

Calories: 510	Cholesterol: 54 mg	Dietary Fiber: 2 g
Calories from Fat: 206	Sodium: 1395 mg	Sugars: 3 g
Total Fat: 23 g	Total Carbohydrates: 49 g	Protein: 25 g
Saturated Fat: 11 g		

Flat Cheese Enchiladas with Eggs

You'll like these flat enchiladas with sauce, onion and
cheese topped with soft poached egg. Mmm good!

4 (7 inch) whole wheat or multigrain tortillas	4 (18 cm)
1 (10 ounce) can mild green or red enchilada sauce	280 g
¼ cup chopped onion	40 g
½ (8 ounce) package reduced-fat shredded cheddar cheese	115 g
1 tablespoon butter	15 ml
4 eggs	

Layer one tortilla, 2 tablespoons (60 ml) sauce, 1 tablespoon (15 ml) chopped onion and 2 tablespoons (60 ml) cheese for each flat enchilada on microwave-safe plates. Cover loosely and heat in microwave on HIGH for 15 to 30 seconds or just until cheese melts. Keep warm while preparing eggs.

Melt butter in non-stick 12-inch (32 cm) skillet over medium heat. Break each egg into small bowl. Slip each egg into skillet. Cover and cook eggs about 2 minutes. Add 4 teaspoons (20 ml) water. Cover, reduce heat to low and cook about 1 minute. Remove carefully and add 1 egg to each flat enchilada.

Serves 4.
Serving size: 1 flat enchilada with egg

TIP: Instead of using skillet, use the microwave oven to poach eggs. Break egg into sprayed custard cup, prick yolk and microwave on HIGH for 20 seconds. Turn cup to evenly cook other side of egg and microwave for 10 seconds.

One Serving

Calories: 331	Cholesterol: 224 mg	Dietary Fiber: 2 g
Calories from Fat: 137	Sodium: 832 mg	Sugars: 4 g
Total Fat: 15 g	Total Carbohydrates: 31 g	Protein: 17 g
Saturated Fat: 6 g		

Breakfast & Brunch

Whole Wheat Crepes

This is a terrific, versatile recipe for any sweet or savory filling.

2 eggs, beaten or ½ cup egg substitute	**125 g**
1½ cups light plain soymilk	**375 ml**
1 tablespoon canola oil	**15 ml**
¾ cup whole wheat flour	**100 g**

Whisk all ingredients and ¼ teaspoon (1 ml) salt in medium bowl until it mixes well.

Preheat sprayed non-stick crepe pan or 10-inch (25 cm) skillet with sloping sides. When drops of water sizzle in pan, quickly pour in scant ¼ cup (60 ml) batter. Rotate pan so batter flows over entire surface.

When the surface looks dry and edges brown, carefully turn crepe with spatula and cook other side just until it is light brown. Spray skillet as needed and frequently stir batter before cooking.

Carefully remove crepe with spatula or invert skillet over wax or parchment paper so crepe will slide out. Place wax paper between crepes if not served immediately. Wrapped airtight, crepes can be refrigerated for 3 days or frozen for longer storage.

Add your favorite filling and serve.

Serves 8.
Serving size: 2 to 3 crepes

TIP: This recipe will take some practice, so expect to use one recipe to learn how to use your skillet to make a perfect crepe. Your family and friends will really be impressed!

One Serving
Nutrition facts are based on egg substitute.

Calories: 144	Cholesterol: 0 mg	Dietary Fiber: 2 g
Calories from Fat: 41	Sodium: 31 mg	Sugars: 13 g
Total Fat: 5 g	Total Carbohydrates: 24 g	Protein: 4 g
Saturated Fat: 0 g		

Three-Cheese Crepes

Crepes are light and paper thin and are folded or rolled with savory and sweet fillings.

¼ cup egg substitute	60 g
1½ cups part-skim ricotta cheese	370 g
1 cup (4 ounces) reduced-fat shredded mozzarella cheese	115 g
¾ cup grated parmesan or romano cheese, divided	75 g
1 (5 ounce/10 count) package refrigerated or frozen 9-inch crepes	145 g/23 cm
2 cups Marinara Sauce (page 239) or tomato pasta sauce	500 ml

Preheat oven to 350° (175° C).

Combine egg substitute, ½ teaspoon (2 ml) salt and ⅛ teaspoon (.5 ml) pepper in medium bowl. Stir in ricotta cheese, mozzarella cheese and ½ cup (50 g) parmesan cheese. Spoon about 2 tablespoons (30 ml) cheese mixture slightly off center on each crepe and roll to enclose cheese filling.

Spread 1 cup (250 ml) Marinara Sauce in sprayed 9 x 13-inch (23 x 33 cm) baking dish. Arrange single layer of filled crepes, seam-side down in sauce. Cover with remaining sauce and sprinkle with remaining parmesan cheese.

Bake uncovered for about 30 minutes or until hot.

Serves 6.

Serving size: 2 crepes with sauce

One Serving

Calories: 287	Cholesterol: 50 mg	Dietary Fiber: 1 g
Calories from Fat: 147	Sodium: 644 mg	Sugars: 3 g
Total Fat: 16 g	Total Carbohydrates: 15 g	Protein: 20 g
Saturated Fat: 9 g		

Cottage Cheese Pancakes

Use egg substitute for these zero-cholesterol pancakes.

6 eggs, beaten or 1½ cups egg substitute	**365 g**
1 cup reduced-fat, small curd cottage cheese, well drained	**225 g**
¼ cup canola oil	**60 ml**
½ cup self-rising flour	**65 g**

Combine eggs, cottage cheese and oil in mixing bowl. Add flour and stir just until moist.

Heat sprayed griddle, or sprayed non-stick 12-inch (32 cm) skillet over medium-high heat until drops of water sizzle on the surface. Pour ¼ cup (60 ml) batter on griddle for each pancake. Turn when pancake is set around edges and holes begin forming on top. Transfer to warmed plate when golden brown.

Serves 6.
Serving size: 2 (3 inch/8 cm) pancakes

TIP: Serve with sliced fresh strawberries and bananas or Nectarine Dessert Sauce (page 264).

One Serving
Nutrition facts are based on egg substitute.

Calories: 279	Cholesterol: 2 mg	Dietary Fiber: 0 g
Calories from Fat: 187	Sodium: 264 mg	Sugars: 1 g
Total Fat: 21 g	Total Carbohydrates: 9 g	Protein: 13 g
Saturated Fat: 2 g		

Pumpkin Pancakes

This is an all-time favorite for holiday breakfasts.

2 cups self-rising flour	250 g
2 tablespoons brown sugar	25 g
1¼ teaspoons ground pumpkin pie spice	6 ml
1¾ cups light plain or vanilla soymilk	425 ml
½ cup canned pumpkin	125 g
1 egg or ¼ cup egg substitute	60 g
2 tablespoons canola oil	30 ml

Combine flour, brown sugar and pumpkin pie spice in large bowl.

In separate bowl, combine soymilk, pumpkin, egg and oil. Add milk mixture to flour mixture and stir just until moist. Batter will be lumpy but do not overmix.

Heat sprayed non-stick griddle or non-stick 12-inch (32 cm) skillet on medium-high heat until drops of water sizzle on the surface. Pour ¼ cup (60 ml) batter onto hot griddle for each pancake.

Turn when edges of pancake set and top of pancake begins to bubble. Cook turned pancake additional 2 to 3 minutes or until golden brown. Transfer to warm plate.

Serves 4.
Serving size: 2 (3 inch/8 cm) diameter pancakes

TIP: Try adding 1 tablespoon (15 ml) finely grated orange peel to the batter.

One Serving
Nutrition facts are based on egg substitute.

Calories: 253	Cholesterol: 0 mg	Dietary Fiber: 3 g
Calories from Fat: 60	Sodium: 637 mg	Sugars: 4 g
Total Fat: 6 g	Total Carbohydrates: 39 g	Protein: 9 g
Saturated Fat: 1 g		

Whole Wheat-Oat Pancakes

These hearty pancakes will give you a jump-start in the morning.

½ cup old-fashioned oats	40 g
1 cup whole wheat flour	130 g
1½ teaspoons baking powder	7 ml
½ cup packed brown sugar	110 g
1¼ cups light plain soymilk or fat-free skim milk	310 ml
½ cup fat-free plain yogurt	115 g

Toast oats in 10-inch (25 cm) skillet over medium heat and stir occasionally until light brown. Cool.

Combine oats, whole wheat flour, baking powder, brown sugar and ¼ teaspoon (1 ml) salt in large bowl. In separate bowl, combine soymilk and yogurt. Stir milk mixture into oat mixture just until it blends well. Batter will be lumpy.

Spray non-stick griddle or 12-inch (32 cm) skillet and heat on medium-high until water droplets sprinkled on griddle bounce. Drop scant ¼ cup (60 ml) batter and spread into round shape. Cook 2 minutes or until bubbles form on surface. Turn pancakes and cook 2 minutes or until brown.

Serves 6.
Serving size: 2 (4 inch/10 cm) pancakes

One Serving

Calories: 222	Cholesterol: 0 mg	Dietary Fiber: 5 g
Calories from Fat: 20	Sodium: 52 mg	Sugars: 18 g
Total Fat: 2 g	Total Carbohydrates: 44 g	Protein: 8 g
Saturated Fat: 0 g		

Zucchini Brunch Pancakes

Choose an easy green salad and fruit dessert to round
out this very nice, savory brunch or supper entree.

3 cups shredded zucchini	375 g
⅓ cup finely chopped onion	55 g
3 eggs, beaten or ¾ cup egg substitute	185 g
¾ cup flour	95 g
½ teaspoon oregano	2 ml
¼ cup olive oil, divided	60 ml

Squeeze zucchini between paper towels to completely remove excess moisture. Transfer to bowl and add onion, eggs, flour, oregano and ¼ teaspoon (1 ml) pepper. Stir to mix.

Add 2 tablespoons (30 ml) oil to non-stick 12-inch (32 cm) skillet and heat on medium-high until water droplets sprinkled on skillet bounce.

Pour in about 3 tablespoons (45 ml) pancake batter and spread to a (4 inch/10 cm) circle. Cook for 3 to 4 minutes on each side. Lift pancakes with spatula and drain on paper towels. Transfer to serving plate and keep warm. Repeat with remaining batter and add oil if needed.

Serves 6.
Serving size: 4 pancakes

TIP: Choose small to medium zucchini with shiny, taut skin and firm flesh. Avoid large, overgrown squash.

One Serving
Nutrition facts are based on egg substitute.

Calories: 173	Cholesterol: 0 mg	Dietary Fiber: 1 g
Calories from Fat: 92	Sodium: 62 mg	Sugars: 1 g
Total Fat: 10 g	Total Carbohydrates: 14 g	Protein: 6 g
Saturated Fat: 1 g		

Whole Wheat-Cornmeal Waffles

These waffles are crunchy and crisp with a slightly
tart flavor. They are worth a little extra effort.

2 eggs, beaten or ½ cup egg substitute	125 g
2 cups reduced-fat buttermilk*	500 ml
½ cup canola oil	125 ml
1¼ cups whole wheat flour	165 g
½ cup stone-ground yellow cornmeal	80 g
1 tablespoon plus 1 teaspoon baking powder	15 ml/5 ml
½ teaspoon baking soda	2 ml
3 tablespoons brown sugar	45 g

Whisk eggs, buttermilk and oil in large bowl. In separate bowl, stir flour, cornmeal, baking powder, baking soda, brown sugar and ½ teaspoon (2 ml) salt.

Add flour mixture to egg mixture and stir just until moist. (Be careful to not overmix.)

Preheat non-stick waffle maker according to package directions. Bake until waffle is brown and crisp.

Serves 6.
Serving size: 2 (4½ inch/10.5 cm) square waffles

TIP: To make buttermilk, mix 1 cup (250 ml) milk with 1 tablespoon (15 ml) lemon juice or vinegar and let milk rest about 10 minutes.

One Serving
Nutrition facts are based on egg substitute.

Calories: 284	Cholesterol: 7 mg	Dietary Fiber: 4 g
Calories from Fat: 114	Sodium: 114 mg	Sugars: 9 g
Total Fat: 13 g	Total Carbohydrates: 35 g	Protein: 10 g
Saturated Fat: 2 g		

Kid Friendly Toast Sticks

Children like these "cooked-in-a-pan" toast sticks.

3 slices whole wheat or whole grain bread	
2 eggs, beaten or ½ cup egg substitute	125 g
¼ cup light plain soymilk or fat-free half-and-half cream	60 ml
2 teaspoons honey or sugar	10 ml
½ teaspoon vanilla	2 ml
1 tablespoon butter, cut in small pieces	15 ml

Cut each bread slice into 3 strips; leave crusts on bread.

Combine eggs, soymilk, honey or sugar, vanilla and ¼ teaspoon (1 ml) salt in shallow dish.

Melt 2 to 3 small pieces of butter in sprayed 10-inch (25 cm) skillet over medium heat. Dip bread strips in egg mixture. Add 3 coated bread strips at a time to skillet.

Be careful not to burn butter. Cook strips, turning once, until both sides are brown. Add more pieces of butter as needed.

Serves 4.
Serving size: 2 sticks

TIP: Serve with maple syrup or honey as a dipping sauce.

One Serving
Nutrition facts are based on egg substitute.

Calories: 120	Cholesterol: 8 mg	Dietary Fiber: 1 g
Calories from Fat: 46	Sodium: 163 mg	Sugars: 4 g
Total Fat: 5 g	Total Carbohydrates: 13 g	Protein: 6 g
Saturated Fat: 2 g		

Panettone French Toast

3 eggs, beaten or ¾ cup egg substitute	185 g
½ cup fat-free half-and-half cream	125 ml
½ cup light plain soymilk	125 ml
2 tablespoons sugar	25 g
1 tablespoon butter	15 ml
3 (¾ inch) large slices panettone bread	3 (1.8 cm)

Whisk eggs, half-and-half cream, soymilk, sugar and ¼ teaspoon (1 ml) in medium bowl until they mix well. Pour into 9 x 9-inch (23 x 23 cm) baking dish.

Melt butter on large non-stick griddle or non-stick 12-inch (32 cm) skillet over medium heat.

Dip panettone slices in egg mixture and turn to lightly soak both sides. Grill slices about 4 minutes on each side or until brown. Cut each slice in half.

Serves 6.
Serving size: ½ slice

TIP: *Panettone is an airy, light and scrumptious sweet yeast bread with raisins, citron, pine nuts and anise. It comes wrapped in paper like a giant cupcake. Remove paper, cut off ends and cut into ¾-inch (1.8 cm) slices. One panettone yields about 6 (¾ inch/1.8 cm) slices.*

One Serving
Nutrition facts are based on egg substitute.

Calories: 146	Cholesterol: 5 mg	Dietary Fiber: 2 g
Calories from Fat: 44	Sodium: 175 mg	Sugars: 7 g
Total Fat: 5 g	Total Carbohydrates: 19 g	Protein: 7 g
Saturated Fat: 1 g		

Cheesy Popovers

These crispy popovers will be a hit for breakfast or lunch.

2 eggs or ½ cup egg substitute	125 g
1 cup fat-free skim milk	250 ml
1 tablespoon melted butter	15 ml
1 cup unbleached white flour	120 g
¾ cup finely shredded sharp cheddar cheese	85 g

Preheat oven to 400° (205° C).

Beat eggs in medium bowl, add milk and butter until it blends. Add flour and ¼ teaspoon (1 ml) salt and beat until smooth.

Spray 6 non-stick muffin cups. Distribute cheese equally in cups. Distribute popover batter evenly over cheese. For even cooking, add ¼ cup (60 ml) water to each unfilled muffin cup.

Bake until puffed and well browned, about 50 minutes. Pierce each popover with a sharp knife to allow steam to escape and cool for 1 minute. Carefully loosen and remove. Serve warm.

Serves 6.
Serving Size: 1 popover

TIP: Batter may also be prepared in a food processor or a blender.

One Serving
Nutrition facts are based on egg substitute.

Calories: 182	Cholesterol: 20 mg	Dietary Fiber: 1 g
Calories from Fat: 67	Sodium: 147 mg	Sugars: 2 g
Total Fat: 8 g	Total Carbohydrates: 18 g	Protein: 10 g
Saturated Fat: 4 g		

Good Morning Bagel

No time for a sit-down breakfast? This takes just a few minutes if you prepare hard-boiled egg the night before.

¼ cup whipped reduced-fat
    cream cheese   60 g
2 bagel halves, toasted
1 egg, hard-boiled, cut
    into 8 slices
2 tablespoons no-sugar
    orange marmalade   40 g

Spread cream cheese on each bagel half. Add 4 slices hard-boiled egg to each bagel half and top with marmalade. Warm each bagel half just a few seconds in microwave oven on MEDIUM.

Serves 2.
Serving size: ½ bagel

TIP: This works well with English muffins.

One Serving

Calories: 304	Sodium: 412 mg
Calories from Fat: 79	Total Carbohydrates: 44 g
Total Fat: 9 g	Dietary Fiber: 1 g
Saturated Fat: 5 g	Sugars: 13 g
Cholesterol: 123 mg	Protein: 9 g

Apple-Cheese Muffins

These yummy muffins will get you going on busy mornings.

2 whole wheat English muffins,
    split, toasted
1 apple with peel, cored, thinly sliced
4 cheddar soy veggie slices or fat-free
    Swiss cheese slices

Arrange apple slices on each muffin half. Top with cheese and broil until it melts.

Serves 4.
Serving size: 1 muffin half

TIP: This is also good with peaches and nectarines.

One Serving

Calories: 135	Sodium: 229 mg
Calories from Fat: 20	Total Carbohydrates: 19 g
Total Fat: 2 g	Dietary Fiber: 3 g
Saturated Fat: 1 g	Sugars: 7 g
Cholesterol: 10 mg	Protein: 11 g

Bran Cereal Muffins

Freeze these muffins and warm in microwave for a hearty breakfast.

2 cups bran cereal flakes, crushed	80 g
1⅓ cups light vanilla soymilk	325 ml
¼ cup canola oil	60 ml
1 egg or ¼ cup egg substitute	60 g
½ cup packed light brown sugar	110 g
1¼ cups unbleached white flour	150 g
1 tablespoon baking powder	15 ml

Preheat oven to 400° (205° C).

Spray or line 12 muffin cups with baking cups.

Combine cereal and soymilk in medium bowl. Let stand about 5 minutes or until cereal softens. Beat in oil and egg with fork.

Add brown sugar to large bowl and remove any hard lumps. Add flour, baking powder and ¼ teaspoon (1 ml) salt to brown sugar and whisk. Pour in cereal mixture and stir with spatula just until mixture becomes moist. Do not overmix. Spoon batter into muffin cups.

Bake for 20 to 25 minutes or until toothpick inserted in centers comes out clean. Remove muffins immediately to wire rack.

Serves 12.
Serving size: 1 muffin

TIP: Most flours available today are pre-sifted and do not require sifting before use. However, it's a good idea to stir through the flour container just before measuring. Spoon flour into dry measuring cup and level with spatula or knife.

One Serving
Nutrition facts are based on egg substitute.

Calories: 176	Cholesterol: 0 mg	Dietary Fiber: 2 g
Calories from Fat: 50	Sodium: 77 mg	Sugars: 140 g
Total Fat: 6 g	Total Carbohydrates: 26 g	Protein: 4 g
Saturated Fat: 0 g		

Granola Muffins

This is healthful granola baked in a muffin. It's a tasty little package.

1⅓ cups self-rising flour	170 g
¾ cup toasted granola	65 g
⅓ cup sugar	70 g
¼ cup egg substitute	60 g
¾ cup plain light soymilk	175 ml
¼ cup oil	60 ml

Preheat oven to 400° (205° C). Spray 12 muffin cups or line with baking cups.

Combine flour, granola and sugar in medium bowl; stir well. Make a well in the center of flour mixture.

In separate bowl, combine egg substitute, soymilk and oil. Add egg mixture to flour mixture. Stir just until moist; batter will be lumpy. Do not over-mix.

Fill muffin cups about two-thirds full. Bake for 18 to 20 minutes or until a toothpick inserted in centers comes out clean. Cool muffins in muffin cups on wire rack for 5 minutes.

Serves 12.
Serving size: 1 muffin

TIP: Be sure to use granola such as oats, nuts and fruits instead of granola cereal.

One Serving

Calories: 174	Cholesterol: 0 mg	Dietary Fiber: 1 g
Calories from Fat: 47	Sodium: 196 mg	Sugars: 7 g
Total Fat: 7 g	Total Carbohydrates: 21 g	Protein: 3 g
Saturated Fat: 1 g		

Tomato-Egg-Cheese Muffin

*This delicious muffin is a much healthier choice
than fast food bacon-egg-cheese biscuits and they taste better too.*

1 cup egg substitute	**245 g**
1 large firm tomato	
2 whole wheat English muffins, halved	
¼ cup reduced-fat shredded cheddar cheese	**30 g**

Pour egg substitute into sprayed non-stick 8-inch (20 cm) skillet over medium-high heat. Add ½ teaspoon (2 ml) salt and ¼ teaspoon (1 ml) pepper. Cook and stir gently until eggs set, but are still moist. Transfer to warm plate and keep warm.

Preheat oven broiler. Remove ends from tomato and cut into 4 (¼ inch/.6 cm) slices. Place tomato slices in baking pan and broil 1 or 2 minutes. Remove from pan and keep tomatoes warm.

Lightly toast English muffin halves in baking pan under broiler. For each serving, top each muffin half with tomato slice, one-fourth scrambled eggs and one-fourth cheese. Broil just until cheese melts. Serve immediately.

Serves 4.
Serving size: 1 muffin half

TIP: To make this really easy, have all the ingredients ready for each step of preparation.

One Serving

Calories: 239	Cholesterol: 30 mg	Dietary Fiber: 3 g
Calories from Fat: 121	Sodium: 374 mg	Sugars: 3 g
Total Fat: 13 g	Total Carbohydrates: 15 g	Protein: 15 g
Saturated Fat: 7 g		

Yogurt Muffins

For a special breakfast, serve these muffins with fresh fruit and whipped cream cheese.

2 cups flour	**250 g**
½ teaspoon baking soda	**2 ml**
½ cup egg substitute	**125 g**
1 cup reduced-fat plain yogurt	**230 g**
⅔ cup packed brown sugar	**150 g**
1 teaspoon vanilla	**5 ml**
½ cup canola oil	**125 ml**

Preheat oven to 400° (205° C).

Whisk flour and baking soda in large bowl.

In separate bowl, whisk egg substitute, yogurt, brown sugar, vanilla and oil.

Add egg mixture to flour mixture and stir just until dry ingredients are moist. Do not overmix.

Spoon batter into 12 sprayed or paper-lined muffin cups. Bake for 12 to 15 minutes or until toothpick inserted in centers of muffins comes out clean.

Serves 12.
Serving size: 1 muffin

TIP: For a cake doughnut taste, dip top of cooked muffins in ½ cup (125 ml) melted butter and then into bowl with ½ cup (50 g) sugar mixed with 1 teaspoon (5 ml) ground cinnamon.

One Serving

Calories: 436	Cholesterol: 0 mg	Dietary Fiber: 1 g
Calories from Fat: 173	Sodium: 79 mg	Sugars: 24 g
Total Fat: 19 g	Total Carbohydrates: 58 g	Protein: 8 g
Saturated Fat: 2 g		

Appetizers
&
Beverages

Contents

Chop Chop

*Serve as an appetizer or salsa
with Tex-Mex dishes.*

1 (4 ounce) can chopped green chilies, drained	115 g
1 (4 ounce) can chopped ripe olives, drained	115 g
2 medium tomatoes, diced	
1 medium green or yellow bell pepper, diced	
½ cup finely chopped red onion	80 g
¼ cup chopped parsley or cilantro	20 g/5 g
½ cup Favorite French Dressing (page 105) or Oregano Dressing (page 109)	125 ml

Combine all ingredients in large
bowl. Serve immediately or
cover and refrigerate.

Serves 16.
Serving size: ¼ cup (60 ml)
Makes 4 cups (1 L).

*TIP: Cilantro [see-LAHN-troh] leaves are
from the coriander plant and have a
pungent fragrance and flavor. Just
before using cilantro, wash and pat
dry with paper towels and use a sharp,
heavy knife to chop.*

One Serving

Calories: 51	Sodium: 146 mg
Calories from Fat: 38	Total Carbohydrates: 3 g
Total Fat: 4 g	Dietary Fiber: 1 g
Saturated Fat: 0 g	Sugars: 2 g
Cholesterol: 0 mg	Protein: 0 g

Corn-Bell Pepper Relish

*This relish is a colorful, flavorful
accompaniment to bean
dishes and veggie burgers.*

1 (10 ounce) package frozen whole kernel corn. thawed, drained	280 g
½ cup chopped green bell pepper	75 g
½ cup chopped red bell pepper	75 g
¼ cup finely chopped red or white onion	40 g
¼ cup Cumin Vinaigrette (page 104)	60 ml
¼ cup chopped parsley or 2 tablespoons chopped cilantro	20 g/5 g

Combine corn, bell peppers,
onion, ½ teaspoon (2 ml) salt
and ¼ teaspoon (1 ml) pepper
in mixing bowl. Stir in Cumin
Vinaigrette and parsley.
Refrigerate at least 1 hour
before serving.

Serves 24.
Serving size: 2 tablespoons (30 ml)
Makes 3 cups (750 ml).

One Serving

Calories: 15	Sodium: 31 mg
Calories from Fat: 1	Total Carbohydrates: 3 g
Total Fat: 0 g	Dietary Fiber: 0 g
Saturated Fat: 0 g	Sugars: 1 g
Cholesterol: 0 mg	Protein: 0 g

Tickled-Pink Pickled Onions

Great relish with just about anything!

2 tablespoons white or white wine vinegar, divided	30 ml
1 large red onion, thinly sliced	
1 tablespoon canola oil	15 ml
½ teaspoon mustard seeds	2 ml
¼ teaspoon cumin seeds	1 ml

Bring to boiling 2 cups (500 ml) water and 1 tablespoon (15 ml) vinegar in 1-quart (1 L) saucepan. Add red onion and return to boiling. Reduce heat to medium and cook uncovered for 2 to 3 minutes. Remove onion with slotted spoon to medium bowl and cool.

Add remaining vinegar, oil, mustard seeds, cumin seeds and ½ teaspoon (2 ml) salt to onion mixture and stir. Serve at room temperature or cover and refrigerate until ready to serve.

Serves 12.
Serving Size: 2 tablespoons (30 ml)
Makes 1½ cups (375 ml).

TIP: Especially good with bean patties and veggie burgers

One Serving

Calories: 17	Sodium: 0 mg
Calories from Fat: 11	Total Carbohydrates: 1 g
Total Fat: 1 g	Dietary Fiber: 0 g
Saturated Fat: 0 g	Sugar: 1 g
Cholesterol: 0 mg	Protein: 0 g

Corn-Cucumber Salsa

Originating in Holland, "seedless" cucumbers are grown in greenhouses and are sold shrink-wrapped. Long and smooth, they have few ridges and very few seeds, making them much more digestible than regular cucumbers.

1½ cups frozen whole kernel corn, thawed, drained	250 g
½ fresh jalapeno or serrano chile, halved, seeded, minced	
½ cup finely chopped seedless cucumber	70 g
¼ cup thinly sliced green onions	25 g
1 tablespoon finely grated orange peel	15 ml
3 tablespoons orange juice	45 ml
1 teaspoon cumin seeds or ¼ teaspoon ground cumin	5 ml/1 ml

Combine all ingredients in mixing bowl and stir well.

Serves 16.
Serving size: 2 tablespoons (30 ml)
Makes 2 cups (500 ml).

TIP: Wear rubber gloves when removing seeds from jalapenos.

One Serving

Calories: 19	Sodium: 1 mg
Calories from Fat: 1	Total Carbohydrates: 4 g
Total Fat: 0 g	Dietary Fiber: 0 g
Saturated Fat: 0 g	Sugars: 0 g
Cholesterol: 0 mg	Protein: 0 g

Fresh Tomatillo Salsa

½ pound fresh tomatillos, husked	230 g
¼ cup coarsely chopped onion	40 g
¼ cup coarsely chopped cilantro, leaves and stems	5 g
½ fresh jalapeno pepper, seeded	

 Rinse and stem tomatillos. Cut large tomatillos in half. Bring 1 quart (1 L) water to a boil in large pot. Add tomatillos and reduce heat. Cover and simmer about 5 to 7 minutes or until tomatillos are tender. Drain; set aside about ½ cup (125 ml) liquid.

 Place tomatillos, onion, cilantro and jalapeno in food processor or blender. Add about 2 tablespoons (30 ml) reserved liquid and ½ teaspoon (2 ml) salt. Cover and process until combined, adding more liquid if needed.

Serves 12.
Serving size: 2 tablespoons (30 ml)
Makes 1½ cups (375 ml).

TIP: Tomatillos [toe-ma-TEE-ohs] are little green tomatoes from Mexico that are loaded with vitamins A and C. They are usually available year-round in Southwestern states or in Mexican food specialty markets.

One Serving

Calories: 11	Cholesterol: 0 mg	Sugars: 1 g
Calories from Fat: 0	Sodium: 0 mg	Protein: 0 g
Total Fat: 0 g	Total Carbohydrates: 2 g	
Saturated Fat: 0 g	Dietary Fiber: 0 g	

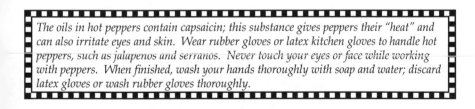

The oils in hot peppers contain capsaicin; this substance gives peppers their "heat" and can also irritate eyes and skin. Wear rubber gloves or latex kitchen gloves to handle hot peppers, such as jalapenos and serranos. Never touch your eyes or face while working with peppers. When finished, wash your hands thoroughly with soap and water; discard latex gloves or wash rubber gloves thoroughly.

Mild Green Chile Salsa

Canned green chilies are really versatile for everyday cooking. It's a good idea to keep several cans in your pantry.

3 medium tomatoes, peeled,
   finely chopped
1 (4 ounce) can chopped
   green chilies, drained   115 g
½ cup finely chopped onion   80 g
1 tablespoon olive oil   15 ml
Juice of 1 lime
1 tablespoon chopped cilantro   15 ml

Combine ingredients and let stand 10 minutes. You can store in refrigerator for 2 to 3 days.

Serves 16.
Serving size: 2 tablespoons (30 ml)
Makes 2 cups (500 ml).

TIP: This is even better with 2 fresh New Mexico (Anaheim) green chiles, roasted, peeled and finely chopped.

One Serving

Calories: 15	Sodium: 1 mg
Calories from	Total Carbohy-
Fat: 0	drates: 2 g
Total Fat: 1 g	Dietary Fiber: 0 g
Saturated Fat: 0 g	Sugars: 1 g
Cholesterol: 0 mg	Protein: 0 g

Pico de Gallo

Great with chips or as a garnish for many dishes, including tacos and fajitas.

1 cup ripe, firm tomato, diced   180 g
1 cup finely chopped onion   160 g
2 garlic cloves, minced
¼ cup coarsely chopped
   cilantro   5 g
Juice of 1 lime

Combine all ingredients and serve.

Serves 16.
Serving size: 2 tablespoons (30 ml)
Makes 2 cups (500 ml).

TIP: For more spice, add 1 small jalapeno pepper, stemmed, seeded and finely chopped or 2 tablespoons (30 ml) chopped canned chipotle pepper.

One Serving

Calories: 6	Sodium: 1 mg
Calories from	Total Carbohy-
Fat: 0	drates: 1 g
Total Fat: 0 g	Dietary Fiber: 0 g
Saturated Fat: 0 g	Sugars: 0 g
Cholesterol: 0 mg	Protein: 0 g

Mango Salsa

Fantastic! You can't stop eating it!

2 large mangoes or 1 (16 ounce) package frozen mango chunks, thawed, drained	455 g
½ cup diced red bell pepper	75 g
3 teaspoons red wine vinegar	15 ml
4 teaspoons lime juice	20 ml
1 teaspoon sugar or sugar substitute	5 ml
1 small fresh jalapeno or serrano chile pepper	

Peel mangoes with serrated knife and slice into ½-inch (1.2 cm) pieces. Combine mango, bell pepper, vinegar, lime juice and sugar in medium bowl.

Slice jalapeno pepper in half and carefully remove seeds. Finely dice one-half and use other half if you want more "hot". Add ½ teaspoon (2 ml) diced pepper at a time to mango mixture and taste. (Avoid making salsa too spicy.) Let salsa stand at room temperature 30 minutes before serving or refrigerate up to 24 hours.

Serves 16.
Serving size: 2 tablespoons (30 ml)
Makes 2 cups (500 ml).

TIP: Wear rubber gloves when removing seeds from jalapenos.

One Serving
Nutrition facts are based on sugar substitute.

Calories: 19	Sodium: 1 mg
Calories from Fat: 0	Total Carbohydrates; 5 g
Total Fat: 0 g	Dietary Fiber: 1 g
Saturated Fat: 0 g	Sugars: 4 g
Cholesterol: 0 mg	Protein: 0 g

Pineapple-Cucumber Salsa

This is a unique combination of ingredients for a salsa. Try it — you'll like it!

1 cup canned crushed pineapple, drained	250 g
½ cup chopped cucumber, seeded	70 g
1 fresh serrano or jalapeno pepper, seeded, minced	
1 teaspoon finely grated lime peel	5 ml
3 tablespoons lime juice	45 ml
2 tablespoons chopped cilantro	30 ml

Combine all ingredients in medium bowl. Serve or refrigerate up to 4 hours.

Serves 16.
Serving size: 2 tablespoons (30 ml)
Makes 1½ cups (375 ml).

TIP: Use the fine side of grater to finely grate lime peel (zest).

One Serving

Calories: 8	Sodium: 0 mg
Calories from Fat: 0	Total Carbohydrates: 2 g
Total Fat: 0 g	Fiber: 0 g
Saturated Fat: 0 g	Sugars: 2 g
Cholesterol: 0 mg	Protein: 0 g

Creamy Spinach-Bell Pepper Dip

1 (10 ounce) package frozen
    chopped spinach, thawed   280 g
1 cup finely chopped red
    bell pepper   150 g
1 cup finely chopped onion   160 g
1 garlic clove, minced
½ cup reduced-fat sour cream   120 g
½ cup reduced-fat
    mayonnaise   115 g

Squeeze spinach between paper towels to completely remove excess moisture. Add all ingredients to medium bowl. Add ½ teaspoon (2 ml) salt and ⅛ teaspoon (.5 ml) pepper. Stir to combine ingredients.

Serves 10.
Serving size: ¼ cup (60 ml)
Makes 2½ cups (625 ml).

TIP: Use fat-free mayonnaise and fat-free sour cream to further reduce calories.

One Serving

Calories: 79	Sodium: 115 mg
Calories from	Total Carbohy-
Fat: 51	drates: 5 g
Total Fat: 6 g	Dietary Fiber: 2 g
Saturated Fat: 2 g	Sugars: 2 g
Cholesterol: 4 mg	Protein: 2 g

Feta-Spinach-Artichoke Dip

Feta cheese adds a piquant flavor to this dip.

1 (13 ounce) can artichoke
    hearts in water, drained   370 g
1 (10 ounce) package frozen
    chopped spinach, thawed   280 g
2 cups reduced-fat
    mayonnaise   450 g
½ - 1 cup crumbled feta or
    blue cheese   75-150 g
2 garlic cloves, minced

Preheat oven to 325° (160° C).

Chop artichoke hearts. Squeeze spinach between paper towels to completely remove excess moisture. Combine all ingredients in medium bowl. Spread in 8 x 8-inch (20 x 20 cm) baking dish.

Bake about 1 hour or until bubbly.

Serves 24.
Serving size: ¼ cup (60 ml)
Makes 6 cups (1.4 L).

TIP: Try with raw vegetables or whole wheat pita or flatbread wedges.

One Serving

Calories: 84	Sodium: 236 mg
Calories from	Total Carbohy-
Fat: 64	drates: 4 g
Total Fat: 7 g	Dietary Fiber: 1 g
Saturated Fat: 1 g	Sugars: 0 g
Cholesterol: 3 mg	Protein: 2 g

Chipotle-Refried Bean Dip

A chipotle [chih-POHT-lay] chile is a dried, smoked jalapeno pepper. Chipotles can be found dried or canned in adobo sauce, a sauce made from ground chiles, herbs and vinegar.

3 tablespoons chopped cilantro	5 g
½ cup finely chopped onion	80 g
1 garlic clove, minced	
1 tablespoon chopped dried chipotle chile (or canned in adobo sauce)	15 ml
2 tablespoons fresh lime juice	30 ml
1 (15 ounce) can fat-free refried beans	425 g

Add cilantro, onion, garlic and chipotle chile to food processor or blender. Cover and process briefly. Transfer to bowl and stir in lime juice, refried beans, ½ teaspoon (2 ml) salt and ⅛ teaspoon (.5 ml) pepper.

Serves 8.
Serving size: ¼ cup (60 ml)
Makes 2 cups (500 ml).

TIP: Roll limes on hard surface to break down inside membranes before juicing.

One Serving

Calories: 50	Sodium: 151 mg
Calories from Fat: 0	Total Carbohydrates: 10 g
Total Fat: 0 g	Dietary Fiber: 3 g
Saturated Fat: 0 g	Sugars: 1 g
Cholesterol: 0 mg	Protein: 3 g

Dill Dip for Vegetables

If available, fresh dill is the best choice for this dip.

2 cups reduced-fat sour cream or nonfat plain yogurt	480 g
¼ cup coarsely chopped red or white onion	40 g
2 tablespoons chopped fresh dill weed, 1 teaspoon dill seed or 1 tablespoon dried dill weed	30 ml/5 ml/15 ml

Combine sour cream, onion, fresh dill weed and ½ teaspoon (2 ml) salt in food processor or blender. Cover and process about 30 seconds.

Serves 10.
Serving size: ¼ cup (60 ml)
Makes 2 cups (500 ml).

TIP: You can easily replace red or white onion with 2 to 3 tablespoons (30 - 45 ml) chopped green onions.

One Serving

Calories: 109	Sodium: 123 mg
Calories from Fat: 77	Total Carbohydrates: 14 g
Total Fat: 9 g	Dietary Fiber: 7 g
Saturated Fat: 15 g	Sugars: 0 g
Cholesterol: 61 mg	Protein: 4 g

Green Chile Guacamole

This is great, fresh guacamole that takes just minutes to make.

3 large Hass avocados
3 roma or plum tomatoes, seeded, chopped
1 (4 ounce) can chopped green chilies, drained 115 g
2 tablespoons lemon juice 30 ml

Peel and slightly mash avocados in mixing bowl, but leave several chunks. Add tomatoes, green chilies, lemon juice and 1 teaspoon (5 ml) salt. Stir ingredients to combine.

Serves 12.
Serving size: ¼ cup (60 ml)
Makes 3 cups (750 ml).

TIP: Hass avocados' skin is pebbly texture and almost black. Purchase heavy, firm, unripe avocados and store in paper bag at room temperature 2 to 3 days to ripen.

One Serving

Calories: 84	Sodium: 70 mg
Calories from	Total Carbohy-
Fat: 66	drates: 5 g
Total Fat: 7 g	Dietary Fiber: 3 g
Saturated Fat: 1 g	Sugars: 0 g
Cholesterol: 0 mg	Protein: 0 g

Blue Cheese Stuffed Celery

Here's a new twist on an old favorite.

½ pound celery (about 4 large stalks) 230 g
¼ cup crumbled blue, gorgonzola or feta cheese 140 g
1 (8 ounce) package reduced-fat cream cheese 230 g
2 teaspoons fat-free skim milk, divided 10 ml

Clean celery and cut off tops and bottoms. With vegetable peeler, remove strings from larger stalks. Cut into 3 to 4-inch (8 cm) pieces.

Combine blue cheese, cream cheese, ½ teaspoon (2 ml) salt and ⅛ teaspoon (.5 ml) pepper until smooth. If needed, add 1 to 2 teaspoons (5 - 10 ml) milk for smoothness.

Lightly pack cheese filling onto celery pieces.

Serves 8 to 10.
Serving size: 2 pieces stuffed celery
Makes 1¼ cups (310 ml) cheese filling.

TIP: For this recipe, you might choose celery hearts. The milder, inner stalks of celery are almost free of strings.

One Serving

Calories: 78	Sodium: 153 mg
Calories from	Total Carbohy-
Fat: 51	drates: 3 g
Total Fat: 6 g	Dietary Fiber: 0 g
Saturated Fat: 4 g	Sugars: 1 g
Cholesterol: 18 mg	Protein: 4 g

Hot Creamy Artichoke Spread

½ cup reduced-fat mayonnaise	115 g
1 (8 ounce) package reduced-fat cream cheese, softened	230 g
⅔ cup freshly grated parmesan or romano cheese	70 g
¼ teaspoon garlic powder or 1 clove garlic, minced	1 ml
1 (14 ounce) can artichoke hearts in water, drained	400 g
½ cup finely chopped green onions	50 g

Preheat oven to 350° (175° C).

Combine mayonnaise, cream cheese, parmesan cheese, garlic powder or garlic clove, ½ teaspoon (2 ml) salt and ¼ teaspoon (1 ml) pepper in food processor. Cover and process briefly. Add artichoke hearts and pulse briefly to leave artichoke chunks in mixture. Stir in green onions.

Transfer to 2-quart (2 L) baking dish. Bake uncovered for 30 minutes or until top browns. Serve hot.

Serves 24.
Serving size: ¼ cup (60 ml)
Makes 6 cups (1.4 L).

TIP: You can replace canned artichoke hearts with 1 (10 ounce/280 g) package frozen artichoke hearts.

One Serving

Calories: 58	Cholesterol: 8 mg	Dietary Fiber: 1 g
Calories from Fat: 36	Sodium: 161 mg	Sugars: 0 g
Total Fat: 4 g	Total Carbohydrates: 3 g	Protein: 3 g
Saturated Fat: 2 g		

Appetizers & Beverages

Caponata Relish

Caponata [kap-oh-NAH-tah] is a Sicilian dish served as a relish or a side dish.

2 cups diced celery	205 g
1½ cups diced onion	240 g
1 medium eggplant with peel, cut in ¾-inch cubes	1.8 cm
⅓ cup red wine vinegar	80 ml
1 (14 ounce) can diced tomatoes	400 g
1 tablespoon olive oil	15 ml
1 (4 ounce) can sliced ripe olives, drained	115 g

Combine celery, onion and 2 tablespoons (30 ml) water in microwave-safe bowl. Microwave on HIGH about 4 to 5 minutes, stirring once. Celery and onions should be very soft. Remove and set aside.

Microwave eggplant cubes in ¼ cup (60 ml) water in microwave-safe bowl on HIGH for about 7 to 9 minutes, stirring twice. Eggplant should be very soft. Remove and set aside.

Combine vinegar, tomatoes, 1 teaspoon (5 ml) salt and ¼ teaspoon pepper in nonstick 12-inch (32 cm) skillet. Cook, stirring occasionally, over medium heat for about 5 minutes. Add oil, celery-onion mixture, eggplant and olives to skillet. Reduce heat and simmer uncovered about 20 minutes or until most liquid evaporates.

Serves 20.
Serving size: ¼ cup (60 ml)
Makes 5 cups (1.2 L).

TIP: Dice means to cut food into uniform pieces, usually ⅛-inch to ¼-inch (.4 cm). Cube usually means to cut food into uniform ½-inch (1.2 cm) cubes.

One Serving

Calories: 29	Cholesterol: 0 mg	Dietary Fiber: 2 g
Calories from Fat: 12	Sodium: 72 mg	Sugars: 1 g
Total Fat: 1 g	Total Carbohydrates: 4 g	Protein: 1 g
Saturated Fat: 0 g		

Cumin-Mayo Spread

½ cup reduced-fat mayonnaise	115 g
1 teaspoon dijon-style mustard	5 ml
¼ teaspoon ground cumin	1 ml

Combine all ingredients in small bowl and mix well.

Serves 8.
Serving Size: 1 tablespoon (15 ml)
Makes ½ cup (125 ml).

TIP: Use with Guacamole Po' Boys (page 139).

One Serving

Calories: 46	Sodium: 106 mg
Calories from Fat: 43	Total Carbohy-drates: 1 g
Total Fat: 5 g	Dietary Fiber: 0 g
Saturated Fat: 1 g	Sugars: 1 g
Cholesterol: 0 mg	Protein: 0 g

All-Purpose Hummus

Hummus is a versatile vegetarian dish and can be served as an appetizer or filling for sandwiches.

1 (15 ounce) can garbanzo beans, rinsed, drained	425 g
¼ cup tahine (sesame paste)	65 g
3 tablespoons lemon juice	45 ml
1 garlic clove, peeled	
¼ teaspoon cumin	1 ml

Combine all ingredients, ½ teaspoon (2 ml) salt and ¼ teaspoon (1 ml) pepper in food processor or blender. Cover and process until smooth.

Serves 12.
Serving size: 2 tablespoons (30 ml)
Makes 1½ cups (375 ml).

TIP: For different texture and flavors, try with other beans such as cannellini or navy beans.

One Serving

Calories: 59	Sodium: 107 mg
Calories from Fat: 16	Total Carbohy-drates: 9 g
Total Fat: 2 g	Dietary Fiber: 2 g
Saturated Fat: 0 g	Sugars: 0 g
Cholesterol: 0 mg	Protein: 2 g

Dippin' Artichokes

Artichokes are delicious and definitely worth trying. Freshly cooked artichoke leaves are wonderful when dipped in lemon-butter sauce.

2 medium artichokes
1 lemon
¼ cup butter   60 g
¼ teaspoon dried tarragon leaves, crushed   1 ml

 Trim away tough outer leaves of artichokes. With heavy, sharp knife cut off 1-inch (2.5 cm) from tops and snip off sharp leaf tips with kitchen shears. Cut lemon in half and rub exposed cut leaves. Squeeze lemon juice from lemon halves and set aside.

Bring 3 quarts (3 L) water to a boil, add artichokes and 1 teaspoon (5 ml) salt. Return water to a boil, reduce heat and keep at slow boil, covered, about 30 minutes or until a leaf pulls out easily. Drain artichokes upside down on paper towels.

Melt butter and add 1 tablespoon (15 ml) lemon juice and tarragon.

Serve artichokes with butter sauce. Pull off one leaf at a time and dip into sauce. Draw base of leaf through your teeth and scrape off tender flesh. After leaves are pulled, remove artichoke heart with spoon or knife. Use a fork to eat the hearts and dip each piece into sauce.

Serves 2.
Serving size: 1 artichoke with butter sauce

TIP: Try dipping cold artichokes into ¼ cup (60 ml) reduced-fat mayonnaise combined with ½ teaspoon (2 ml) finely grated orange peel (zest).

One Serving

Calories: 264   Cholesterol: 61 mg   Dietary Fiber: 7 g
Calories from Fat: 207   Sodium: 124 mg   Sugars: 0 g
Total Fat: 23 g   Total Carbohydrates: 14 g   Protein: 4 g
Saturated Fat: 15 g

Marinated Vegetables

Hearts of palm are the inner edible portion of the stem of the swamp cabbage palm tree, Florida's official state tree. The stems resemble white asparagus without the tips and are a boon to dieters.

1 (16 ounce) carton fresh mushrooms	455 g
1 (6 ounce) can large pitted ripe olives, drained	170 g
1 (14 ounce) can artichoke hearts, drained, quartered	400 g
1 (14 ounce) jar hearts of palm, drained	400 g
1 (15 ounce) jar baby corn, drained	425 g
½ cup Classic Italian Dressing (page 107)	125 ml

Clean mushrooms with damp cloth and cut large ones in half.

Combine mushrooms, olives, artichoke hearts, hearts of palm and baby corn in large bowl.

Pour Classic Italian Dressing over vegetables and toss to coat. Refrigerate 6 hours or overnight.

Serves 16.
Serving size: ½ cup (125 ml)
Makes 8 cups (1.9 L).

TIP: It works out best if all mushrooms are uniform in size.

One Serving

Calories: 78	Sodium: 299 mg
Calories from Fat: 36	Total Carbohydrates: 7 g
Total Fat: 12 g	Dietary Fiber: 3 g
Saturated Fat: 1 g	Sugars: 1 g
Cholesterol: 0 mg	Protein: 2 g

Peperonata

Peperonata is an Italian dish used hot as a condiment or cold as an antipasto.

2 cups thinly sliced yellow onions	230 g
1 cup slivered green bell pepper	95 g
1 cup slivered red bell pepper	95 g
3-6 garlic cloves, minced	

Add all ingredients to sprayed non-stick 10-inch (25 cm) skillet, cook over medium-high heat for 5 minutes and stir occasionally.

Add ¼ cup (60 ml) water and cook over medium-low heat, covered, about 20 to 25 minutes or until vegetables are very tender. Uncover and cook until liquid has evaporated. Season with ½ teaspoon (2 ml) salt and ¼ teaspoon (1 ml) pepper.

Serves 8.
Serving size: ¼ cup (60 ml)
Makes 2 cups (500 ml).

TIP: This is great served with toasted Italian or French bread slices.

One Serving

Calories: 26	Sodium: 3 mg
Calories from Fat: 1	Total Carbohydrates: 6 g
Total Fat: 0 g	Dietary Fiber: 1 g
Saturated Fat: 0 g	Sugars: 3 g
Cholesterol: 0 mg	Protein: 1 g

Nancy's Stuffed Mushrooms

A friend gave me this recipe and I have used it a hundred times.

1 (16 ounce) package large (1½ - 2 inch diameter) fresh mushrooms	**455 g/3 cm**
¼ cup finely chopped onion	**40 g**
¼ cup chopped ripe olives	**35 g**
¼ cup grated parmesan cheese	**25 g**
1 tablespoon reduced-fat mayonnaise	**15 ml**
⅔ cup fine breadcrumbs	**80 g**

Preheat oven to 425° (220° C).

Clean mushrooms with damp cloth, remove stems and set aside caps. Finely chop stems to make 1 cup. Cook and stir chopped mushroom stems and onion in sprayed 10-inch (25 cm) skillet over medium heat and stir until tender.

Transfer cooked mushroom mixture and liquid to medium bowl and add olives, cheese, mayonnaise and breadcrumbs. Stir and add ½ teaspoon (2 ml) salt and ⅛ teaspoon (.5 ml) pepper.

Place mushroom caps on wax paper. Spray both sides with non-stick cooking spray. Arrange stem-side up on baking sheet. Spoon filling into mushroom caps.

Bake about 8 to 10 minutes or until hot.

Serves 12.
Serving size: 2 stuffed mushrooms

TIP: You may have to purchase two packages of mushrooms to get uniform size. Also, spraying caps before baking will prevent drying during baking.

One Serving

Calories: 54	Cholesterol: 4 mg	Dietary Fiber: 0 g
Calories from Fat: 32	Sodium: 128 mg	Sugars: 2 g
Total Fat: 4 g	Total Carbohydrates: 2 g	Protein: 4 g
Saturated Fat: 0 g		

Spinach Quesadillas

Easy, delicious quesadillas for skillet or electric quesadilla maker

1 (10 ounce) package frozen chopped spinach, thawed	280 g
½ cup part-skim ricotta cheese	125 g
¼ cup roasted red pepper strips	25 g
¼ cup thinly sliced green onions	25 g
4 (7 inch) flour tortillas	4 (18 cm)

Squeeze spinach between paper towels to completely remove excess moisture. Add spinach, ricotta cheese, red pepper and green onion to medium bowl. Add ½ teaspoon (2 ml) salt and ¼ teaspoon (1 ml) pepper and mix lightly.

On one side of each tortilla, mound 2 to 3 tablespoons (30 - 45 ml) spinach mixture and lightly pack. Fold tortilla gently in half.

Cook folded tortillas in sprayed non-stick 12-inch (32 cm) skillet over medium heat until light brown, about 5 minutes. Turn carefully with spatula and cook other side for about 3 minutes.

To use electric quesadilla maker, use 2 tortillas with filling and cook according to manufacturer's directions.

Slide hot quesadillas onto serving plates and serve.

Serves 4.
Serving size: 1 quesadilla

TIP: When making folded quesadillas or rolled enchiladas, regular flour tortillas are easier to handle than whole wheat tortillas. However, warming makes the whole wheat tortillas more pliable.

One Serving

Calories: 208	Cholesterol: 10 mg	Dietary Fiber: 4 g
Calories from Fat: 59	Sodium: 384 mg	Sugars: 1 g
Total Fat: 6 g	Total Carbohydrates: 28 g	Protein: 10 g
Saturated Fat: 2 g		

Kid Friendly Quesadillas

It's fun to assemble the ingredients on a tray so kids can make their own quesadillas.

2 (10 inch) whole wheat,
    multigrain or vegetable-
    based tortillas   2 (25 cm)
Canola oil non-stick cooking spray
½ cup reduced-fat lightly packed
    shredded Monterey
    Jack cheese, divided   60 g

Preheat oven broiler.

Place tortillas on wax paper and lightly spray tortillas on both sides. Transfer to baking sheet and broil 4 inches from broiler until warm, about 1 minute.

Remove baking sheet and spread ¼ cup (30 g) cheese evenly on each tortilla. Broil until cheese melts and cut each tortilla into 4 wedges.

Serves 4.
Serving size: 2 wedges

One Serving

Calories: 181	Sodium: 398 mg
Calories from Fat: 181	Total Carbohy-drates: 38 g
Total Fat: 15 g	Dietary Fiber: 2 g
Saturated Fat: 7 g	Sugars: 2 g
Cholesterol: 37 mg	Protein: 20 g

Nutty Butter Balls

These tasty tidbits will disappear before you can get them all made!

¼ cup peanut butter   75 g
2 tablespoons nonfat dry
    milk powder   15 g
¼ cup chopped unsalted
    dry-roasted peanuts   45 g

Combine peanut butter and milk powder in small bowl. Form mixture into 1-inch (2.5 cm) balls. Roll balls in chopped peanuts. Serve or refrigerate.

Serves 4.
Serving size: 2 balls (1 inch/2.5 cm)
Makes 8 balls.

TIP: You can also use soy or almond butter instead of peanut butter.

One Serving

Calories: 217	Sodium: 28 mg
Calories from Fat: 156	Total Carbohy-drates: 30 g
Total Fat: 18 g	Fiber: 2 g
Saturated: 4 g	Sugars: 4 g
Cholesterol: 0 mg	Protein: 10 g

Microwave Toasted Pecans

These delicious pecans will disappear quickly at a party.

2 cups pecan halves	230 g
2 tablespoons butter, melted	30 g
1½ teaspoons seasoning salt	7 ml

Combine pecans, butter and seasoning salt in microwave-safe baking dish. Microwave on HIGH for 1 minute.

Stir pecans with wooden spoon until thoroughly coated. Return to microwave and cook on HIGH for 4 to 5 minutes. Stop and stir once or twice. Spread on paper towels to cool.

Serves 16.
Serving size: 2 tablespoons (30 ml)

TIP: To toast pecans in conventional oven, combine pecans, butter and seasoning salt. Arrange in a single layer on baking sheet. Bake at 250° (120° C) for 1 hour, stirring every 15 minutes.

One Serving

Calories: 98	Sodium: 148 mg
Calories from Fat: 93	Total Carbohydrates: 2 g
Total Fat: 10 g	Dietary Fiber: 1 g
Saturated Fat: 2 g	Sugars: 1 g
Cholesterol: 4 mg	Protein: 1 g

Pita Crisps

Here's a simple way to economize by making your own pita crisps. Let the kids help.

2 large whole wheat pita breads	
Olive oil non-stick cooking spray	
½ teaspoon garlic salt	2 ml
2 tablespoons dried dill weed	30 ml

Preheat oven to 400° (205° C).

Slice each pita in half. On wax paper, spray pita halves on both sides. Combine garlic and dill weed in small mixing bowl and sprinkle tops of pita halves. Cut each half into 8 wedges.

Arrange pita wedges on sprayed baking sheet and bake 8 to 10 minutes or until light brown and crisp. Store in airtight container.

Serves 10 to 12.
Serving size: 3 pita wedges

One Serving

Calories: 21	Sodium: 43 mg
Calories from Fat: 2	Total Carbohydrates: 4 g
Total Fat: 0 g	Dietary Fiber: 1 g
Saturated Fat: 0 g	Sugars: 0 g
Cholesterol: 0 mg	Protein: 1 g

Banana Smoothie

What a healthy, delicious drink!

1 medium banana
¼ cup fat-free skim milk — 60 ml
¼ cup fat-free plain yogurt — 60 g
1 teaspoon honey — 5 ml
½ teaspoon vanilla — 2 ml

Combine all ingredients in blender and mix until smooth and creamy.

Serves 1.
Serving size: 1 smoothie

One Serving

Calories: 168	Sodium: 54 mg
Calories from Fat: 0	Total Carbohy-drates: 39 g
Total Fat: 0 g	Dietary Fiber: 3 g
Saturated Fat: 0 g	Sugars: 26 g
Cholesterol: 0 mg	Protein: 5g

Orange Smoothie

This makes a nutritious snack when you need a lift.

1 (1 quart) carton frozen reduced-fat vanilla yogurt — 910 g
½ cup frozen orange juice concentrate, thawed — 125 ml
½ cup light plain soymilk — 125 ml

Combine all ingredients in food processor or blender.

Cover and process about 45 seconds until thick and smooth. Stop food processor once or twice to scrape sides.

Serves 4.
Serving size: 1 cup (250 ml)

TIP: Try different frozen fruit juice concentrates to make your own favorite concoction.

One Serving

Calories: 345	Sodium: 175 mg
Calories from Fat: 59	Total Carbohy-drates: 69 g
Total Fat: 7 g	Dietary Fiber: 1 g
Saturated Fat: 4 g	Sugars: 67 g
Cholesterol: 20 mg	Protein: 10 g

Fresh Strawberry Smoothie

*Fortunately, fresh strawberries
are available almost year-round
and this is so good!*

1 pint (2 cups) fresh strawberries	360 g
1 cup light plain soymilk	250 ml
2 (6 ounce) cartons reduced-fat strawberry or vanilla yogurt	2 (170 g)

Set aside a few whole strawberries for garnish.

Cut out hulls (stem ends) from remaining strawberries. Add trimmed strawberries, soymilk and yogurt to blender or food processor. If desired, add about ½ cup crushed ice. Cover and process about 30 seconds until smooth. Garnish with whole strawberries.

Serves 4.
Serving size: 1 cup (250 ml)

TIP: Try with fat-free skim milk and reduced-fat frozen yogurt. Frozen strawberries also work well.

One Serving

Calories: 136	Sodium: 84 mg
Calories from Fat: 13	Total Carbohydrates: 25 g
Total Fat: 2 g	Dietary Fiber: 2 g
Saturated Fat: 0 g	Sugars: 20 g
Cholesterol: 0 mg	Protein: 7 g

Tropical Smoothie

*Pineapple, orange and banana
combine for an icy cold treat.
Pretend you're back in the islands.*

2 ripe bananas	
1 cup unsweetened pineapple juice, chilled	250 ml
½ cup orange juice, chilled	125 ml
1 cup reduced-fat frozen vanilla yogurt	230 g

Peel bananas, cut into 2-inch (5 cm) pieces and wrap in plastic wrap. Freeze for at least 1 hour.

Combine all ingredients in food processor or blender and process until smooth.

Pour into glasses and serve at once.

Serves 2 to 3.
Serving size: 1 cup (250 ml)

One Serving

Calories: 199	Sodium: 53 mg
Calories from Fat: 7	Total Carbohydrates: 45 g
Total Fat: 1 g	Dietary Fiber: 3 g
Saturated Fat: 0 g	Sugars: 30 g
Cholesterol: 0 mg	Protein: 4 g

Tofu Honey Smoothie

Here's a healthy treat for smoothie lovers.

2 medium ripe bananas
1 (16 ounce) carton
 silken tofu 455 g
½ cup crushed ice 115 ml
3 tablespoons honey 65 g
¼ teaspoon almond extract
 or vanilla 1 ml

Peel bananas and cut into 1-inch (2.5 cm) pieces. Cover tightly with plastic wrap and freeze at least 2 hours.

Combine all ingredients in blender or food processor and process until smooth.

Serves 4.
Serving size: 1 cup (250 ml)

One Serving

Calories: 161	Sodium: 73 mg
Calories from Fat: 22	Total Carbohydrates: 27 g
Total Fat: 4 g	Dietary Fiber: 2 g
Saturated Fat: 0 g	Sugars: 20 g
Cholesterol: 0 mg	Protein: 9 g

Orange Nog

Traditionally, nog, the nickname for eggnog, is any beverage made with beaten egg, milk and usually liquor.

1 (1 pint) carton frozen
 reduced-fat vanilla yogurt 455 g
⅓ cup frozen orange juice
 concentrate 75 ml
¼ cup egg substitute 60 g
2 cups fat-free skim milk 500 ml
Ground nutmeg

Mix yogurt, orange juice concentrate and egg substitute in food processor or blender. Gradually add milk while processing. Pour into 4 glasses and sprinkle nutmeg on top.

Serves 4.
Serving size: 1 cup (250 ml)

TIP: For a less rich taste, omit the egg substitute.

One Serving

Calories: 231	Sodium: 145 mg
Calories from Fat: 7	Total Carbohydrates: 47 g
Total Fat: 1 g	Dietary Fiber: 1 g
Saturated Fat: 0 g	Sugars: 40 g
Cholesterol: 0 mg	Protein: 9 g

Hot Cranberry Percolator Punch

9 cups reduced-calorie cranberry juice	2.1 L
9 cups unsweetened pineapple juice	2.1 L
1 cup packed brown sugar	220 g
4½ teaspoons whole cloves	22 ml
4 cinnamon sticks, broken in pieces	

Combine cranberry juice, pineapple juice, 4½ cups (1.1 L) water and brown sugar in 30-cup (7.1 L) automatic coffeemaker.

Add cloves, cinnamon sticks and ¼ teaspoon (1 ml) salt to coffeemaker basket. Brew according to manufacturer's directions and serve piping hot.

Makes about 23 cups.
Serving size: 1 cup (250 ml)

One Serving

Calories: 105	Sodium: 8 mg
Calories from Fat: 0	Total Carbohydrates: 26 g
Total Fat: 0 g	Dietary Fiber: 0 g
Saturated Fat: 0 g	Sugars: 23 g
Cholesterol: 0 mg	Protein: 0 g

Chai Tea

Chai is black tea brewed with a combination of spices diluted with milk and sugar. The spices usually consist of cinnamon, cardamom, cloves, pepper and ginger. Honey brings out the flavor of the spices.

1½ sticks cinnamon	
6 whole cloves	
¼-inch fresh ginger root, thinly sliced	.6 cm
1 cup 2% reduced-fat milk	250 ml
4 teaspoons honey	20 ml
2 English breakfast or Earl Grey tea bags	

Combine cinnamon, cloves, ginger root and 2 cups (480 ml) water in 2-quart (2 L) saucepan. Bring to a boil. Reduce heat to simmer and cover. Simmer for 10 minutes.

Stir in milk and honey and heat to simmer. Add tea bags, remove from heat and cover. Steep for 5 minutes and strain. Whisk until frothy.

Serves 3.
Serving size: 1 cup (250 ml)

TIP: No time to make chai from scratch? Look for tea bags with chai spices or bottled chai spice blend.

One Serving

Calories: 103	Sodium: 51 mg
Calories from Fat: 27	Total Carbohydrates: 18 g
Total Fat: 3 g	Dietary Fiber: 0 g
Saturated Fat: 2 g	Sugars: 18 g
Cholesterol: 10 mg	Protein: 4 g

Spiced Chai Tea

Very refreshing and you can vary ingredients to suit your particular taste preferences. Ground spices speed preparation of this tea.

4 regular black tea bags
2 cups fat-free skim milk or
    light plain soymilk   500 ml
1 tablespoon honey   15 ml
¼ teaspoon ground ginger   1 ml
¼ teaspoon ground nutmeg   1 ml
¼ teaspoon ground
    cinnamon   1 ml

Bring 2 cups (500 ml) water in 2-quart (2 L) saucepan to a boil over medium-high heat. Add tea bags and reduce heat. Simmer uncovered 2 minutes. Discard tea bags.

Stir in remaining ingredients and heat to a boil. Whisk to blend spices.

Serves 4.
Serving size: 1 cup (250 ml)

TIP: Treat yourself to a cup of spiced chai tea instead of a high-calorie dessert.

One Serving

Calories: 58	Sodium: 52 mg
Calories from	Total Carbohy-
Fat: 0	drates: 10 g
Total Fat: 0 g	Dietary Fiber: 0 g
Saturated Fat: 0 g	Sugars: 10 g
Cholesterol: 0 mg	Protein: 4 g

Mexican Hot Chocolate

Definitely worth a little preparation time. Even if you omit the egg products, you still have a delicious hot chocolate.

6 cups light plain soymilk
    or fat-free skim milk   1.4 L
1 cinnamon stick
1 teaspoon vanilla   5 ml
6 (1 ounce) squares unsweetened
    chocolate, grated   6 (30 g)
1 egg yolk
2 egg whites, beaten until stiff
Coarse brown sugar

Combine soymilk, cinnamon stick and vanilla in non-stick 2-quart (2 L) saucepan over medium-low heat. Bring to simmer and stir in chocolate. Do not boil.

Stir chocolate mixture until it mixes thoroughly, add egg yolk and whisk rapidly. Whisk in egg whites all at once. Sweeten with brown sugar. Serve immediately.

Serves 6.
Serving size: 1 cup (250 ml)

TIP: You can substitute natural sugar or turbinado for brown sugar, if you like. Golden turbinado is raw sugar that is steam cleaned. The crystals have a texture like kosher salt.

One Serving

Calories: 288	Sodium: 161 mg
Calories from	Total Carbohy-
Fat: 192	drates: 21 g
Total Fat: 21 g	Dietary Fiber: 8 g
Saturated Fat: 10 g	Sugars: 2 g
Cholesterol: 35 mg	Protein: 16 g

Salads
&
Salad
Dressings

Contents

Apple, Grape and Walnut Salad

Colorful, crunchy and fresh flavors make this salad stand out.

2 cups diced Granny Smith apples with peels	250 g
1 cup halved seedless green or red grapes	155 g
½ cup Craisins®	60 g
¼ cup toasted walnut pieces	65 g
1 cup reduced-fat vanilla yogurt	230 g

Combine apple, grapes, Craisins® and walnuts. Fold in yogurt.

Serves 4.
Serving size: 1 cup (250 ml)

TIP: Toasting brings out the flavors of nuts and seeds. Place nuts or seeds on baking sheet and bake at 225° (110° C) for 10 minutes. Be careful not to burn them.

One Serving

Calories: 205	Sodium: 43 mg
Calories from Fat: 49	Total Carbohydrates: 37 g
Total Fat: 6 g	Dietary Fiber: 3 g
Saturated Fat: 1 g	Sugars: 31 g
Cholesterol: 3 mg	Protein: 5 g

Apple-Raisin Slaw

Crunchy slaw of apple and celery is sweetened with raisins for a very pleasant salad.

1 (10 ounce) package coleslaw mix	280 g
1 large red delicious apple with peel, diced	
2 large celery stalks, sliced diagonally	
⅓ cup dark or golden raisins	50 g
½ cup reduced-fat mayonnaise	115 g
2 teaspoons lemon juice	10 ml

Combine slaw, apple, celery and raisins in large bowl. Combine mayonnaise and lemon juice in small bowl and pour over slaw mixture. Toss lightly.

Serves 6 to 8.
Serving size: ¾ cup (175 ml)

One Serving

Calories: 73	Sodium: 36 mg
Calories from Fat: 25	Total Carbohydrates: 13 g
Total Fat: 3 g	Dietary Fiber: 2 g
Saturated Fat: 1 g	Sugars: 8 g
Cholesterol: 3 mg	Protein: 1 g

Next time you purchase grapes, place a few clusters in the freezer. When you need a lift, the frozen grapes will pick you right up!

Banana-Apple Salad

Fresh and dried fruit with the delicious crunch of toasted nuts are very good together.

4 ripe firm bananas, peeled, sliced

2 teaspoons grated orange peel   10 ml

2 tablespoons orange juice   30 ml

3 medium red delicious apples with peels, diced

¼ cup pecan pieces, toasted   30 g

½ cup dark raisins   80 g

½ cup reduced-fat vanilla yogurt   115 g

Combine bananas, orange peel and orange juice in mixing bowl. Stir to coat bananas. Add apples, nuts and raisins and gently stir. Refrigerate until serving time. Spoon yogurt onto each serving.

Serves 4 to 6.
Serving size: ¾ cup (175 ml)

TIP: *If you don't like raisins, substitute Craisins® or sweetened dried cherries. Toasting brings out the flavors of nuts and seeds. Place nuts or seeds on baking sheet and bake at 225° (110° C) for 10 minutes. Be careful not to burn them.*

One Serving

Calories: 200	Sodium: 16 mg
Calories from Fat: 33	Total Carbohy-drates: 43 g
Total Fat: 4 g	Dietary Fiber: 5 g
Saturated Fat: 1 g	Sugars: 29 g
Cholesterol: 1 mg	Protein: 3 g

New Waldorf Salad

2 cups diced red or golden delicious apples   250 g

1 cup diced celery   105 g

½ cup Craisins®   60 g

½ cup coarsely chopped pecans or walnuts, toasted   60 g

2 tablespoons reduced-fat mayonnaise   30 g

½ teaspoon lemon juice   2 ml

1 cup reduced-fat frozen whipped topping, thawed   75 g

Combine apple, celery, Craisins® and nuts in large bowl.

In separate bowl, combine mayonnaise and lemon juice and fold in whipped topping. Add whipped topping mixture to apple mixture and toss lightly. Refrigerate until serving time.

Serves 6.
Serving size: ¾ cup (175 ml)

TIP: *Toasting brings out the flavors of nuts and seeds. Place nuts or seeds on baking sheet and bake at 225° (110° C) for 10 minutes. Be careful not to burn them.*

One Serving

Calories: 167	Sodium: 33 mg
Calories from Fat: 88	Total Carbohy-drates: 20 g
Total Fat: 10 g	Dietary Fiber: 3 g
Saturated Fat: 2 g	Sugars: 15 g
Cholesterol: 2 mg	Protein: 2 g

Grapefruit-Red Onion Salad

Grapefruit sections or sliced oranges work equally well in this salad.

Bibb lettuce leaves
1 (24 ounce) jar pink grapefruit
   sections, drained   680 g
½ medium red onion,
   thinly sliced
¼ cup Poppy Seed Dressing
   (page 110)   60 ml

Line salad plates with lettuce leaves. Arrange grapefruit sections and onions on leaves. Drizzle with Poppy Seed Dressing and serve.

Serves 4 to 6.
Serving size: 1 cup (250 ml)

TIP: Replace bibb lettuce with red or green leafy lettuce, if you like.

One Serving

Calories: 97	Sodium: 8 mg
Calories from Fat: 56	Total Carbohydrates: 12 g
Total Fat: 6 g	Dietary Fiber: 0 g
Saturated Fat: 1 g	Sugars: 8 g
Cholesterol: 0 mg	Protein: 0 g

Double Pineapple Salad

1 (8 ounce) can crushed
   pineapple with juice   230 g
½ cup golden raisins   80 g
1 (15 ounce) can chunk pineapple
   with juice, drained   425 g
2 cups diced celery   205 g
1 (8 ounce) container reduced-fat
   frozen whipped topping,
   thawed   230 g

Drain crushed pineapple and set aside juice.

Combine juice and raisins in 1-quart (1 L) saucepan and bring to a boil. Remove from heat, let stand 10 minutes to plump raisins; then drain.

Combine drained chunk pineapple, raisins and celery in large bowl. In separate bowl, combine crushed pineapple and whipped topping and add to pineapple chunk mixture. Toss lightly. Cover and refrigerate until serving time.

Serves 6 to 8.
Serving size: ¾ cup (175 ml)

TIP: You can turn this salad into a dessert if you replace celery and raisins with chopped dates and macadamia nuts. It makes a delicious pineapple dessert.

One Serving

Calories: 99	Sodium: 29 mg
Calories from Fat: 12	Total Carbohydrates: 22 g
Total Fat: 1 g	Dietary Fiber: 2 g
Saturated Fat: 1 g	Sugars: 19 g
Cholesterol: 0 mg	Protein: 1 g

Orange-Romaine Salad

4 cups torn romaine lettuce
    leaves   160 g
1 medium navel orange,
    peeled, thinly sliced
½ cucumber, thinly sliced
½ medium onion, diced or slivered
½ green bell pepper, diced or
    slivered
½ cup canola oil   125 ml
⅓ cup red wine vinegar   75 ml

Combine lettuce, orange, cucumber, onion and bell pepper in large bowl. Combine oil, vinegar, ½ teaspoon (2 ml) salt and ⅛ teaspoon (.5 ml) pepper in small bowl.

Pour vinegar mixture over lettuce mixture and toss.

Serves 8.
Serving size: 1 cup (250 ml)

One Serving

Calories: 64	Sodium: 1 mg
Calories from Fat: 62	Total Carbohydrates: 0 g
Total Fat: 7 g	Dietary Fiber: 0 g
Saturated Fat: 1 g	Sugars: 0 g
Cholesterol: 0 mg	Protein: 0 g

Favorite Creamy Fruit Salad

This popular recipe shows up repeatedly at family gatherings and church socials.

1 (8 ounce) carton reduced-fat
    small curd cottage
    cheese, drained   230 g
1 (3 ounce) package
    sugar-free fat-free gelatin   85 g
1 (8 ounce) container frozen
    reduced-fat whipped
    topping, thawed   230 g
1 (8 ounce) can crushed
    pineapple, drained   230 g

Combine cottage cheese and gelatin. Fold in whipped topping and pineapple. Refrigerate at least 1 hour before serving.

Serves 6.
Serving size: ¾ cup (175 ml)

TIP: Orange and lime gelatin are favorites for this salad. If you use orange gelatin, replace pineapple with 1 (8 ounce/230 g) can mandarin oranges, drained.

One Serving

Calories: 101	Sodium: 315 mg
Calories from Fat: 21	Total Carbohydrates: 10 g
Total Fat: 2 g	Dietary Fiber: 1 g
Saturated Fat: 2 g	Sugars: 10 g
Cholesterol: 3 mg	Protein: 10 g

Pear-Walnut-Cheese Salad

Fresh lemon juice	
2 medium pears, cored, sliced	
8 cups butter lettuce or mixed salad greens	440 g
2 tablespoons walnut pieces, toasted	20 g
¼ cup cheddar cheese crumbles	35 g
4 teaspoons canola oil	20 ml
3 teaspoons red wine vinegar	15 ml

Sprinkle lemon juice over pear slices to prevent discoloration.

Combine lettuce, walnuts, cheese, oil and vinegar in large bowl and toss. Divide into individual servings and arrange pear slices on top.

Serves 6 to 8.
Serving size: 1½ cups (375 ml)

TIP: Toasting brings out the flavors of nuts and seeds. Place nuts or seeds on baking sheet and bake at 225° (110° C) for 10 minutes. Be careful not to burn them.

One Serving

Calories: 111	Sodium: 31 mg
Calories from Fat: 65	Total Carbohydrates: 10 g
Total Fat: 7 g	Dietary Fiber: 3 g
Saturated Fat: 2 g	Sugars: 5 g
Cholesterol: 9 mg	Protein: 4 g

Cottage Cheese Scramble

Radishes and water chestnuts add a very pleasing crunchiness to this salad.

2 tablespoons thinly sliced green onions	15 g
2 radishes, thinly sliced	
½ cup cucumber, peeled, quartered, thinly sliced	60 g
½ cup sliced water chestnuts, rinsed, drained	70 g
2 cups reduced-fat cottage cheese, well drained	250 g
2 tablespoons reduced-fat sour cream	30 g

Combine green onions, radishes, cucumber, water chestnuts and cottage cheese. Add ½ teaspoon (2 ml) salt and ¼ teaspoon (1 ml) pepper. Stir in sour cream. (You may need to drain before serving.)

Serves 4.
Serving size: ½ cup (125 ml)

One Serving

Calories: 119	Sodium: 471 mg
Calories from Fat: 28	Total Carbohydrates: 7 g
Total Fat: 3 g	Dietary Fiber: 1 g
Saturated Fat: 2 g	Sugars: 4 g
Cholesterol: 10 mg	Protein: 15 g

Jack Cheese Salad

1½ cups diced or shredded Monterey Jack cheese	170 g
¼ cup sliced green onions	25 g
1 cup sliced celery	105 g
1 tablespoon reduced-fat mayonnaise	15 ml
2 tablespoons Italiano Vinaigrette (page 107)	30 ml

Combine cheese, green onions and celery in medium bowl. In smaller bowl, combine mayonnaise and Italiano Vinaigrette. Pour mayonnaise mixture over cheese mixture and toss.

Serves 4 to 6.
Serving size: ½ cup (125 ml)

One Serving

Calories: 197	Sodium: 195 mg
Calories from Fat: 157	Total Carbohy- drates: 2 g
Total Fat: 18 g	Dietary Fiber: 0 g
Saturated Fat: 7 g	Sugars: 1 g
Cholesterol: 30 mg	Protein: 8 g

Mushroom-Cheese-Walnut Salad

6 cups romaine lettuce leaves, torn in bite-size pieces	280 g
1 cup sliced fresh mushrooms	75 g
2 tablespoons thinly sliced green onions	15 g
2 tablespoons walnut pieces, toasted	20 g
2 tablespoons crumbled blue cheese	20 g
8 cherry tomatoes, halved	
2 tablespoons Favorite French Dressing (page 105)	30 ml

Combine lettuce, mushrooms, green onions and walnuts in large bowl and toss lightly. When ready to serve, add blue cheese, tomatoes and Favorite French Dressing and toss.

Serves 6 to 8.
Serving size: 1 cup (250 ml)

TIP: Toasting brings out the flavors of nuts and seeds. Place nuts or seeds on baking sheet and bake at 225° (110° C) for 10 minutes. Be careful not to burn them.

One Serving

Calories: 77	Sodium: 63 mg
Calories from Fat: 61	Total Carbohy- drates: 2 g
Total Fat: 7 g	Dietary Fiber: 1 g
Saturated Fat: 2 g	Sugars: 1 g
Cholesterol: 3 mg	Protein: 3 g

Garden Pasta Salad

8 ounces (2 cups) whole wheat rotini (spirals)	230 g
½ cup frozen whole corn kernels, thawed	85 g
½ cup finely diced red bell pepper	75 g
½ cup finely diced carrots	65 g
¼ cup finely sliced green onions	25 g
⅓ cup Mayo-Mustard Dressing (page 109)	75 ml

 Prepare rotini according to package directions. Drain and transfer to large bowl and cool.

 Add corn, bell pepper, carrots and green onions. Stir Mayo -Mustard Dressing into pasta to moisten.

Serves 6.
Serving size: 1 cup (250 ml)
Makes 6 cups (1.4 L).

One Serving

Calories: 153	Sodium: 72 mg
Calories from Fat: 33	Total Carbohy-drates: 26 g
Total Fat: 4 g	Dietary Fiber: 4 g
Saturated Fat: 0 g	Sugars: 1 g
Cholesterol: 0 mg	Protein: 4 g

Picnic Macaroni Salad

1 (12 ounce) package whole wheat elbow macaroni	340 g
1 cup thinly sliced celery	105 g
½ cup sliced green onions	50 g
1 cup cheddar cheese crumbles or ½-inch cubes	135 g/1.2 cm
¼ cup chopped sweet pickles	40 g
⅓ cup Mayo-Mustard Dressing (page 109)	75 ml
2 cups halved cherry tomatoes	280 g

 Prepare macaroni according to package directions. Drain and cool. To further drain, spread macaroni between paper towels and gently roll.

 Combine macaroni, celery, green onions, cheese and pickles in large bowl. Fold in just enough Mayo-Mustard Dressing to moisten macaroni mixture. Cover and refrigerate 6 hours or overnight. Add tomatoes before serving.

Serves 12.
Serving size: ¾ cup (175 ml)
Makes 9 cups (2.1 L)

One Serving

Calories: 171	Sodium: 155 mg
Calories from Fat: 50	Total Carbohy-drates: 24 g
Total Fat: 5 g	Dietary Fiber: 3 g
Saturated Fat: 2 g	Sugars: 3 g
Cholesterol: 10 mg	Protein: 6 g

Southwestern Wagon Wheel Salad

Wagon wheel macaroni is also known as rotelle.

4 cups wagon wheel macaroni or whole wheat elbow macaroni	300 g
1 (16 ounce) can pinto beans, drained, rinsed	455 g
1 cup frozen whole kernel corn, thawed, drained	165 g
½ cup finely chopped green, red or yellow bell pepper	75 g
½ cup chopped or sliced kalamata olives	65 g
1 cup Pico de Gallo (page 54)	250 ml

Prepare macaroni according to package directions. Drain and cool.

Combine macaroni, pinto beans, corn, bell pepper and olives in large bowl and toss.

Before serving, add Pico de Gallo and toss again.

Serves 8.
Serving size: ¾ cup (175 ml)
Makes 6 cups (1.4 L).

One Serving

Calories: 277	Sodium: 254 mg
Calories from Fat: 8	Total Carbohydrates: 55 g
Total Fat: 1 g	Dietary Fiber: 9 g
Saturated Fat: 0 g	Sugars: 1 g
Cholesterol: 0 mg	Protein: 11 g

Vegetable Medley Bowtie Salad

Bowtie is also known as farfalle pasta. In Italian, farfalle is taken from the word for butterfly.

8 ounces (2 cups) bowtie pasta	230 g
2 cups bite-size broccoli florets	145 g
1 cup bite-size cauliflower florets	100 g
1 cup diced green or red bell pepper	150 g
1 cup frozen whole kernel corn, thawed, drained	165 g
⅓ cup Creamy Goddess Dressing (page 104)	75 ml

Prepare pasta according to package directions. Just before pasta is done, add broccoli, cauliflower and bell pepper to boiling water. Cook 1 to 2 minutes.

Drain pasta and vegetables and combine with corn in large bowl. Toss lightly with small amount of Creamy Goddess Dressing to moisten.

Serves 9.
Serving size: 1 cup (250 ml)
Makes 9 cups (2.1 L).

One Serving

Calories: 148	Sodium: 6 mg
Calories from Fat: 9	Total Carbohydrates: 28 g
Total Fat: 1 g	Dietary Fiber: 4 g
Saturated Fat: 0 g	Sugars: 1 g
Cholesterol: 0 mg	Protein: 4 g

Asparagus with Basil Vinaigrette

1 pound or 20 spears fresh asparagus, trimmed	455 g
2 tablespoons Basil Vinaigrette (page 102)	30 ml
1 egg, hard-boiled, chopped	

Add asparagus and ½ cup (125 ml) water to non-stick 12-inch (32 cm) skillet. Bring to a boil over medium-high heat.

Cover and cook 3 to 5 minutes, just until stalks become tender. Drain and spread stalks on paper towels to cool.

Arrange asparagus on serving platter and drizzle with Basil Vinaigrette. Sprinkle with chopped egg.

Serves 4.
Serving size: 5 asparagus spears

One Serving

Calories: 87	Sodium: 20 mg
Calories from Fat: 54	Total Carbohydrates: 5 g
Total Fat: 6 g	Dietary Fiber: 2 g
Saturated Fat: 1 g	Sugars: 2 g
Cholesterol: 53 mg	Protein: 4 g

Pronto Southwest Salad

This hearty rice salad combines the goodness of black beans, corn and spicy green chile sauce.

2 cups cooked brown rice	390 g
1 (16 ounce) can black beans, drained, rinsed	455 g
1 cup frozen whole kernel corn, thawed	165 g
½ - 1 cup Green Chile Sauce (page 238) or bottled mild salsa verde	125 - 250 ml
Lime wedges	

Combine rice, black beans, corn and Green Chile Sauce and stir until they mix. Serve with lime wedges.

Serves 6.
Serving size: 1 cup (250 ml)

TIP: In a hurry? Use precooked microwave brown rice pouches.

One Serving

Calories: 184	Sodium: 281 mg
Calories from Fat: 15	Total Carbohydrates: 37 g
Total Fat: 2 g	Dietary Fiber: 5 g
Saturated Fat: 0 g	Sugars: 1 g
Cholesterol: 0 mg	Protein: 6 g

Kidney Bean Salad

Some different ingredients add zest to this traditional dish.

1 (15 ounce) can dark kidney beans, drained, rinsed	425 g
2 cups chopped celery	205 g
1 tablespoon finely chopped red onion	15 ml
½ cup chopped walnuts, toasted	65 g
4 small sweet pickles, chopped	
2 tablespoons canola oil	30 ml
1½ tablespoons red wine vinegar	22 ml

Combine beans, celery, red onion, nuts and pickles in large bowl. Combine oil, vinegar, ½ teaspoon (2 ml) salt and ⅛ teaspoon (.5 ml) pepper in small bowl. Mix oil and vinegar and pour over bean mixture. Stir well before serving.

Serves 6.
Serving size: ¾ cup (175 ml)
Makes 4½ cups (1.1 L).

TIP: Toasting brings out the flavors of nuts and seeds. Place nuts or seeds on baking sheet and bake at 225° (110° C) for 10 minutes. Be careful not to burn them.

One Serving

Calories: 179	Sodium: 265 mg
Calories from Fat: 81	Total Carbohydrates: 20 g
Total Fat: 56 g	Dietary Fiber: 5 g
Saturated Fat: 1 g	Sugars: 3 g
Cholesterol: 0 mg	Protein: 7 g

Fruit-Nut-Broccoli Slaw

Broccoli is one of the most popular vegetables and is a relative of cabbage, brussels sprouts and cauliflower.

⅓ cup reduced-fat mayonnaise	75 g
2 tablespoons white wine vinegar	30 ml
⅛ teaspoon ground ginger	.5 ml
1 (8 ounce) package broccoli-slaw mix	230 g
⅓ cup Craisins®	40 g
½ cup pecans or walnuts, toasted	60 g

Combine mayonnaise, vinegar, ginger, ¼ teaspoon (1 ml) salt and stir until they mix.

Combine broccoli slaw and Craisins® in large bowl. Add mayonnaise mixture and mix well.

Cover and refrigerate at least 1 hour. Garnish with nuts.

Serves 6.
Serving size: ¾ cup (175 ml)
Makes 4½ cups (1.1 L).

TIP: Toasting brings out the flavors of nuts and seeds. Place nuts or seeds on baking sheet and bake at 225° (110° C) for 10 minutes. Be careful not to burn them.

One Serving

Calories: 125	Sodium: 25 mg
Calories from Fat: 77	Total Carbohydrates: 11 g
Total Fat: 9 g	Dietary Fiber: 1 g
Saturated Fat: 1 g	Sugars: 6 g
Cholesterol: 3 mg	Protein: 2 g

Broccoli-Grape Salad

Cashews are a delicious addition to this salad.

1 (16 ounce) package bite-size broccoli florets	455 g
2 cups halved seedless red or green grapes	300 g
1½ cups thinly sliced celery	150 g
½ cup reduced-fat mayonnaise	115 g
¼ cup sugar or sugar substitute	50 g
½ teaspoon white vinegar	2 ml
¼ cup coarsely chopped cashews	30 g

Combine broccoli florets, grapes and celery in large bowl. Combine mayonnaise, sugar and vinegar in small bowl. Pour mayonnaise mixture over broccoli mixture and toss lightly. Sprinkle with cashews.

Serves 8.
Serving size: ¾ cup (175 ml)
Makes 6½ cups (1.5 L).

One Serving
Nutrition facts are based on sugar substitute.

Calories: 140	Sodium: 48 mg
Calories from Fat: 53	Total Carbohy-drates: 20 g
Total Fat: 6 g	Dietary Fiber: 1 g
Saturated Fat: 1 g	Sugars: 14 g
Cholesterol: 3 mg	Protein: 4 g

Crunchy Cashew-Rice Salad

⅓ cup cashews	40 g
1 (8 ounce) can sliced water chestnuts, drained, rinsed	230 g
½ cup chopped red onion	80 g
½ cup chopped green bell pepper	75 g
¼ cup raisins or Craisins®	40 g/30 g
2 cups cooked brown rice	390 g
¼ - ½ cup Ginger-Sesame Dressing (page 106)	60 - 125 ml

Toast cashews in non-stick 12-inch (32 cm) skillet over medium heat about 3 to 4 minutes and stir frequently. Be careful not to burn.

Transfer cashews to large bowl. Add water chestnuts, red onion, bell pepper, raisins and rice and stir to blend. Add Ginger-Sesame Dressing and toss to coat.

Serves 6.
Serving size: ¾ cup (175 ml)
Makes 4½ cups (1.1 L).

TIP: If you want some more crunch, add 1 cup (160 g) cooked snow peas for color and crisp texture.

One Serving

Calories: 202	Sodium: 32 mg
Calories from Fat: 74	Total Carbohy-drates: 25 g
Total Fat: 35 g	Dietary Fiber: 8 g
Saturated Fat: 2 g	Sugars: 3 g
Cholesterol: 0 mg	Protein: 8 g

Broccoflower Salad

*Broccoflower is a cross between broccoli and
cauliflower and looks like a chartreuse
cauliflower. Raw, it tastes like cauliflower;
cooked, the taste is more like broccoli.*

1 (1½ pound) head broccoflower, trimmed	680 g
1 cup shredded carrots	110 g
1 cup diced red bell pepper	150 g
¼ cup chopped green onions	25 g
2 tablespoons orange juice	30 ml
1 tablespoon olive oil	15 ml
1 tablespoon pine nuts, toasted	15 ml

Trim broccoflower and cut into
small florets. Combine florets,
carrots, bell pepper and green
onions in large bowl.

Combine orange juice and oil
in small bowl. Drizzle over
vegetables and toss lightly.
Sprinkle with pine nuts.

Serves 5.
Serving size: 1 cup (250 ml)
Makes 5 cups (1.2 L).

*TIP: Toasting brings out the flavors of
nuts and seeds. Place nuts or seeds
on baking sheet and bake at 225°
(110° C) for 10 minutes. Be careful
not to burn them.*

One Serving

Calories: 93	Sodium: 45 mg
Calories from Fat: 42	Total Carbohydrates: 9 g
Total Fat: 4 g	Dietary Fiber: 2 g
Saturated Fat: 0 g	Sugars: 1 g
Cholesterol: 0 mg	Protein: 5 g

Creamy Cauliflower-Broccoli Salad

*To save time, look for fresh broccoli and
cauliflower florets in one convenient
package. They're a lifesaver.*

5 - 6 cups (1 large head, trimmed) bite-size cauliflower florets	600 g
5 - 6 cups (1 pound, trimmed) bite-size broccoli florets	455 g
3 cups (1 pound) diced carrots	455 g
2 zucchini (6 inches in length), sliced	2 (15 cm)
1 red onion, sliced, separated into rings	
½ - ¾ cup Creamy Sweet-Sour Dressing (page 112)	125-175 ml

Combine cauliflower and
broccoli florets, carrots, zucchini
and red onion in large bowl.
Toss vegetables with Creamy
Sweet-Sour Dressing to coat.
Refrigerate at least 4 hours
before serving.

Serves 8.
Serving size: 1 cup (250 ml)
Makes 8 cups (1.9 L).

*TIP: Two heads of broccoflower could
be used to replace broccoli and
cauliflower.*

One Serving

Calories: 79	Sodium: 113 mg
Calories from Fat: 21	Total Carbohydrates: 13 g
Total Fat: 2 g	Dietary Fiber: 5 g
Saturated Fat: 0 g	Sugars: 5 g
Cholesterol: 0 mg	Protein: 3 g

Cauliflower Salad Nicoise

This is a unique twist on the typical Salad Nicoise usually made with potatoes and green beans.

2 cups frozen cut green beans	**250 g**
½ teaspoon garlic powder	
or 1 garlic clove, minced	**2 ml**
2 cups bite-size cauliflower	
florets	**200 g**
¼ cup diced red onion	**40 g**
¼ cup sliced Spanish green	
olives	**35 g**
½ cup Lemony Vinaigrette	
(page 108)	**125 ml**

Steam green beans in electric steamer or in saucepan with steamer basket until tender. Plunge into ice water to stop cooking. Drain.

Sprinkle garlic on green beans in large bowl and stir. Add cauliflower, red onion and olives and toss. Drizzle with Lemony Vinaigrette.

Serves 6.
Serving size: 1 cup (250 ml)
Makes 6 cups (1.4 L).

One Serving

Calories: 112	Sodium: 93 mg
Calories from	Total Carbohy-
Fat: 83	drates: 5 g
Total Fat: 9 g	Dietary Fiber: 2 g
Saturated Fat: 1 g	Sugars: 1 g
Cholesterol: 0 mg	Protein: 1 g

Carrot-Raisin Salad

This recipe has stood the test of time and is a very satisfying combination of fruit and vegetable.

3 large carrots (2½ cups),	
peeled, shredded	**275 g**
½ cup dark raisins	**80 g**
½ cup reduced-fat	
mayonnaise	**115 g**
1 teaspoon fresh lemon juice	**5 ml**

Combine all ingredients. Serve or cover and refrigerate.

Serves 6.
Serving size: ½ cup (125 ml)
Makes 3 cups (750 ml).

TIP: Pineapple is really good in this salad, too. If you have some, add ⅓ cup (85 g) crushed drained pineapple.

One Serving

Calories: 103	Sodium: 52 mg
Calories from	Total Carbohy-
Fat: 33	drates: 18 g
Total Fat: 4 g	Dietary Fiber: 2 g
Saturated Fat: 1 g	Sugars: 11 g
Cholesterol: 5 mg	Protein: 1 g

Celery Seed Coleslaw

This is a great potluck favorite and so easy to prepare.

1 (16 ounce) package coleslaw mix	455 g
2 tablespoons diced pimento or roasted red pepper	25 g
½ cup Celery Seed Dressing (page 102)	125 ml

Add coleslaw mix to large bowl and toss. Add pimento and drizzle with Celery Seed Dressing. Cover, refrigerate at least 8 hours and toss several times.

Serves 9.
Serving size: ¾ cup (175 ml)
Makes 7 cups (1.7 L).

One Serving

Calories: 82	Sodium: 19 mg
Calories from Fat: 54	Total Carbohydrates: 10 g
Total Fat: 6 g	Dietary Fiber: 1 g
Saturated Fat: 1 g	Sugars: 9 g
Cholesterol: 0 mg	Protein: 1 g

Corn-Green Chile Salad

This creamy dish makes a great salad or a dip.

2 (11 ounce) cans shoe-peg corn, rinsed, drained	2 (315 g)
½ cup chopped onion	80 g
1 (8 ounce) package shredded Monterey Jack cheese	230 g
3 tablespoons diced green chilies, drained	45 g
1 cup reduced-fat mayonnaise	225 g
½ cup reduced-fat sour cream	120 g

Combine corn, onion, cheese and green chilies in medium bowl. Combine mayonnaise and sour cream in large bowl. Add corn mixture and stir. Refrigerate until serving time. You may need to drain before serving.

Serves 10.
Serving size: ½ cup (125 ml)
Makes 5 cups (1.2 L).

One Serving

Calories: 200	Sodium: 295 mg
Calories from Fat: 121	Total Carbohydrates: 14 g
Total Fat: 14 g	Dietary Fiber: 1 g
Saturated Fat: 6 g	Sugars: 3 g
Cholesterol: 31 mg	Protein: 7 g

Creamy Dilled Cucumbers

Seedless greenhouse cucumbers are wonderful in this recipe.

2 pounds cucumbers with peels, thinly sliced	910 g
1 cup reduced-fat sour cream	240 g
3 tablespoons white wine vinegar	45 ml
½ teaspoon dried dill weed	2 ml
1 teaspoon sugar or sugar substitute	5 ml

Combine sliced cucumbers and 2 teaspoons (10 ml) salt in colander. Set aside to drain for 30 minutes. Transfer cucumbers to paper towels and pat dry.

Combine sour cream, vinegar, dill weed and sugar in large bowl. Add cucumbers and toss lightly to coat.

Serve immediately.

Serves 8.
Serving size: ½ cup (125 ml)
Makes 4 cups (1 L).

TIP: Fresh dill weed is always preferable to dried dill weed for the best flavor. Replace dried dill weed with 2 tablespoons (30 ml) fresh dill weed, if you have it.

One Serving
Nutrition facts are based on sugar substitute.

Calories: 74	Sodium: 23 mg
Calories from Fat: 38	Total Carbohydrates: 7 g
Total Fat: 4 g	Dietary Fiber: 0 g
Saturated Fat: 3 g	Sugars: 3 g
Cholesterol: 11 mg	Protein: 2 g

Eggplant Salad

1 (1½ pound) large eggplant	680 g
1 tablespoon olive oil	15 ml
1 tablespoon lemon juice	15 ml
1 garlic clove, minced	
1 cup finely chopped green bell pepper	150 g
1 cup reduced-fat plain yogurt	230 g
Romaine lettuce leaves	

Preheat oven to 400° (205° C).

Pierce skin of eggplant with fork. Bake eggplant in roasting pan or broiler pan for 1 hour or until very soft. Cool. Cut in half and scoop flesh into large bowl. Mash flesh with fork.

Add olive oil, lemon juice, garlic, bell pepper, yogurt, ½ teaspoon (2 ml) salt and ¼ teaspoon (1 ml) pepper and stir. Cover and refrigerate 2 hours.

For individual servings, mound eggplant on lettuce leaves.

Serves 6.
Serving size: ¾ cup (175 ml)
Makes 4½ cups (1.1 L).

TIP: You can serve this as an appetizer with raw vegetables and pita wedges.

One Serving

Calories: 98	Sodium: 31 mg
Calories from Fat: 25	Total Carbohydrates: 15 g
Total Fat: 3 g	Dietary Fiber: 6 g
Saturated Fat: 1 g	Sugars: 9 g
Cholesterol: 2 mg	Protein: 4 g

Jicama Chopped Salad

*Jicama is a wonderful vegetable
native to Mexico and South America.
It has a sweet, juicy texture
similar to a water chestnut.*

1 pound jicama	455 g
1 large cucumber, halved lengthwise, seeded	
2 medium navel oranges, peeled	
6 medium radishes, trimmed, coarsely chopped	
½ medium red onion, diced	
Juice of 2 limes (about ⅓ cup)	75 ml
⅓ cup chopped fresh cilantro	10 g

Peel and halve jicama. Cut into ½-inch (1.2 cm) cubes. Dice seeded cucumber. Slice oranges and cut into ½-inch (1.2 cm) pieces.

Combine jicama, cucumber, oranges, radishes, red onion and lime juice in large bowl. Cover and refrigerate about 20 minutes. Sprinkle with cilantro.

Serves 7.
Serving size: 1 cup (250 ml)
Makes 7 cups (1.7 L).

TIP: The best way to serve this salad, is to mound chopped iceberg lettuce on a serving platter and spoon salad on top of lettuce.

One Serving
Calories: 79	Sodium: 3 mg
Calories from Fat: 0	Total Carbohydrates: 8 g
Total Fat: 0 g	Dietary Fiber: 3 g
Saturated Fat: 0 g	Sugars: 4 g
Cholesterol: 0 mg	Protein: 0 g

Mediterranean Salad

6 cups mixed greens	300 g
¼ red onion, thinly sliced	
¼ cup pitted medium ripe olives	35 g
½ medium cucumber, peeled, seeded, cut in bite-size chunks	
2 cups halved cherry tomatoes	280 g
¼ cup Feta Cheese Dressing (page 105)	60 ml

Combine mixed greens, red onion, olives, cucumber and tomatoes in large bowl. Drizzle with Feta Cheese Dressing and toss lightly.

Serves 8.
Serving size: 1 cup (250 ml)
Makes 8 cups (1.9 L).

One Serving
Calories: 35	Sodium: 172 mg
Calories from Fat: 11	Total Carbohydrates: 4 g
Total Fat: 1 g	Dietary Fiber: 1 g
Saturated Fat: 1 g	Sugars: 0 g
Cholesterol: 4 mg	Protein: 2 g

Mixed Greens-Beet Salad

A colorful and nutritious salad.

2 (3 ounce) packages mixed baby greens	2 (85 g)
½ cup diced pickled beets, drained	115 g
¼ cup Citrus Dressing (page 103)	60 ml
¼ cup cheddar cheese crumbles	35 g

 Lightly toss greens, beets and Citrus Dressing in large bowl. Sprinkle with cheese crumbles.

Serves 6.
Serving size: 1 cup (250 ml)
Makes 6 cups (1.4 L).

TIP: If mixed baby greens are not available, use 4 cups (200 g) of any type lettuce torn into bite-size pieces.

One Serving

Calories: 53	Sodium: 131 mg
Calories from Fat: 16	Total Carbohydrates: 8 g
Total Fat: 2 g	Dietary Fiber: 2 g
Saturated Fat: 1 g	Sugars: 3 g
Cholesterol: 6 mg	Protein: 3 g

Orange-Onion-Mushroom Salad

8 cups fresh spinach	240 g
2 navel oranges, peeled, sliced	
1 cup sliced mushrooms	75 g
1 cup red onion rings	115 g
½ cup walnut pieces, toasted	65 g
2 tablespoons Balsamic Vinaigrette (page 101)	30 ml

 Remove large stems from spinach and transfer leaves to large bowl. Cut orange slices into bite-size pieces. Add orange pieces, mushrooms, red onion rings and walnuts to spinach. Drizzle with Balsamic Vinaigrette and toss.

Serves 6.
Serving size: 1 cup (250 ml)
Makes 6 cups (1.4 L).

TIP: Toasting brings out the flavors of nuts and seeds. Place nuts or seeds on baking sheet and bake at 225° (110° C) for 10 minutes. Be careful not to burn them.

One Serving

Calories: 69	Sodium: 2 mg
Calories from Fat: 51	Total Carbohydrates: 2 g
Total Fat: 6 g	Dietary Fiber: 1 g
Saturated Fat: 0 g	Sugars: 1 g
Cholesterol: 0 mg	Protein: 3 g

Clean fresh mushrooms by wiping them with a damp cloth, or use a soft mushroom brush. If you choose to lightly rinse mushrooms, be sure to dry immediately. Store mushrooms in a paper bag in the refrigerator; they deteriorate more quickly if stored in a plastic bag.

Potluck Potato Salad

2 pounds new (red) potatoes with peels	910 g
⅓ cup finely chopped onion	55 g
1 cup finely chopped celery (2 - 3 stalks)	105 g
6 eggs, hard-boiled, chopped	
½ cup finely chopped sweet pickles	120 g
3 tablespoons diced pimento, drained	40 g
½ cup Mayo-Mustard Dressing (page 109)	125 ml

 Scrub potatoes and bring to a boil in large pan with enough water to cover. Reduce heat and simmer 20 to 25 minutes or until tender. Drain and cool. Peel and cube potatoes.

 Combine potatoes, onion, celery, eggs, sweet pickles and pimento in large bowl and stir in Mayo-Mustard Dressing to moisten. Cover and refrigerate 4 to 6 hours before serving.

Serves 12.
Serving size: ½ cup (125 ml)
Makes 6 cups (1.4 L).

One Serving

Calories: 126	Sodium: 144 mg
Calories from Fat: 47	Total Carbohydrates: 15 g
Total Fat: 5 g	Dietary Fiber: 3 g
Saturated Fat: 1 g	Sugars: 2 g
Cholesterol: 106 mg	Protein: 6 g

New Potato-Beet Salad

You'll love this new twist on potato salad!

1½ pounds new (red) potatoes	680 g
¼ cup Favorite French Dressing (page 105)	60 ml
1 cup reduced-fat sour cream	240 g
3 tablespoons thinly sliced green onions	20 g
1 cup diced pickled beets, drained	230 g

 Scrub new potatoes, peel and cut in halves (or quarters if large). Boil potatoes in enough water to cover until tender, about 25 minutes, in medium saucepan.

 Drain and transfer to large bowl. Add Favorite French Dressing and toss gently. Let cool about 15 to 20 minutes.

 In separate bowl, combine sour cream and green onions. Pour over potatoes and stir gently. Before serving, spoon beets on top. If desired, stir beets in for a striking magenta-colored salad.

Serves 5.
Serving size: 1 cup (250 ml)
Makes 5 cups (1.2 L).

One Serving

Calories: 271	Sodium: 164 mg
Calories from Fat: 110	Total Carbohydrates: 34 g
Total Fat: 12 g	Dietary Fiber: 6 g
Saturated Fat: 5 g	Sugars: 0 g
Cholesterol: 17 mg	Protein: 8

Yellow Rice and Vegetable Salad

Saffron is a pungent, aromatic spice used to flavor and tint foods. Just a tiny amount goes a long way. This is a very colorful rice dish.

1 (10 ounce) package saffron-seasoned long grain rice mix	280 g
½ cup diced red onion	80 g
½ cup diced green or red bell pepper	75 g
½ cup frozen petite peas, thawed	75 g
⅓ cup sliced Spanish green olives	85 g
2 tablespoons Favorite French Dressing (page 105)	30 ml

🥦 Cook rice according to package directions. Cool about 10 minutes.

🥦 Combine rice, onion, bell pepper, peas and green olives in large bowl. Pour Favorite French Dressing over mixture and toss.

Serves 5.
Serving size: 1 cup (250 ml)
Makes 5 cups (1.1 L).

TIP: Saffron is marketed in both powdered form and in threads. Thousands of years ago, saffron was used to make medicines and to dye cloth.

One Serving

Calories: 268	Sodium: 1040 mg
Calories from Fat: 54	Total Carbohydrates: 48 g
Total Fat: 6 g	Dietary Fiber: 3 g
Saturated Fat: 1 g	Sugars: 2 g
Cholesterol: 0 mg	Protein: 5 g

Quinoa Garden Salad

Quinoa [KEEN wah] is considered a complete protein because it contains all 8 essential amino acids and has more protein than any other grain.

1 cup quinoa	170 g
1 cup diced tomato	180 g
1 cup diced seedless cucumber	135 g
½ cup diced red onion	80 g
½ cup diced cheddar cheese or crumbles	135 g
2 tablespoons Italiano Vinaigrette (page 107)	30 ml

🥦 Rinse quinoa in wire mesh strainer. Pour into 2-quart (2 L) saucepan and add 2 cups (500 ml) water. Bring to a boil, reduce heat and simmer covered 10 to 15 minutes or until quinoa absorbs water. Remove from heat and cool.

🥦 Combine tomato, cucumber, red onion and cheese in large bowl. Add cooled quinoa and Italiano Vinaigrette and toss.

Serves 6.
Serving size: 1 cup (250 ml)
Makes 6 cups (1.4 L).

TIP: Tiny bead-shaped ivory-colored quinoa resembles white rice but takes half the time to cook. It has a delicate flavor and a light texture.

One Serving

Calories: 172	Sodium: 64 mg
Calories from Fat: 28	Total Carbohydrates: 23 g
Total Fat: 5 g	Dietary Fiber: 3 g
Saturated Fat: 2 g	Sugars: 2 g
Cholesterol: 10 mg	Protein: 6 g

Family Reunion Sauerkraut Salad

Sauerkraut is an excellent source of vitamin C and has refreshing tartness.

4 cups refrigerated sauerkraut, rinsed, drained	570 g
1 medium red bell pepper, chopped	
1 large onion, diced	
1 cup diced celery	105 g
2 tablespoons cider vinegar	30 ml
¼ cup canola oil	60 ml
½ cup sugar	100 g

🥦 Combine sauerkraut, bell pepper, onion and celery in large bowl.

🥦 Combine cider vinegar, oil and sugar in saucepan and cook over low heat. Cook and stir until sugar dissolves. Pour vinegar mixture over sauerkraut mixture. Mix thoroughly, cover and refrigerate for at least 4 hours before serving.

Serves 8.
Serving size: ½ cup (125 ml)
Makes 4 cups (1 L).

One Serving

Calories: 105	Sodium: 229 mg
Calories from Fat: 32	Total Carbohy- drates: 17 g
Total Fat: 4 g	Dietary Fiber: 3 g
Saturated Fat: 0 g	Sugars: 15 g
Cholesterol: 0 mg	Protein: 1 g

Horseradish Coleslaw

Anyone who likes the taste of horseradish will really like this coleslaw.

1 (16 ounce) package coleslaw mix	455 g
1 large red delicious apple with peel, cored, diced	
¾ cup reduced-fat sour cream	180 g
2 tablespoons light plain soymilk	30 ml
2 teaspoons prepared horseradish	10 ml

🥦 Combine slaw and apple in large bowl. In separate bowl, combine sour cream, soymilk and horseradish. Add ½ teaspoon (2 ml) salt and ¼ teaspoon (1 ml) pepper.

🥦 Pour sour cream mixture over slaw and diced apple and toss lightly. Refrigerate at least 1 hour before serving.

Serves 8.
Serving size: 1 cup (250 ml)
Makes 8 cups (1.9 L).

One Serving

Calories: 53	Sodium: 20 mg
Calories from Fat: 30	Total Carbohy- drates: 4 g
Total Fat: 3 g	Dietary Fiber: 0 g
Saturated Fat: 2 g	Sugars: 2 g
Cholesterol: 8 mg	Protein: 2 g

Snappy Slaw

1 (20 ounce) package coleslaw mix	570 g
2 cups fresh sugar snap peas, trimmed	200 g
1 (8 ounce) jar baby corn, rinsed, drained	230 g
1 cup red onion rings	115 g
¼ cup Tangy Lime Vinaigrette (page 108)	60 ml

Combine coleslaw, peas, corn and onion rings in large bowl and toss. Drizzle with Tangy Lime Vinaigrette and toss again.

Serves 8.
Serving size: 1 cup (250 ml)
Makes 8 cups (1.9 L).

One Serving

Calories: 87	Sodium: 112 mg
Calories from Fat: 30	Total Carbohydrates: 11 g
Total Fat: 3 g	Dietary Fiber: 3 g
Saturated Fat: 1 g	Sugars: 5 g
Cholesterol: 0 mg	Protein: 2 g

Toasted Noodle Coleslaw

This is a variation of the popular ramen noodle salads.

½ cup sliced or slivered almonds	90 g
2 - 3 tablespoons sesame seeds	30 - 45 ml
3 ounces Oriental thin noodles	85 g
1 (20 ounce) package coleslaw mix	570 g
¼ cup thinly sliced green onions	25 g
½ cup thinly sliced fresh mushrooms	40 g
⅓ cup Sweet-Sour Dressing (page 111)	75 ml

Toast nuts, sesame seeds and noodles in sprayed non-stick 10-inch (25 cm) skillet over medium heat. Shake skillet to evenly brown. Cool.

Combine coleslaw, onions and mushrooms in large bowl. Add toasted noodle mixture and Sweet-Sour Dressing and toss.

Serves 8 to 10.
Serving size: ¾ cup (175 ml)
Makes 6 cups (1.4 L).

One Serving

Calories: 131	Sodium: 74 mg
Calories from Fat: 75	Total Carbohydrates: 11 g
Total Fat: 9 g	Dietary Fiber: 3 g
Saturated Fat: 1 g	Sugars: 3 g
Cholesterol: 0 mg	Protein: 4 g

Spanish Slaw

2 (20 ounce) bags angel hair shredded cabbage	2 (570 g)
¼ cup canola or olive oil	60 ml
2 tablespoons apple cider vinegar	30 ml
1½ tablespoons diced pimentos, drained	22 ml

🥦 Add shredded cabbage to large bowl and toss.

🥦 In separate bowl, combine oil, cider vinegar and 1 teaspoon (5 ml) each of salt and black pepper. Pour over cabbage. Add pimentos and toss to mix. Refrigerate at least 2 hours.

Serves 6.
Serving size: ½ cup (125 ml)
Makes 3 cups (750 ml).

TIP: Black pepper is a key ingredient in this slaw. You'll love it.

One Serving

Calories: 48	Sodium: 13 mg
Calories from Fat: 32	Total Carbohy-drates: 4 g
Total Fat: 4 g	Dietary Fiber: 2 g
Saturated Fat: 0 g	Sugars: 2 g
Cholesterol: 0 mg	Protein: 1 g

Spinach-Pecan Salad

6 cups fresh spinach	180 g
¼ cup thinly sliced green onions	25 g
¼ cup olive oil	60 ml
1 - 2 tablespoons fresh lemon juice	15 - 30 ml
½ cup chopped pecans, toasted	60 g

🥦 Wash spinach, remove stems and tear leaves into bite-size pieces. Combine spinach and green onions in large bowl.

🥦 Combine oil and lemon juice in small bowl and drizzle over spinach mixture. Toss to coat and top with pecans.

Serves 6.
Serving size: 1 cup (250 ml)
Makes 6 cups (1.4 L).

TIP: Toasting brings out the flavors of nuts and seeds. Place nuts or seeds on baking sheet and bake at 225° (110° C) for 10 minutes. Be careful not to burn them.

One Serving

Calories: 112	Sodium: 73 mg
Calories from Fat: 97	Total Carbohy-drates: 2 g
Total Fat: 11 g	Dietary Fiber: 2 g
Saturated Fat: 1 g	Sugars: 0 g
Cholesterol: 0 mg	Protein: 2 g

Petite Pea-Spinach Salad

6 cups fresh spinach	180 g
1 (10 ounce) package frozen petite peas, slightly thawed	280 g
1 (5 ounce) can sliced water chestnuts, rinsed, drained	145 g
⅓ cup Balsamic Vinaigrette (page 101)	80 ml
1 egg, hard-boiled, white portion only, chopped	

Wash spinach, remove stems, tear leaves into bite-size pieces and dry in salad spinner basket. Combine spinach, peas and water chestnuts in large bowl and toss. Before serving, add Balsamic Vinaigrette and toss. Sprinkle chopped egg white on top.

Serves 6.
Serving size: 1 cup (250 ml)
Makes 6 cups (1.4 L).

One Serving

Calories: 52	Total Carbohydrates: 8 g
Calories from Fat: 6	
Total Fat: 1 g	Dietary Fiber: 2 g
Saturated Fat: 0 g	Sugars: 4 g
Cholesterol: 26 mg	Protein: 2 g
Sodium: 51 mg	

Spinach-Melon-Avocado Salad

6 cups fresh spinach	180 g
1 cup bite-size chunks cantaloupe	180 g
½ cup alfalfa or broccoli sprouts	15 g
¼ cup thinly sliced green onions	25 g
1 medium ripe Hass avocado	
⅓ cup Citrus Honey Dressing (page 103)	75 ml

Wash spinach, remove stems, tear leaves into bite-size pieces and dry in salad spinner basket.

Combine spinach, cantaloupe, sprouts and green onions in large bowl. Peel and pit avocado and cut in bite-size chunks. Arrange avocado chunks on top of spinach mixture and drizzle with Citrus-Honey Dressing.

Serves 8.
Serving size: 1 cup (250 ml)
Makes 8 cups (1.9 L).

One Serving

Calories: 68	Sodium: 60 mg
Calories from Fat: 32	Total Carbohydrates: 8 g
Total Fat: 4 g	Dietary Fiber: 2 g
Saturated Fat: 1 g	Sugars: 5 g
Cholesterol: 0 mg	Protein: 1 g

Sunflower Salad

Italian balsamic vinegar is one of the best things to come out of Italy. This is a great reason to use it.

1 small head iceberg lettuce, shredded
5 large navel oranges, peeled, sliced
1 medium red onion, thinly sliced
⅓ cup canola oil   75 ml
2 - 3 tablespoons balsamic
   vinegar   30 - 45 ml
1 teaspoon sugar or sugar
   substitute   5 ml
½ cup sunflower seeds   65 g

Spread shredded lettuce on round platter. Arrange orange and red onion slices alternately in circle on top of lettuce.

Mix oil, vinegar, sugar, ½ teaspoon (2 ml) salt and ⅛ teaspoon (.5 ml) pepper in small bowl and drizzle over salad. Sprinkle sunflower seeds on top.

Serves 8.
Serving size: 1 cup (250 ml)
Makes 8 cups (1.9 L).

One Serving
Nutrition facts are based on sugar substitute.

Calories: 218	Sodium: 3 mg
Calories from	Total Carbohy-
Fat: 59	drates: 12 g
Total Fat: 7 g	Dietary Fiber: 2 g
Saturated Fat: 1 g	Sugars: 8 g
Cholesterol: 0 mg	Protein: 2 g

French Bread-Tomato Salad

Here's a robust and flavorful combination of bread and salad ingredients.

1 (14 ounce) can whole tomatoes
   or 6 roma tomatoes, peeled 400 g
1 garlic clove, minced
2 teaspoons balsamic vinegar   10 ml
3 tablespoons olive oil   45 ml
1 loaf whole wheat or plain
   `French bread
Parsley

Add tomatoes to food processor and process until tomatoes and juice mix well. Add garlic, vinegar, olive oil, 1 teaspoon (5 ml) salt and ¼ teaspoon (1 ml) pepper and pulse briefly. Transfer to large bowl.

Tear bread into 1½-inch (3 cm) pieces to make 3 cups (105 g). (Crusts can stay on or be removed.) Add bread to tomato mixture. Lightly stir until bread absorbs tomato mixture. Serve immediately or it will become soggy. Garnish with parsley.

Serves 6.
Serving size: ½ cup (125 ml)
Makes 3 cups (750 ml).

One Serving

Calories: 215	Sodium: 440 mg
Calories from	Total Carbohy-
Fat: 70	drates: 29 g
Total Fat: 8 g	Dietary Fiber: 2 g
Saturated Fat: 1 g	Sugars: 3 g
Cholesterol: 0 mg	Protein: 6 g

Tofu-Vegetable Greek Salad

Lots of vegetarian cuisine can be traced to foods and recipes originating in Greece.

1 (14 ounce) carton firm tofu	400 g
⅓ cup Oregano Dressing (page 109)	75 g
2 teaspoons sesame oil	10 ml
1 cup halved cherry tomatoes	140 g
1 medium cucumber, peeled, cubed	
½ cup chopped red onion	80 g
1 (4 ounce) can sliced ripe olives	115 g

Blot tofu with paper towels to remove excess moisture. Cut into ½-inch (1.2 cm) cubes. Pour Oregano Dressing over cubed tofu and marinate for at least 1 hour.

Combine oil and marinated tofu in non-stick 12-inch (32 cm) skillet over medium heat. Gently stir tofu until it browns. Cool.

Combine cooled tofu cubes, tomatoes, cucumber, red onion and any remaining dressing from marinade in large bowl and toss lightly. Refrigerate until time to serve. When ready to serve, garnish with ripe olives.

Serves 6.
Serving size: 1 cup (250 ml)
Makes 6 cups (1.4 L).

TIP: Spoon salad over fresh spinach leaves. Use crumbled feta cheese as a garnish.

One Serving

Calories: 88	Cholesterol: 0 mg	Dietary Fiber: 1 g
Calories from Fat: 44	Sodium: 210 mg	Sugars: 0 g
Total Fat: 6 g	Total Carbohydrates: 3 g	Protein: 5 g
Saturated Fat: 0 g		

Marinated Tomatoes

8 firm ripe tomatoes	
¼ cup parsley, chopped	20 g
1 garlic clove, minced	
1 teaspoon sugar or sugar substitute	5 ml
¼ cup canola oil	60 ml
2 tablespoons cider vinegar	30 ml
2 teaspoons mustard	10 ml

Peel tomatoes with serrated knife and cut out stem ends. Slice crosswise several times and push back into shape. Place in large shallow serving dish.

Combine remaining ingredients in airtight container. Cover and shake well. Pour over tomatoes and cover tomatoes loosely. Let stand at room temperature up to 30 minutes before serving.

Serves 8.
Serving size: 1 tomato

One Serving
Nutrition facts are based on sugar substitute.

Calories: 61	Sodium: 11 mg
Calories from Fat: 34	Total Carbohydrates: 7 g
Total Fat: 4 g	Dietary Fiber: 1 g
Saturated Fat: 0 g	Sugars: 1 g
Cholesterol: 0 mg	Protein: 1 g

Zucchini-Apple Salad

3 medium red or golden delicious apples, cored, sliced	
½ medium red onion, halved, sliced	
1 cup chopped or slivered green or red bell pepper	150 g
4 cups (1 pound) thinly sliced zucchini	455 g
¼ cup Basil Vinaigrette (page 102)	60 ml

Combine apples, red onion, bell pepper and zucchini in large bowl. Drizzle with Basil Vinaigrette and toss lightly.

Serves 6 to 8.
Serving size: ¾ cup (175 ml)
Makes 6 cups (1.4 L).

One Serving

Calories: 75	Sodium: 7 mg
Calories from Fat: 32	Total Carbohydrates: 10 g
Total Fat: 3 g	Dietary Fiber: 2 g
Saturated Fat: 1 g	Sugars: 8 g
Cholesterol: 0 mg	Protein: 1 g

When using sugar substitute, always read package instructions for measuring the correct equivalent amount to sugar.

Zucchini Olé Salad

4 cups (1 pound) thinly sliced zucchini	455 g
2 tablespoons thinly sliced green onions	15 g
⅓ cup diced green chilies, drained	80 g
⅓ cup sliced ripe olives, drained	45 g
1 cup cubed cheddar cheese	115 g
⅓ cup Cumin Vinaigrette (page 104)	75 ml

Combine zucchini, green onions, green chilies, olives and cheese in large bowl. Drizzle with Cumin Vinaigrette and toss.

Serves 6.
Serving size: 1 cup (250 ml)
Makes 6 cups (1.4 L).

One Serving

Calories: 171	Sodium: 200 mg
Calories from Fat: 121	Total Carbohydrates: 4 g
Total Fat: 13 g	Dietary Fiber: 1 g
Saturated Fat: 5 g	Sugars: 1 g
Cholesterol: 23 mg	Protein: 7 g

Balsamic Vinaigrette

½ cup olive or canola oil	125 ml
⅓ cup dark balsamic vinegar	75 ml
½ teaspoon dried basil leaves	2 ml
1 teaspoon dijon-style mustard	5 ml

Combine ingredients in airtight container. Cover and shake.

Serves 12.
Serving size: 1 tablespoon (15 ml)
Makes ¾ cup (175 ml).

TIP: This is great with Grapefruit-Red Onion Salad (page 77), Grilled Portobello Burgers, (page 142), Orange-Onion-Mushroom Salad (page 91), Petite Pea-Spinach Salad (page 97) and Fruited Lentil Pilaf Salad (page 186).

One Serving

Calories: 86	Sodium: 2 mg
Calories from Fat: 81	Total Carbohydrates: 1 g
Total Fat: 9 g	Dietary Fiber: 0 g
Saturated Fat: 1 g	Sugars: 1 g
Cholesterol: 0 mg	Protein: 0

Basil Vinaigrette

½ cup canola or olive oil	125 ml
2 tablespoons lemon juice	30 ml
2 tablespoons white wine vinegar	30 ml
1 teaspoon sugar or sugar substitute	5 ml
1 teaspoon dried basil leaves, crushed	5 ml

Combine all ingredients in airtight container and add ½ teaspoon (2 ml) salt. Cover and shake.

Serves 12.
Serving size: 1 tablespoon (15 ml)
Makes ¾ cup (175 ml).

TIP: Try this with Asparagus with Basil Vinaigrette (page 83), Hummus-Gorgonzola Wraps (page 146) and Zucchini-Apple Salad (page 100).

One Serving
Nutrition facts are based on sugar substitute.

Calories: 81	Sodium: 1 mg
Calories from Fat: 81	Total Carbohydrates: 0 g
Total Fat: 9 g	Dietary Fiber: 0 g
Saturated Fat: 1 g	Sugars: 0 g
Cholesterol: 0 mg	Protein: 0 g

Celery Seed Dressing

1 teaspoon dry mustard	5 ml
1 teaspoon paprika	5 ml
1 teaspoon celery seed	5 ml
⅛ teaspoon onion salt	.5 ml
⅔ cup honey	230 g
⅓ cup white wine vinegar	75 ml
1 tablespoon fresh lemon juice	15 ml
¾ cup canola oil	175 ml

Combine dry mustard, paprika, celery seed and onion salt. Combine honey, vinegar, lemon juice and spice mixture in food processor or blender. Cover, process and pour oil in top in slow stream until mixture thickens.

Serves 24.
Serving size: 1 tablespoon (15 ml)
Makes 1½ cups (375 ml).

TIP: Use with Celery Seed Coleslaw (page 88).

One Serving

Calories: 88	Sodium: 10 mg
Calories from Fat: 61	Total Carbohydrates: 8 g
Total Fat: 7 g	Dietary Fiber: 0 g
Saturated Fat: 1 g	Sugars: 8 g
Cholesterol: 0 mg	Protein: 0 g

Citrus Dressing

3 tablespoons fresh orange juice	45 ml
1 tablespoon fresh lemon juice	15 ml
2 tablespoons canola oil	30 ml
2 teaspoons sugar or sugar substitute	10 ml

 Combine all ingredients in airtight container. Cover and shake.

Serves 8.
Serving size: 1 tablespoon (15 ml)
Makes ½ cup (125 ml).

TIP: Use with Mixed Greens-Beet Salad (page 91).

One Serving
Nutrition facts are based on sugar substitute.

Calories: 64	Sodium: 0 mg
Calories from Fat: 61	Total Carbohydrates: 1 g
Total Fat: 1 g	Dietary Fiber: 0 g
Saturated Fat: 0 g	Sugars: 0 g
Cholesterol: 0 mg	Protein: 0 g

Citrus-Honey Dressing

This dressing especially complements cantaloupe and honeydew melons.

¼ cup honey	85 g
1 teaspoon finely grated orange peel	5 ml
½ cup orange juice	125 ml
1 teaspoon finely grated lime peel	5 ml
2 tablespoons lime juice	30 ml

Combine all ingredients in airtight container. Cover and shake before serving.

Serves 8
Serving size: 2 tablespoons (30 ml)
Makes 1 cup (250 ml).

TIP: Use with Melon Medley (page 12), Spinach-Melon-Avocado Salad (page 97) and Mixed Greens-Beet Salad (page 91).

One Serving

Calories: 38	Sodium: 1 mg
Calories from Fat: 1	Total Carbohydrates: 10 g
Total Fat: 0 g	Dietary Fiber: 0 g
Saturated Fat: 0 g	Sugars: 9 g
Cholesterol: 0 mg	Protein: 0 g

Creamy Goddess Dressing

1 cup reduced-fat mayonnaise or soy mayonnaise	225 g
½ cup reduced-fat sour cream	120 g
⅓ cup finely chopped parsley	20 g
3 tablespoons finely chopped chives or green onions	20 g
3 tablespoons tarragon vinegar	45 ml
1 tablespoon lemon juice	15 ml

 Mix all ingredients in small bowl until smooth.

Serves 28.
Serving size: 1 tablespoon (15 ml)
Makes 1¾ cups (425 ml).

TIP: Use with Vegetable Medley Bowtie Salad (page 82) and California BLT Sandwich (page 139).

One Serving

Calories: 36	Sodium: 64 mg
Calories from Fat: 30	Total Carbohydrates: 1 g
Total Fat: 3 g	Dietary Fiber: 0 g
Saturated Fat: 1 g	Sugars: 0 g
Cholesterol: 2 mg	Protein: 0 g

Cumin Vinaigrette

2 tablespoons lemon juice	30 ml
¼ cup canola oil	60 ml
⅛ teaspoon ground cumin	.5 ml

Combine lemon juice, oil, cumin, ½ teaspoon (2 ml) salt and ¼ teaspoon (1 ml) pepper in airtight container. Cover and shake before serving.

Serves 5.
Serving size: 1 tablespoon (15 ml)
Makes ⅓ cup (75 ml).

TIP: Use with Zucchini Olé Salad (page 101) and Corn-Bell Pepper Relish (page 51).

One Serving

Calories: 96	Sodium: 0 mg
Calories from Fat: 97	Total Carbohydrates: 0 g
Total Fat: 11 g	Dietary Fiber: 0 g
Saturated Fat: 2 g	Sugars: 0 g
Cholesterol: 0 mg	Protein: 0 g

Feta Cheese Dressing

This is a tangy and flavorful dressing for a variety of salads.

¼ cup fresh lemon juice	60 ml
⅓ cup olive oil	75 ml
1 teaspoon dried basil leaves, crushed	5 ml
3 tablespoons crumbled feta cheese	30 g

Combine lemon juice, oil, basil, ½ teaspoon (2 ml) salt and ¼ teaspoon (1 ml) pepper in airtight container. Cover and shake. Add feta cheese, cover and shake again.

Serves 12.
Serving size: 1 tablespoon (15 ml)
Makes ¾ cup (175 ml).

TIP: Use with Couscous Vegetable Salad (page 192), Fava Bean Pasta Salad (page 179) and Mediterranean Salad (page 90).

One Serving

Calories: 67	Sodium: 67 mg
Calories from Fat: 65	Total Carbohydrates: 0 g
Total Fat: 7 g	Dietary Fiber: 0 g
Saturated Fat: 2 g	Sugars: 0 g
Cholesterol: 5 mg	Protein: 1 g

Favorite French Dressing

This salad dressing is so versatile it will go with just about anything!

½ cup canola oil	125 ml
¼ cup red wine vinegar	60 ml
1 teaspoon sugar or sugar substitute	5 ml
¾ teaspoon dry mustard	4 ml
¼ teaspoon paprika	1 ml
⅛ teaspoon cayenne	.5 ml

Combine all ingredients and ½ teaspoon (2 ml) salt in airtight container. Cover and shake.

Serves 12.
Serving size: 1 tablespoon (15 ml)
Makes ¾ cup (175 ml).

TIP: Use with Chop Chop (page 51), Mushroom-Cheese-Walnut Salad (page 80), New Potato-Beet Salad (page 92) and Yellow Rice and Vegetable Salad (page 93).

One Serving

Calories: 82	Sodium: 67 mg
Calories from Fat: 65	Total Carbohydrates: 0 g
Total Fat: 7 g	Dietary Fiber: 0 g
Saturated Fat: 2 g	Sugars: 0 g
Cholesterol: 5 mg	Protein: 0 g

Fruit Salad Dressing

¾ cup canola oil	175 ml
¼ cup fresh orange juice	60 ml
3 tablespoons fresh lemon juice	45 ml
1 tablespoon cider vinegar	15 ml
⅓ cup sugar or sugar substitute	70 g
1 teaspoon paprika	5 ml
⅛ teaspoon onion powder	.5 ml

 Combine all ingredients and 1 teaspoon (5 ml) salt in airtight container. Cover and shake.

Serves 21.
Serving size: 1 tablespoon (15 ml)
Makes 1⅔ cups (400 ml).

One Serving
Nutrition facts are based on sugar substitute.

Calories: 69	Sodium: 0 mg
Calories from Fat: 70	Total Carbohy-drates: 0 g
Total Fat: 8 g	Dietary Fiber: 0 g
Saturated Fat: 1 g	Sugars: 0 g
Cholesterol: 0 mg	Protein: 0 g

Ginger-Sesame Dressing

⅓ cup olive oil	75 ml
2 tablespoons sesame oil	30 ml
2 tablespoons rice vinegar or white wine vinegar	30 ml
1 tablespoon honey or pure maple syrup	15 ml
1 tablespoon reduced-sodium soy sauce	15 ml
1 teaspoon grated fresh ginger	5 ml
1 tablespoon toasted sesame seeds	15 ml

 Combine all ingredients in airtight container. Cover and shake.

Serves 12.
Serving size: 1 tablespoon (15 ml)
Makes ¾ cup (175 ml).

TIP: Use with Crunchy Cashew-Rice Salad (page 85).

One Serving

Calories: 88	Sodium: 51 mg
Calories from Fat: 77	Total Carbohy-drates: 3 g
Total Fat: 9 g	Dietary Fiber: 0 g
Saturated Fat: 1 g	Sugars: 3 g
Cholesterol: 0 mg	Protein: 0 g

Classic Italian Dressing

¾ cup canola or olive oil	175 ml
⅓ cup apple cider vinegar	75 ml
2 teaspoons sugar or sugar substitute	10 ml
½ teaspoon celery salt	2 ml
¼ teaspoon dry mustard	1 ml
¼ teaspoon dry cayenne	1 ml
¼ teaspoon garlic powder or 1 clove garlic, minced or pressed	1 ml

Mix all ingredients with ½ teaspoon (2 ml) salt in airtight container. Cover and shake.

Serves 21.
Serving size: 1 tablespoon (15 ml)
Makes 1⅓ cups (325 ml).

TIP: Use with Marinated Vegetables (page 63).

One Serving
Nutrition facts are based on sugar substitute.

Calories: 69	Sodium: 12 mg
Calories from Fat: 69	Total Carbohydrates: 0 g
Total Fat: 8 g	Fiber: 0 g
Saturated Fat: 1 g	Sugars: 0 g
Cholesterol: 0 mg	Protein: 0 g

Italiano Vinaigrette

⅔ cup olive oil	150 ml
⅓ cup red wine vinegar	75 ml
2 garlic cloves, minced	
1 teaspoon dried Italian herbs, crushed	5 ml
⅛ teaspoon cayenne	.5 ml
2 teaspoons sugar or sugar substitute	10 ml

Combine all ingredients in airtight container. Cover and shake.

Serves 16.
Serving size: 1 tablespoon (15 ml)
Makes 1 cup (250 ml).

TIP: Add 2 tablespoons (30 g) reduced-fat mayonnaise for a creamy dressing. Use with Quinoa Garden Salad (page 93) and Jack Cheese Salad (page 80).

One Serving
Nutrition facts are based on sugar substitute.

Calories: 91	Sodium: 1 mg
Calories from Fat: 91	Total Carbohydrates: 0 g
Total Fat: 10 g	Dietary Fiber: 0 g
Saturated Fat: 1 g	Sugars: 0 g
Cholesterol: 0 mg	Protein: 0 g

Lemony Vinaigrette

¼ cup olive or canola oil	60 ml
3 tablespoons fresh lemon juice	45 ml

  Combine oil, lemon juice, 2 tablespoons (30 ml) water and ¼ teaspoon (1 ml) salt in airtight container. Cover and shake well.

Serves 5.
Serving size: 1 tablespoon (15 ml)
Makes ⅓ cup (75 ml).

TIP: Use with Cauliflower Salad Nicoise (page 87), Lemony Lentil Pilaf (page 186) and Tofu Tabbouleh (page 223).

One Serving

Calories: 96	Sodium: 0 mg
Calories from Fat: 97	Total Carbohy-drates: 0 g
Total Fat: 11 g	Dietary Fiber: 0 g
Saturated Fat: 2 g	Sugars: 0 g
Cholesterol: 0 mg	Protein: 0 g

Tangy Lime Vinaigrette

¼ cup olive oil	60 ml
2 tablespoons lime juice	30 ml
1 teaspoon finely grated lime peel	5 ml
2 tablespoons snipped parsley	10 g

  Combine all ingredients and ¼ teaspoon (1 ml) salt in airtight container. Cover and shake.

Serves 4.
Serving size: 2 tablespoons (30 ml)
Makes ½ cup (125 ml).

TIP: Use with Snappy Slaw (page 95).

One Serving

Calories: 120	Sodium: 0 g
Calories from Fat: 122	Total Carbohy-drates: 0 g
Total Fat: 14 g	Dietary Fiber: 0 g
Saturated Fat: 2 g	Sugars: 0 g
Cholesterol: 0 mg	Protein: 0 g

Mayo-Mustard Dressing

This is great with potato and macaroni salads.

1¼ cups reduced-fat mayonnaise	280 g
1 tablespoon mustard	15 ml
¼ - ½ teaspoon Creole seasoning or seasoning salt	1 - 2 ml

Mix mayonnaise, mustard, Creole seasoning, 1 teaspoon (5 ml) salt and ¼ teaspoon (1 ml) pepper in small bowl.

Serves 24.
Serving size: 1 tablespoon (15 ml)
Makes 1½ cups (375 ml).

TIP: Use with Avocado-Cheese Sandwich (page 138), Picnic Macaroni Salad (page 81), Potluck Potato Salad (page 92) and Garden Pasta Salad (page 81).

One Serving

Calories: 40	Sodium: 88 mg
Calories from Fat: 36	Total Carbohydrates: 1 g
Total Fat: 4 g	Dietary Fiber: 0 g
Saturated Fat: 1 g	Sugars: 1 g
Cholesterol: 0 mg	Protein: 0 g

Oregano Dressing

¼ cup olive oil	60 ml
2 tablespoons fresh lemon juice	30 ml
½ teaspoon dried oregano, crushed	2 ml
⅛ teaspoon garlic salt	.5 ml

Combine all ingredients plus ⅛ teaspoon (.5 ml) pepper in airtight container. Cover and shake.

Serves 5.
Serving size: 1 tablespoon (15 ml)
Makes ⅓ cup (75 ml).

TIP: Use with Mediterranean Salad (page 90) and Tofu-Vegetable Greek Salad (page 99).

One Serving

Calories: 96	Sodium: 25 mg
Calories from Fat: 96	Total Carbohydrates: 0 g
Total Fat: 11 g	Dietary Fiber: 0 g
Saturated Fat: 2 g	Sugars: 0 g
Cholesterol: 0 mg	Protein: 0 g

Poppy Seed Dressing

This sweet, tangy flavor goes well with fruit salads.

2 tablespoons minced onion	20 g
⅓ cup sugar or sugar substitute	70 g
1 teaspoon dry mustard	5 ml
⅓ cup white wine vinegar or white vinegar	75 ml
½ cup canola oil	125 ml
1 tablespoon poppy seeds	15 ml

Combine onion, sugar, dry mustard, vinegar and oil in food processor or blender. Cover and blend about 20 seconds. Pour into airtight container, add poppy seeds, cover and shake. Store in refrigerator.

Serves 12.
Serving size: 1 tablespoon (15 ml)
Makes 1½ cups (375 ml).

TIP: Use with Grapefruit-Red Onion Salad (page 77).

One Serving
Nutrition facts are based on sugar substitute.

Calories: 42	Sodium: 0 mg
Calories from Fat: 42	Total Carbohydrates: 0 g
Total Fat: 5 g	Dietary Fiber: 0 g
Saturated Fat: 1 g	Sugars: 0 g
Cholesterol: 0 mg	Protein: 0 g

Rice Vinegar Dressing

Rice vinegar is made from rice wine (sake) and has a mild, sweet flavor.

⅓ cup canola oil	75 ml
2 tablespoons reduced-sodium soy sauce	30 ml
2 tablespoons rice vinegar or white wine vinegar	30 ml
1 teaspoon sugar or sugar substitute	5 ml

Combine oil, soy sauce, vinegar and sugar in airtight container. Cover and shake well.

Serves 8.
Serving size: 1 tablespoon (15 ml)
Makes ½ cup (125 ml).

TIP: Use with Broccoli-Carrot Pasta Salad (page 188).

One Serving
Nutrition facts are based on sugar substitute.

Calories: 84	Sodium: 150 mg
Calories from Fat: 80	Total Carbohydrates: 0 g
Total Fat: 9 g	Dietary Fiber: 0 g
Saturated Fat: 1 g	Sugars: 0 g
Cholesterol: 0 mg	Protein: 0 g

Soy Sauce-Red Pepper Dressing

2 tablespoons apple cider vinegar	30 ml
2 tablespoons honey or maple syrup	45 g/30 ml
2 tablespoons reduced-sodium soy sauce	30 ml
¼ teaspoon crushed red pepper	1 ml

Combine all ingredients in airtight container. Cover and shake well.

Serves 5.
Serving size: 1 tablespoon (15 ml)
Makes ⅓ cup (75 ml).

One Serving

Calories: 58	Sodium: 241 mg
Calories from Fat: 0	Total Carbohydrates: 15
Total Fat: 0 g	Dietary Fiber: 0 g
Saturated Fat: 0 g	Sugars: 14 g
Cholesterol: 0 mg	Protein: 0 g

Sweet-Sour Dressing

½ cup canola oil	125 ml
2 tablespoons apple cider or white distilled vinegar	30 ml
¼ cup sugar or sugar substitute	50 g
4 teaspoons reduced-sodium soy sauce	60 ml

Combine all ingredients and ½ teaspoon (2 ml) salt in airtight container. Cover and shake.

Serves 24.
Serving size: 1 tablespoon (15 ml)
Makes 1½ cups (375 ml).

TIP: Use with Toasted Noodle Coleslaw (page 95).

One Serving
Nutrition facts are based on sugar substitute.

Calories: 42	Sodium: 100 mg
Calories from Fat: 41	Total Carbohydrates: 0 g
Total Fat: 5 g	Dietary Fiber: 0 g
Saturated Fat: 1 g	Sugars: 0 g
Cholesterol: 0 mg	Protein: 0 g

Creamy Sweet-Sour Dressing

⅔ cup reduced-fat mayonnaise	150 g
½ cup cider vinegar	120 ml
¼ cup sugar or sugar substitute	50 g

Mix all ingredients with ½ teaspoon (2 ml) salt in small bowl.

Serves 28.
Serving size: 1 tablespoon (15 ml)
Makes 1¾ cups (425 ml).

TIP: Use with Creamy Cauliflower-Broccoli Salad (page 86).

One Serving
Nutrition facts are based on sugar substitute.

Calories: 18	Cholesterol: 0 mg	Dietary Fiber: 0 g
Calories from Fat: 15	Sodium: 37 mg	Sugars: 0 g
Total Fat: 2 g	Total Carbohydrates: 0 g	Protein: 0 g
Saturated Fat: 0 g		

Soups
&
Sandwiches

Contents

Black-Eyed Pea Soup

If you eat this soup on New Year's Day, you'll have good luck in the new year.

½ cup chopped onion	80 g
1 garlic clove, minced	
1 (15 ounce) can black-eyed peas with liquid, divided	425 g
1 (14 ounce) can diced tomatoes with liquid	400 g
1 (4 ounce) can diced green chilies with liquid, divided	115 g

Cook and stir onion and garlic in large, heavy, sprayed saucepan over medium heat until tender.

Add 1 cup (240 g) black-eyed peas to food processor or blender. Gradually add 1 cup (250 ml) water and process until smooth. Add processed mixture to onions and garlic.

Stir in remaining black-eyed peas, tomatoes, ¼ cup (60 g) green chilies and ½ teaspoon (2 ml) salt.

Cook on low heat until hot. Taste for flavor and add remaining green chilies, if you like.

Serves 6.
Serving size: 1 cup (250 ml)
Makes 6 cups (1.4 L).

One Serving

Calories: 81	Sodium: 414 mg
Calories from Fat: 0	Total Carbohydrates: 15 g
Total Fat: 0 g	Dietary Fiber: 4 g
Saturated Fat: 0 g	Sugars: 2 g
Cholesterol: 0 mg	Protein: 4 g

Sweet Potato and Black-Eyed Pea Soup

This delicious, hearty soup is uniquely flavored with curry powder.

1 tablespoon canola oil or butter	15 ml
1 (16 ounce) package frozen seasoning blend (onion, celery, peppers)	455 g
2 (14 ounce) cans vegetable broth	2 (400 g)
1 medium sweet potato, peeled, cubed	
1 (15 ounce) can black-eyed peas, rinsed, drained	425 g
1 teaspoon curry powder	5 ml

Combine oil or butter and seasoning blend in large, heavy pan over medium-high heat. Cook and stir until vegetables are tender.

Add broth and bring to a boil. Add sweet potato, reduce heat, cover and simmer until tender, about 8 to 10 minutes. Add black-eyed peas, curry powder and ½ teaspoon salt.

Uncover and simmer about 5 minutes.

Serves 6.
Serving size: 1 cup (250 ml)
Makes 6 cups (1.4 L).

One Serving

Calories: 126	Sodium: 800 mg
Calories from Fat: 21	Total Carbohydrates: 21 g
Total Fat: 2 g	Dietary Fiber: 5 g
Saturated Fat: 0 g	Sugars: 3 g
Cholesterol: 0 mg	Protein: 3 g

Okra, Tomato and Black-Eyed Pea Soup

Canned and frozen vegetables make this soup a snap to make.

2 teaspoons olive oil	10 ml
1 (16 ounce) package frozen seasoning blend (onion, celery, peppers)*	455 g
1 (14 ounce) can vegetable broth	400 g
1 (15 ounce) can black-eyed peas, rinsed, drained	425 g
1 (16 ounce) package frozen cut okra, thawed	455 g
1 (14 ounce) can diced tomatoes with liquid	400 g
¼ teaspoon crushed red pepper	1 ml

Combine oil, seasoning blend and 1 teaspoon (5 ml) salt in large, heavy saucepan over medium-high heat. Cook and stir until vegetables are tender, about 5 minutes.

Add broth, black-eyed peas, okra, tomatoes, red pepper and ½ cup (125 ml) water. Bring to a boil. Reduce heat, cover and simmer about 20 to 30 minutes or until okra is tender.

Serves 6.
Serving size: 1 cup (250 ml)
Makes 6 cups (1.4 L).

TIP: Seasoning blend is frozen chopped onion, celery and peppers and is a great convenience.

One Serving

Calories: 100	Cholesterol: 0 mg	Dietary Fiber: 5 g
Calories from Fat: 11	Sodium: 483 mg	Sugars: 4 g
Total Fat: 2 g	Total Carbohydrates: 17 g	Protein: 4 g
Saturated Fat: 0 g		

Hearty Hoppin' John Soup

Children in the old South were very fond of black-eyed peas and rice. They would hop around the kitchen waiting for the dish to cook. So goes the story of this recipe.

3 cups vegetable broth	750 ml
1 (10 ounce) package frozen black-eyed peas, thawed, drained	280 g
1 (10 ounce) package frozen chopped mustard or collard greens, thawed, drained	280 g
2 cups cooked brown rice	390 g
¼ teaspoon crushed red pepper	1 ml

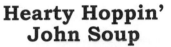 Bring broth to a boil in large, heavy saucepan over medium-high heat. Add black-eyed peas and greens, reduce heat and simmer covered until tender.

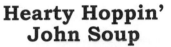 Add brown rice, red pepper and ½ teaspoon (2 ml) salt and heat.

Serves 6.
Serving size: 1 cup (250 ml)
Makes 6 cups (1.4 L).

One Serving

Calories: 156	Sodium: 482 mg
Calories from Fat: 10	Total Carbohydrates: 30 g
Total Fat: 1 g	Dietary Fiber: 5 g
Saturated Fat: 0 g	Sugars: 1 g
Cholesterol: 0 mg	Protein: 7 g

Slow-Cooker Pea Soup with Pistou

1½ cups dry split peas, rinsed, drained	300 g
½ cup chopped onion	80 g
½ cup chopped carrot	65 g
½ cup chopped celery	50 g
6 tablespoons Pistou (page 241)	90 ml

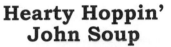 Combine peas, onion, carrot, celery, 1 teaspoon (5 ml) salt and ¼ teaspoon (1 ml) pepper in 4-quart (4 L) slow cooker. Pour in 4 cups (1 L) water.

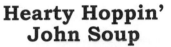 Cover and cook on LOW heat setting for 8 to 10 hours or on HIGH setting for 4 to 5 hours.

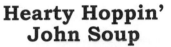 When all vegetables are tender, transfer in portions to food processor. Process until smooth.

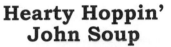 Spoon 1 tablespoon (15 ml) Pistou on top of each serving.

Serves 6.
Serving size: 1 cup (250 ml)
Males 6 cups (1.4 L).

One Serving

Calories: 214	Sodium: 73 mg
Calories from Fat: 24	Total Carbohydrates: 35 g
Total Fat: 3 g	Dietary Fiber: 14 g
Saturated Fat: 0 g	Sugars: 7 g
Cholesterol: 2 mg	Protein: 14 g

Lentil Soup

No vegetarian cookbook would be complete without a recipe for lentil soup.

1 cup brown lentils, rinsed, drained	195 g
1 cup chopped onion	160 g
1 cup chopped celery	105 g
1 cup chopped carrots	130 g
1 teaspoon crushed dried oregano leaves	5 ml
5 teaspoons apple cider vinegar	25 ml

🍵 Combine lentils, ½ teaspoon (2 ml) salt and ⅛ teaspoon (.5 ml) pepper in 6 cups (1.4 L) water large, heavy saucepan and bring to a boil. Reduce heat and simmer about 30 to 40 minutes or until lentils are tender.

🍵 Add onion, celery, carrots and oregano and simmer until vegetables are tender.

🍵 To brighten the taste, stir ½ teaspoon (2 ml) apple cider vinegar into each serving.

Serves 10.
Serving size: 1 cup (250 ml)
Makes 10 cups (2.4 L).

One Serving

Calories: 82	Sodium: 25 mg
Calories from	Total Carbohy-
Fat: 0	drates: 15 g
Total Fat: 0 g	Dietary Fiber: 7 g
Saturated Fat: 0 g	Sugars: 2 g
Cholesterol: 0 mg	Protein: 5 g

Italian Cannellini Soup

This is a delicious recipe for trying Italian cannellini beans.

1 (15 ounce) can cannellini or navy beans with liquid, divided	425 g
1 medium onion, finely chopped	
1 garlic clove, minced	
¼ teaspoon crushed dried thyme	1 ml
1 (10 ounce) package frozen cut leaf spinach, thawed	280 g
1 tablespoon fresh lemon juice	15 ml

🍵 Add 1 cup (260 g) beans with liquid to food processor and process until smooth. Set aside.

🍵 Cook and stir onion and garlic in sprayed, large heavy pan over medium heat until tender.

🍵 Add remaining beans, processed beans, thyme, ¼ teaspoon (1 ml) pepper and 2 cups (500 ml) water. Bring to a boil and add spinach. Reduce heat and gently boil uncovered about 15 minutes.

🍵 Stir in lemon juice before serving.

Serves 6.
Serving size: 1 cup (250 ml)
Makes 6 cups (1.4 L).

TIP: A nice touch is to serve this soup with freshly grated parmesan cheese.

One Serving

Calories: 100	Sodium: 368 mg
Calories from	Total Carbohy-
Fat: 11	drates: 19 g
Total Fat: 1 g	Dietary Fiber: 5 g
Saturated Fat: 0 g	Sugars: 1 g
Cholesterol: 0 mg	Protein: 2 g

White Bean-Tomatillo Chili

Tomatillos are a tart, green tomato-like fruit with papery husks, frequently used in Southwestern cooking.

1 pound tomatillos, husked, rinsed, coarsely chopped	455 g
1 (14 ounce) can vegetable broth	400 g
1 (4 ounce) can chopped mild green chilies, drained	115 g
1 teaspoon ground cumin	5 ml
2 (16 ounce) cans navy or cannellini beans, drained, rinsed, mashed	2 (455 g)

Combine tomatillos, 1 teaspoon (5 ml) salt, broth, green chilies, cumin and 1 cup (250 ml) water in large, heavy pan. Bring to a boil, reduce heat to low and simmer covered about 15 minutes. Stir in beans and heat through.

Serves 8.
Serving size: 1 cup (250 ml)
Makes 8 cups (1.9 L).

TIP: Garnish with chopped cilantro leaves.

One Serving

Calories: 151	Sodium: 740 mg
Calories from Fat: 8	Total Carbohydrates: 29 g
Total Fat: 0 g	Dietary Fiber: 6 g
Saturated Fat: 0 g	Sugars: 3 g
Cholesterol: 0 mg	Protein: 0 g

Southwest Black Bean Soup

Here's a quick and tasty supper soup.

2 (15 ounce) cans black beans with liquid	2 (425 g)
1 (15 ounce) can diced tomatoes with liquid	425 g
2½ teaspoons chili powder	12 ml
½ teaspoon cumin	2 ml
¼ teaspoon garlic powder	1 ml

Combine beans, tomatoes and 1 cup (250 ml) water in large, heavy pan. Bring to a boil, add spices and 1 teaspoon (5 ml) salt. Reduce heat, cover and simmer about 10 minutes.

Serves 8.
Serving size: ¾ cup (175 ml)
Makes 6 cups (1.4 L).

One Serving

Calories: 137	Sodium: 411 mg
Calories from Fat: 11	Total Carbohydrates: 26 g
Total Fat: 1 g	Dietary Fiber: 5 g
Saturated Fat: 0 g	Sugars: 1 g
Cholesterol: 0 mg	Protein: 6 g

Cuban Black Bean Soup

2 cups finely chopped onions	320 g
2 cups (2 medium) finely chopped green bell peppers	300 g
2 garlic cloves, minced	
½ teaspoon ground cumin	2 ml
1 teaspoon dried crushed oregano leaves	5 ml
2 tablespoons red wine vinegar	30 ml
2 (15 ounce) cans black beans, drained, rinsed	2 (425 g)

Combine onion, bell pepper and garlic in large, heavy sprayed pan over medium heat. Cook and stir until tender. Add 3 cups (750 ml) water, cumin, oregano, vinegar and beans.

Bring to a boil, reduce heat and simmer covered for 30 minutes.

Serves 8.
Serving size: ¾ cup (175 ml)
Makes 6 cups (1.4 L).

TIP: Garnish with 1 tablespoon (15 ml) salsa on each serving.

One Serving

Calories: 255	Sodium: 504 mg
Calories from Fat: 18	Total Carbohydrates: 48 g
Total Fat: 2 g	Dietary Fiber: 12 g
Saturated Fat: 0 g	Sugars: 2 g
Cholesterol: 0 mg	Protein: 9 g

Cream of Broccoli Soup

1 (16 ounce) bag frozen chopped broccoli	455 g
1 (14 ounce) can vegetable broth, divided	400 g
1 tablespoon butter	15 ml
1 tablespoon unbleached white flour	15 ml
1 cup light plain soymilk	250 ml

Cook broccoli according to package directions. Drain and set aside 1 cup (185 g).

Add remaining broccoli and ¾ cup (175 ml) broth to food processor. Cover and process about 1 minute.

Melt butter in large, heavy pan over medium heat and stir in flour. Add ½ teaspoon (2 ml) salt and ⅛ teaspoon (.5 ml) pepper and cook until mixture bubbles. Add soymilk, cook and stir until mixture thickens.

Stir in processed broccoli, unprocessed broccoli and remaining broth and cook until hot.

Serves 4.
Serving size: 1 cup (250 ml)
Makes 4 cups (1 L).

One Serving

Calories: 118	Sodium: 232 mg
Calories from Fat: 39	Total Carbohydrates: 16 g
Total Fat: 4 g	Dietary Fiber: 5 g
Saturated Fat: 2 g	Sugars: 4 g
Cholesterol: 8 mg	Protein: 7 g

Broccoli-Cheese Soup

Everybody likes broccoli with cheese.

4 cups frozen chopped broccoli, divided	620 g
1 (14 ounce) can vegetable broth	400 g
1 tablespoon butter	15 ml
1 tablespoon unbleached white flour	15 ml
1 cup light plain soymilk	250 ml
½ cup shredded sharp cheddar cheese	60 g

Cook broccoli according to package directions, drain and set aside 1 cup (185 g).

Combine remaining broccoli and 1 cup (250 ml) broth or water in food processor or blender. Cover and process until smooth.

Melt butter in large, heavy saucepan over medium heat and stir in flour. Add ½ teaspoon salt (2 ml) and ⅛ teaspoon (.5 ml) pepper. Cook until mixture bubbles.

Add soymilk, cook and stir until mixture thickens. Stir in remaining broccoli, processed broccoli, remaining broth and cheese. Cook over low heat until cheese melts.

Serves 5.
Serving size: 1 cup (250 ml)
Makes 5 cups (1.2 L).

One Serving

Calories: 134	Cholesterol: 18 mg	Dietary Fiber: 2 g
Calories from Fat: 67	Sodium: 450 mg	Sugars: 3 g
Total Fat: 7 g	Total Carbohydrates: 11 g	Protein: 8 g
Saturated Fat: 4 g		

Barley-Vegetable Soup

Oats, peas, beans, and barley grow,
Oats, peas, beans and barley grow,
Can you or I or anyone know
How oats, peas, beans and barley grow?

6 cups vegetable broth	1.4 L
¼ cup pearl barley	50 g
1½ cups frozen seasoning blend (onions, celery and peppers)	215 g
1 garlic clove, minced	
1 cup sliced carrots	125 g
¼ cup chopped parsley	20 g

Bring broth to a boil in large, heavy saucepan. Add barley, reduce heat and simmer 1 hour.

Add seasoning blend and garlic to sprayed non-stick 10-inch (25 cm) skillet. Cook and stir over medium-high heat until vegetables are tender.

Add seasoning blend mixture, carrots, ½ teaspoon (2 ml) salt and ¼ teaspoon (1 ml) pepper to broth. Bring to a boil, reduce heat and simmer covered until carrots are tender, about 10 minutes. Stir in chopped parsley.

Servings 6.
Serving size: 1 cup (250 ml)
Makes 6 cups (1.4 L).

TIP: Toasting the barley before adding it to the broth will give it a light, nutty flavor. Place the barley in a non-stick skillet over medium heat and shake constantly until grain is golden.

One Serving

Calories: 44	Cholesterol: 0 mg	Dietary Fiber: 2 g
Calories from Fat: 0	Sodium: 969 mg	Sugars: 3 g
Total Fat: 0 g	Total Carbohydrates: 8 g	Protein: 0 g
Saturated Fat: 0 g		

Cheesy Cauliflower Soup

4 cups fresh cauliflower florets	285 g
1 (14 ounce) can vegetable broth, divided	400 g
1 tablespoon butter	15 ml
1 tablespoon flour	15 ml
1 cup fat-free skim milk or light plain soymilk	250 ml
½ cup shredded sharp cheddar cheese	60 g

▦ Bring 2 cups (500 ml) water to a boil in 4-quart (4 L) saucepan. Add cauliflower and cook until tender. Drain and set aside 1 cup (240 ml) cauliflower.

▦ Combine remaining cauliflower and ¾ cup (175 ml) vegetable broth in food processor. Cover and process for about 1 minute.

▦ Melt butter in large, heavy pan over medium heat. Add flour, ½ teaspoon (2 ml) salt and ⅛ teaspoon (.5 ml) pepper. Cook and stir until mixture bubbles. Add skim milk and cook and stir until mixture thickens. Stir in cheese.

▦ Add processed cauliflower, unprocessed cauliflower and remaining broth to cheese sauce. Cook over low heat until hot.

Serves 8.
Serving size: ¾ cup (175 ml)
Makes 6 cups (1.4 L).

One Serving

Calories: 78	Cholesterol: 12 mg	Dietary Fiber: 2 g
Calories from Fat: 34	Sodium: 266 mg	Sugars: 2 g
Total Fat: 4 g	Total Carbohydrates: 7 g	Protein: 3 g
Saturated Fat: 2 g		

Carrot-Ginger Soup

1 teaspoon olive oil	5 ml
1 large onion, halved, thinly sliced	
3 cups shredded carrots*	330 g
2 teaspoons freshly grated ginger	10 ml
2 (14 ounce) cans vegetable broth	2 (400 g)

🍲 Combine oil and onion in large, heavy saucepan over medium heat. Cook and stir until onion is tender.

🍲 Add carrots and ginger, cook and stir about 3 to 4 minutes.

🍲 Add vegetable broth, ½ teaspoon (2 ml) salt and ⅛ teaspoon (.5 ml) pepper. Bring to a boil, reduce heat and simmer covered for about 10 to 15 minutes.

Serves 6.
Serving size: 1 cup (250 ml)
Makes 6 cups (1.4 L).

TIP: FYI – 3 cups (330 g) shredded carrots equal to about 3 medium carrots.

One Serving

Calories: 48	Sodium: 586 mg
Calories from Fat: 7	Total Carbohy- drates: 9 g
Total Fat: 0 g	Dietary Fiber: 2 g
Saturated Fat: 0 g	Sugars: 5 g
Cholesterol: 0 mg	Protein: 0 g

Corn Chowder

This is so good it will disappear quickly!

1 medium onion, chopped	
1 (14 ounce) can vegetable broth	400 g
2 (15 ounce) cans cream-style corn	2 (425 g)
1 (2 ounce) jar diced pimentos with liquid	60 g
1 cup fat-free half-and-half cream	250 ml

🍲 Cook and stir onion in sprayed, large heavy pan until tender. Add broth, corn, pimentos, ½ teaspoon (2 ml) salt and ⅛ teaspoon (.5 ml) pepper. Bring to a boil, reduce heat and simmer about 10 minutes. Gradually stir in half-and-half. Do not boil, but heat thoroughly and serve.

Serves 6.
Serving size: ¾ cup (175 ml)
Makes 5 cups (1.2 L).

TIP: If you want a little spice, replace pimentos with 1 (4 ounce/115 g) can chopped green chilies with liquid.

One Serving

Calories: 148	Sodium: 756 mg
Calories from Fat: 14	Total Carbohy- drates: 33 g
Total Fat: 2 g	Dietary Fiber: 3 g
Saturated Fat: 0 g	Sugars: 6 g
Cholesterol: 0 mg	Protein: 5 g

French Onion Soup

2 tablespoons butter	30 g
2 cups thinly sliced yellow onions	230 g
2 (14 ounce) cans vegetable broth or 3 cups water	2 (400 g)/750 ml
2 teaspoons white cooking wine	10 ml
⅛ teaspoon white pepper*	.5 ml
6 slices French bread	
1 cup shredded Swiss cheese	110 g

 Melt butter in 4-quart (4 L) saucepan over low heat and add onions. Cover and cook over medium-low heat, stirring frequently, for 10 to 12 minutes.

 Stir in broth or water, cooking wine and white pepper. Bring to a boil and reduce heat. Simmer covered for 10 minutes.

 Toast bread lightly. Sprinkle with cheese and place under broiler until cheese melts.

 Top soup servings with bread. Serve immediately.

Serves 6.
Serving size: 1 cup (250 ml) soup
        with bread
Makes 6 cups (1.4 L).

TIP: White pepper is used to avoid black specks in the soup. Black pepper may be used, if you like.

One Serving

Calories: 226	Sodium: 599 mg
Calories from Fat: 96	Total Carbohy-drates: 24 g
Total Fat: 11 g	Dietary Fiber: 2 g
Saturated Fat: 6 g	Sugars: 4 g
Cholesterol: 30 mg	Protein: 9 g

Brown Rice-Mushroom Soup

This simple recipe brings out the wonderful flavor of mushrooms.

2 teaspoons olive oil	10 ml
½ cup finely chopped onion	80 g
1 garlic clove, minced	
1 (8 ounce) package sliced fresh mushrooms	230 g
⅛ teaspoon crushed dried thyme	.5 ml
1 cup cooked brown rice	195 g

 Combine oil, onion and garlic in large, heavy saucepan over medium heat. Cook and stir until tender. Add mushrooms and cook, stirring occasionally, until tender, about 8 to 10 minutes.

 Stir in thyme, ½ teaspoon (2 ml) salt and ⅛ teaspoon (.5 ml) pepper. Add cooked rice, 3 cups (750 ml) water and bring to a boil. Reduce heat, cover and simmer about 5 minutes.

Serves 4.
Serving size: 1 cup (250 ml)
Makes 4 cups (1 L).

One Serving

Calories: 95	Sodium: 6 mg
Calories from Fat: 27	Total Carbohy-drates: 15 g
Total Fat: 3 g	Dietary Fiber: 2 g
Saturated Fat: 0 g	Sugars: 2 g
Cholesterol: 0 mg	Protein: 3 g

Hearty Potato Soup

5 medium russet potatoes, peeled, cubed	
½ cup chopped onion	80 g
1 (14 ounce) can vegetable broth, divided	400 g
1 tablespoon butter	15 ml
1 tablespoon unbleached white flour	15 ml
1 cup fat-free skim milk, divided	250 ml

Combine potatoes and onion with enough water to cover in 4-quart (4 L) saucepan. Bring to a boil, reduce heat and simmer covered for about 15 to 20 minutes or until potatoes are tender. Drain and set aside 1 cup (160 g) potatoes.

Add remaining drained potato-onion mixture and ¾ cup (175 ml) broth to food processor. Process in batches about 1 minute or until smooth.

Melt butter in large, heavy saucepan over medium heat and stir in flour. Add ½ teaspoon (2 ml) salt and ⅛ teaspoon (.5 ml) pepper. Cook and stir until mixture bubbles. Add skim milk, cook and stir until it thickens.

Stir in processed potatoes, unprocessed potatoes and remaining broth and cook until hot.

Serves 10.
Serving size: ¾ cup (175 ml)
Makes 8 cups (1.9 L).

TIP: Garnish each serving with sliced green onions and shredded sharp cheddar cheese.

One Serving

Calories: 115	Cholesterol: 4 mg	Dietary Fiber: 2 g
Calories from Fat: 12	Sodium: 183 mg	Sugars: 3 g
Total Fat: 1 g	Total Carbohydrates: 23 g	Protein: 3 g
Saturated Fat: 1 g		

Leek and Potato Soup

3 medium (red) potatoes
   with peels, cut in 1-inch
   chunks   3 (2.5 cm)
3 cups chopped leeks, white
   portion only   270 g
½ cup chopped celery   50 g
½ cup diced carrot   65 g
3 cups fat-free skim milk 750 ml
3 tablespoons melted butter 45 g

Combine 1 cup (250 ml) water, potatoes, leeks, celery, carrot, ½ teaspoon (2 ml) salt and ¼ teaspoon (1 ml) pepper in large, heavy saucepan and bring to a boil. Cover, reduce heat to simmer and cook until vegetables are tender, about 20 to 30 minutes. Add water as needed.

Drain vegetables and transfer to food processor. Add skim milk and process until mixture is smooth. Return to pan, add melted butter and cook on low heat until hot.

Serves 6.
Serving size: 1 cup (250 ml)
Makes 6 cups (1.4 L).

One Serving
Calories: 179
Calories from
   Fat: 55
Total Fat: 6 g
Saturated Fat: 4 g
Cholesterol: 18 mg
Sodium: 99 mg
Total Carbohy-
   drates: 26 g
Dietary Fiber: 3 g
Sugars: 9 g
Protein: 6 g

Sweet Potato and Corn Chowder

1 (14 ounce) can vegetable
   broth   400 g
1 large sweet potato, peeled,
   diced
1 cup frozen whole kernel corn 165 g
1 cup light plain soymilk   250 ml

Bring broth in large, heavy pan over medium-high heat to a boil and add sweet potato. Reduce heat, cover and simmer about 20 minutes or until sweet potato is tender.

Add corn and simmer about 6 to 8 minutes or until corn is tender. Add soymilk, ½ teaspoon (2 ml) salt and ⅛ teaspoon (.5 ml) pepper and simmer until hot.

Serves 5.
Serving size: ¾ cup (175 ml)
Makes 4 cups (1 L).

One Serving
Calories: 93
Calories from
   Fat: 12
Total Fat: 1 g
Saturated Fat: 0 g
Cholesterol: 0 mg
Sodium: 378 mg
Total Carbohy-
   drates: 18 g
Dietary Fiber: 3 g
Sugars: 3 g
Protein: 4 g

Holiday Sweet Potato Soup

Creamy and smooth, this sweet potato soup is sweetened with
brown sugar and flavored with grated orange peel.

4 medium sweet potatoes, scrubbed	
3½ cups fat-free skim milk, divided	**875 ml**
½ cup packed brown sugar	**110 g**
3 - 4 tablespoons freshly grated orange peel	**17 - 22 g**

Prick skin of sweet potatoes with fork. Place 2 sweet potatoes in covered dish in microwave and cook on HIGH for 4 minutes. Remove from microwave and turn potatoes with oven mitt. Return to microwave and cook an additional 4 minutes. Remove and set aside to cool.

Repeat cooking procedure with remaining 2 sweet potatoes.

When potatoes are cool, peel and mash. Spoon about 1 cup (250 ml) potatoes into food processor at a time. Use small amount of skim milk to help liquefy. Process in batches until very smooth. Repeat until all potatoes are processed.

Transfer potatoes to large, heavy saucepan. Stir in remaining milk, ½ teaspoon (2 ml) salt and brown sugar. Heat slowly over low heat and stir continuously. Top each serving with about 1 teaspoon (5 ml) grated orange peel.

Serves 8.
Serving size: 1 cup (250 ml)
Makes 8 cups (1.9 L).

One Serving

Calories: 160	Cholesterol: 2 mg	Dietary Fiber: 2 g
Calories from Fat: 2	Sodium: 121 mg	Sugars: 21 g
Total Fat: 0 g	Total Carbohydrates: 34 g	Protein: 5 g
Saturated Fat: 0 g		

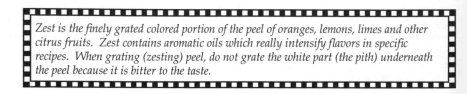

Zest is the finely grated colored portion of the peel of oranges, lemons, limes and other citrus fruits. Zest contains aromatic oils which really intensify flavors in specific recipes. When grating (zesting) peel, do not grate the white part (the pith) underneath the peel because it is bitter to the taste.

Curried Pumpkin Soup

*This is a great warm-up
on those cold, wintry days.*

1 cup finely chopped onion	160 g
1 (14 ounce) can vegetable broth	400 g
1 (15 ounce) can solid-pack pumpkin	425 g
1 teaspoon curry powder	5 ml
1 cup fat-free half-and-half cream	250 ml

- Cook and stir onion in sprayed 4-quart (4 L) saucepan until tender.

- Add broth, pumpkin, curry powder and half-and-half cream. If you want a thinner consistency, add ½ cup (125 ml) water. Stir and heat slowly over low heat.

Serves 6.
Serving size: 1 cup (250 ml)
Makes 6 cups (1.4 L).

TIP: Garnish with chopped green onions or chopped peanuts.

One Serving

Calories: 40	Sodium: 297 mg
Calories from Fat: 8	Total Carbohydrates: 6 g
Total Fat: 1 g	Dietary Fiber: 1 g
Saturated Fat: 0 g	Sugars: 2 g
Cholesterol: 0 mg	Protein: 2 g

Spinach-Tortellini Soup

½ cup finely chopped onion	80 g
1 garlic clove, minced	
1 (14 ounce) can vegetable broth	400 g
1 (14 ounce) can Italian seasoned tomatoes	400 g
1 teaspoon dry crushed Italian herbs	5 ml
1 (9 ounce) package refrigerated cheese-stuffed tortellini	255 g
1 (10 ounce) package frozen cut leaf spinach, thawed	280 g

- Cook and stir onion and garlic in sprayed, large heavy pan over medium heat until tender.

- Add broth, tomatoes, 1 teaspoon (5 ml) salt, ¼ teaspoon (1 ml) pepper, Italian herbs and 3 cups (750 ml) water. Bring to a boil and add tortellini and spinach.

- Reduce heat to medium and cook, stirring occasionally, until pasta is tender.

Serves 6.
Serving size: 1 cup (250 ml)
Makes 6 cups (1.4 L).

TIP: Serve with crusty Italian bread and be sure to pass the parmesan cheese.

One Serving

Calories: 168	Sodium: 582 mg
Calories from Fat: 30	Total Carbohydrates: 26 g
Total Fat: 3 g	Dietary Fiber: 4 g
Saturated Fat: 2 g	Sugars: 3 g
Cholesterol: 18 mg	Protein: 9 g

Blender Gazpacho

Gazpacho is a cool and refreshing dish for hot summer days. It's really delightful and tastes a little bit like a luxury.

1 (14 ounce) can diced tomatoes with liquid	400 g
1 medium cucumber, peeled, seeded, diced	
½ cup diced green pepper	75 g
¼ cup diced onion	40 g
1 tablespoon olive oil	15 ml
1 tablespoon red wine vinegar	15 ml

Combine all ingredients and add ½ teaspoon (2 ml) salt and ⅛ teaspoon (.5 ml) pepper in food processor or blender. Cover and process 1 to 2 minutes until smooth. Refrigerate and serve.

Serves 8.
Serving size: ½ cup (125 ml)
Makes 4 cups (1 L).

TIP: A nice touch for entertaining is to serve gazpacho in stemmed crystal glasses.

One Serving

Calories: 38	Sodium: 97 mg
Calories from Fat: 16	Total Carbohydrates: 3 g
Total Fat: 2 g	Dietary Fiber: 1 g
Saturated Fat: 0 g	Sugars: 2 g
Cholesterol: 0 mg	Protein: 1 g

Pantry Minestrone Soup

1 (16 ounce) package frozen seasoning blend (onion, peppers, celery)	455 g
2 (14 ounce) cans vegetable broth	2 (400 g)
1 (14 ounce) can Italian-seasoned stewed or diced tomatoes	400 g
1 (16 ounce) package frozen bite-size mixed vegetables with green beans, thawed	455 g
3 ounces whole wheat spaghetti, broken	85 g
1 (15 ounce) can dark kidney beans, rinsed, drained	425 g
1 teaspoon dry crushed Italian herbs	5 ml

Add seasoning blend to sprayed, large heavy pan; cook and stir over medium heat until tender.

Add broth, tomatoes, mixed vegetables, spaghetti and 1 cup (250 ml) water. Bring to a boil and cook over medium heat until vegetables and spaghetti are tender, about 15 minutes.

Add beans, herbs, 1 teaspoon (5 ml) salt and ¼ teaspoon (1 ml) pepper and simmer 5 to 10 minutes.

Serves 6.
Serving size: 1 cup (250 ml)
Makes 6 cups (1.4 L).

One Serving

Calories: 226	Sodium: 923 mg
Calories from Fat: 13	Total Carbohydrates: 44 g
Total Fat: 2 g	Dietary Fiber: 9 g
Saturated Fat: 0 g	Sugars: 4 g
Cholesterol: 0 mg	Protein: 9 g

Minestrone with Baby Spinach

This Italian favorite is a meal in a bowl and wonderful.

1 medium onion, chopped	
2 garlic cloves, minced	
1 (15 ounce) can red kidney beans with liquid	425 g
1 (16 ounce) package frozen bite-size mixed vegetables with green beans, thawed	455 g
1 teaspoon dry crushed Italian herbs	5 ml
1 (6 ounce) can tomato paste	168 g
2 cups baby spinach or finely shredded cabbage	60 g/70 g

 Cook and stir onion and garlic in sprayed, large heavy saucepan until tender. Add 8 cups (1.9 L) water, kidney beans and mixed vegetables. Stir in herb seasoning and bring to a boil. Reduce heat, cover and simmer for 30 minutes.

 Stir in tomato paste and simmer for additional 15 minutes. Add spinach or cabbage, cover and cook about 5 minutes or until greens are tender.

Serves 10.
Serving size: 1 cup (250 ml)
Makes 10 cups (2.4 L).

TIP: If you want to make a heartier soup, add 1 cup (140 g) cooked whole wheat small pasta. Pass parmesan cheese around the table to top it off.

One Serving

Calories: 98	Cholesterol: 0 mg	Dietary Fiber: 5 g
Calories from Fat: 7	Sodium: 168 mg	Sugars: 2 g
Total Fat: 1 g	Total Carbohydrates: 20 g	Protein: 5 g
Saturated Fat: 0 g		

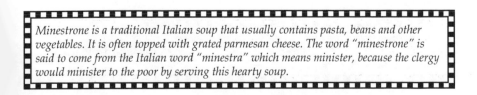

Minestrone is a traditional Italian soup that usually contains pasta, beans and other vegetables. It is often topped with grated parmesan cheese. The word "minestrone" is said to come from the Italian word "minestra" which means minister, because the clergy would minister to the poor by serving this hearty soup.

Vegetable Broth with Leeks

3 - 4 parsley sprigs and stems
1 bay leaf or 1 teaspoon dried thyme, crushed   5 ml
1 tablespoon olive oil   15 ml
1 medium onion, sliced
1 leek white part only, sliced
1 carrot, peeled, sliced
6 garlic cloves, minced

Tie parsley and bay leaf or thyme in 5 x 5-inch (13 x 13 cm) cheesecloth square.

Combine oil, onion, leek, carrot and garlic in large, heavy pan over medium-high heat and cook and stir about 10 minutes.

Add 6 cups (1.4 L) water, cheesecloth bag with herbs, 1 teaspoon (5 ml) salt and ¼ teaspoon (1 ml) pepper. Bring to a boil, reduce heat and simmer covered for 45 to 60 minutes or until vegetables are almost mushy.

Strain into large plastic container and discard vegetables and cheesecloth bag. Store tightly covered in refrigerator up to 4 days or freeze in plastic freezer containers, with about 1 inch (2.5 cm) of space at top to allow for expansion.

Serves 4.
Serving size: 1 cup (250 ml)
Makes 4 cups (1 L).

TIP: Dried parsley, thyme and bay leaf tied in cheesecloth, known as bouquet garni *or herb bouquet, is available in some supermarkets.*

One Serving

Calories: 39	Cholesterol: 0 mg	Dietary Fiber: 1 g
Calories from Fat: 31	Sodium: 0 mg	Sugars: 1 g
Total Fat: 4 g	Total Carbohydrates: 2 g	Protein: 0 g
Saturated Fat: 0 g		

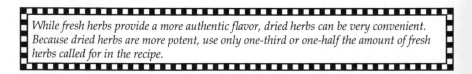

While fresh herbs provide a more authentic flavor, dried herbs can be very convenient. Because dried herbs are more potent, use only one-third or one-half the amount of fresh herbs called for in the recipe.

Skinny Vegetable Soup

2 teaspoons olive oil	10 ml
1 (16 ounce) package frozen seasoning blend (onion, celery, bell peppers*)	455 g
2 medium sliced carrots	
1 cup fresh or frozen whole green beans	125 g
1 small head green cabbage, trimmed, cut in wedges	
1 (6 ounce) can tomato paste	170 g
1 medium zucchini with peel, thinly sliced	

Combine oil, seasoning blend and carrots in large, heavy pan over medium heat. Cook and stir until vegetables are tender.

Add green beans, cabbage, tomato paste and 8 cups (1.9 L) water. Bring to a boil, reduce heat and simmer covered 15 to 20 minutes or until beans and cabbage are tender. Add ½ teaspoon (2 ml) salt and ⅛ teaspoon (.5 ml) pepper.

Stir in zucchini and boil gently for 3 to 4 minutes or until zucchini is tender.

Serves 12.
Serving size: 1 cup (250 ml)
Makes 12 cups (2.9 L).

*TIP: You can make fresh seasoning blend with 1 cup (160 g) chopped onion, ½ cup (50 g) chopped celery and ½ cup (75 g) chopped bell pepper. The frozen package is a really great timesaver when you need it.

One Serving

Calories: 78	Cholesterol: 0 mg	Dietary Fiber: 6 g
Calories from Fat: 12	Sodium: 49 mg	Sugars: 7 g
Total Fat: 1 g	Total Carbohydrates: 15 g	Protein: 3g
Saturated Fat: 0 g		

Roasted Vegetable Broth

Roasting the vegetables will give you a rich, flavorful broth you'll love.

5 carrots, scrubbed, cut in 1-inch pieces	5 (2.5 cm)
3 medium onions, quartered	
10 garlic cloves, peeled	
2 small turnips, peeled, cut in chunks	
2 red bell peppers, seeded, quartered	
2 tablespoons olive oil	30 ml
1 teaspoon dried thyme	5 ml

Preheat oven to 400° (205° C).

Spread carrots, onions, garlic, turnips and bell peppers in 2 shallow roasting pans. Drizzle with olive oil and sprinkle thyme on top.

Transfer to oven, roast vegetables for 1 hour and stir occasionally.

Transfer hot vegetables to large stockpot, add 4½ quarts (4.25 L) water and bring to a boil. Add 1 to 2 teaspoons (5-10 ml) salt and ½ teaspoon (2 ml) pepper. Reduce heat, cover and simmer for 1 hour.

Strain broth into large container and discard vegetables. Cool broth and cover tightly. Refrigerate about 4 days or freeze, leaving about 1 inch (2.5 cm) at top of freezer container to allow for expansion.

Serves 16.
Serving size: 1 cup (250 ml)
Makes 4 quarts (3.8 L).

TIP: If you like sun-dried tomatoes, add 1 cup (55 g) to stockpot.

One Serving

Calories: 29	Cholesterol: 0 mg	Dietary Fiber: 1 g
Calories from Fat: 16	Sodium: 13 mg	Sugars: 1 g
Total Fat: 2 g	Total Carbohydrates: 3 g	Protein: 0 g
Saturated Fat: 0 g		

Vegetable Gumbo

*There are as many different gumbos
as can be imagined. This version
is full of vegetables.*

2 teaspoons canola oil	10 ml
1 (16 ounce) package frozen seasoning blend (onions, celery, peppers)	455 g
2 (14 ounce) cans vegetable broth	2 (400 g)
1 (14 ounce) can diced tomatoes	400 g
1 (16 ounce) package frozen gumbo vegetables, thawed	455 g
1 teaspoon Creole seasoning	5 ml

🥣 Combine oil and seasoning
blend in large, heavy pan over
medium-high heat. Cook and
stir until vegetables are tender.
Add vegetable broth, tomatoes,
gumbo vegetables, Creole
seasoning and 1 teaspoon
(5 ml) salt.

🥣 Bring to a boil, reduce heat and
simmer covered until gumbo
vegetables are tender.

Serves 10.
Serving size: 1 cup (250 ml)
Makes 10 cups (2.4 L)

*TIP: Serve over brown rice and pass the file
powder and hot red pepper sauce.*

One Serving

Calories: 61	Sodium: 425 mg
Calories from Fat: 9	Total Carbohydrates: 10 g
Total Fat: 1 g	Dietary Fiber: 4 g
Saturated Fat: 0 g	Sugars: 4 g
Cholesterol: 0 mg	Protein: 2 g

Vegetable Stew and Dumplings

*This recipe is quick and easy
for feeding hungry folks.*

1 (14 ounce) can diced tomatoes	400 g
1 (16 ounce) package frozen vegetables for stew	455 g
²/₃ cup reduced-fat biscuit mix	80 g
¼ teaspoon dried thyme, crushed	1 ml
3 tablespoons fat-free skim milk	45 ml

🥣 Combine tomatoes and 4 cups
(1 L) water in large, heavy pan
and bring to a boil.

🥣 Add stew vegetables, 1 teaspoon
(5 ml) salt and ½ teaspoon (2 ml)
pepper and boil 2 to 3 minutes.

🥣 Combine baking mix, thyme and
skim milk to form soft dough.
Drop dough by tablespoonfuls
on top of boiling vegetables.
Reduce heat to a low boil and
cook uncovered 10 minutes.

🥣 Cover and cook 10 minutes or
until vegetables are tender.

Serves 6.
Serving size: 1 cup (250 ml)
Makes 6 cups (1.4 L)

One Serving

Calories: 169	Sodium: 374 mg
Calories from Fat: 3	Total Carbohydrates: 36 g
Total Fat: 0 g	Dietary Fiber: 5 g
Saturated Fat: 0 g	Sugars: 17 g
Cholesterol: 0 mg	Protein: 5 g

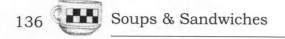

Vermicelli-Bell Pepper Soup

1 tablespoon olive oil	15 ml
8 ounces (2 cups) broken vermicelli	230 g
2 garlic cloves, minced	
¾ cup chopped green bell pepper	115 g
½ cup chopped fresh tomato	90 g
1½ cups vegetable broth	375 ml
¼ cup finely chopped parsley	20 g

Combine oil and vermicelli in non-stick 12-inch (32 cm) skillet over medium-high heat. Cook and stir until pasta browns. (Be careful not to burn it.) Remove and set aside.

In same skillet, add garlic, bell pepper, ½ teaspoon (2 ml) salt and ¼ teaspoon (1 ml) pepper. Cook and stir over medium heat until bell pepper is tender. Add tomato and stir.

Add broth and cook over low heat until liquid is absorbed. Add vermicelli and cook until tender. Sprinkle with parsley.

Serves 6.
Serving size: 1 cup (250 ml)
Makes 6 cups (1.4 L).

TIP: If you like hot and spicy, add one minced jalapeno or serrano pepper. Wear rubber gloves when handling hot peppers.

One Serving

Calories: 146	Cholesterol: 0 mg	Dietary Fiber: 2 g
Calories from Fat: 41	Sodium: 236 mg	Sugars: 1 g
Total Fat: 5 g	Total Carbohydrates: 27 g	Protein: 5 g
Saturated Fat: 0 g		

If you have taken a bite of a dish with peppers too "hot" for your taste, swish some milk around in your mouth to reduce the burning sensation.

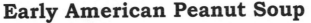

Early American Peanut Soup

Variations of peanut soup have been found in American cookbooks since about 1850.

2 tablespoons butter	30 g
2 tablespoons finely chopped onion	15 g
2 tablespoons flour	15 g
3 cups vegetable broth	750 ml
½ cup peanut butter	145 g
2 teaspoons lemon juice	10 ml
2 tablespoons chopped, unsalted dry-roasted peanuts	20 g

Melt butter in 3-quart (3 L) saucepan over low heat and add onion. Cook and stir until tender.

Stir in flour and cook until mixture bubbles. Add broth, cook and stir until it thickens. Reduce heat and simmer for 30 minutes.

Remove from heat, strain broth and return to pan. Stir in peanut butter, lemon juice and ¼ teaspoon salt until smooth. Heat and garnish with chopped peanuts.

Serves 4.
Serving size: 1 cup (250 ml)
Makes 4 cups (1 L).

TIP: If you have some celery, add ½ cup (50 g) thinly sliced celery with the chopped onion. It gives a nice flavor and texture. Celery is a great addition to most soups.

One Serving

Calories: 84	Cholesterol: 4 mg	Dietary Fiber: 1 g
Calories from Fat: 48	Sodium: 178 mg	Sugars: 1 g
Total Fat: 7 g	Total Carbohydrates: 4 g	Protein: 3 g
Saturated Fat: 3 g		

Avocado-Cheese Sandwich

This classic vegetarian sandwich is found frequently on restaurant menus.

1 tablespoon Mayo-Mustard Dressing (page 109)	15 ml
2 slices hearty whole grain or whole wheat bread	
2 thin slice Monterey Jack cheese	
2 thin slices tomatoes	
3 slices ripe Hass avocado	
¼ cup shredded romaine lettuce or leaf lettuce	15 g
1 - 2 tablespoons alfalfa or broccoli sprouts	15 - 30 ml

Spread Mayo-Mustard Dressing thinly on bread slices. Add cheese and tomatoes and a small amount of salt and pepper. Top with avocado, lettuce and sprouts. Cut in half or quarters.

Serves 1.
Serving size: 1 sandwich

TIP: Add a sprinkling of roasted sunflower seeds for a nice crunch.

One Serving

Calories: 477	Sodium: 766 mg
Calories from Fat: 280	Total Carbohy-drates: 30 g
Total Fat: 31 g	Dietary Fiber: 5 g
Saturated Fat: 8 g	Sugars: 4 g
Cholesterol: 25 mg	Protein: 15 g

Guacamole-Chick Sandwich

This is a fun open-faced sandwich with a feast of flavors!

1 (10 ounce) package frozen meatless "chicken" patties	280 g
4 slices sourdough bread	
3 - 4 tablespoons reduced-fat mayonnaise	45 - 60 g
1 large tomato, thinly sliced	
1 cup shredded romaine lettuce	40 g
¼ cup Green Chile Guacamole (page 58)	60 ml
1 cup alfalfa or broccoli sprouts	40 g

Microwave or bake patties according to package directions.

For each sandwich, spread 1 slice of bread with mayonnaise. Add 1 cooked patty, tomato slices, ¼ cup (10 g) lettuce and 1 tablespoon (15 ml) Green Chile Guacamole; top with ¼ cup (10 g) sprouts.

Serves 4.
Serving size: 1 sandwich

One Serving

Calories: 325	Sodium: 783 mg
Calories from Fat: 117	Total Carbohy-drates: 30 g
Total Fat: 133 g	Dietary Fiber: 8 g
Saturated Fat: 2 g	Sugars: 2 g
Cholesterol: 0 mg	Protein: 23 g

Guacamole Po' Boys

A hearty po' boy sandwich with a great combination of ingredients.

3 (7 inch) whole wheat sub rolls, halved	3 (18 cm)
½ cup Cumin-Mayo Spread (page 61)	125 ml
6 thin slices provolone cheese	
1 cup Green Chile Guacamole (page 58) or refrigerated organic guacamole	250 ml
2 medium tomatoes, thinly sliced	
1 large red onion, sliced, separated	
1 small head iceberg lettuce, shredded	

Place rolls cut side down and lightly toast in sprayed non-stick 12-inch (32 cm) skillet over medium heat.

For each sandwich, spread both halves of toasted roll with Cumin-Mayo Spread and arrange 2 slices cheese on one. Spoon about 3 tablespoons (45 ml) Green Chile Guacamole on top of cheese. Add slices of tomato, onion rings, lettuce and other half roll. Cut sandwich in half and serve.

Serves 6.
Serving size: ½ sandwich

One Serving

Calories: 300	Sodium: 550 mg
Calories from Fat: 168	Total Carbohy-drates: 22 g
Total Fat: 18 g	Dietary Fiber: 3 g
Saturated Fat: 6 g	Sugars: 2 g
Cholesterol: 16 mg	Protein: 8 g

California BLT Sandwich

8 slices sourdough bread	
8 slices veggie soy bacon	
1 cup alfalfa or broccoli sprouts	40 g
1 cup sliced ripe Hass avocado	150 g
1 ripe medium tomato, sliced	
Red lettuce leaves	
Creamy Goddess Dressing (page 104)	

For each sandwich, add 2 slices soy bacon, ¼ cup (10 g) sprouts, 2 to 3 avocado slices, 1 or 2 tomato slices, lettuce leaves and Creamy Goddess Dressing to 1 slice bread and top with another slice bread. Cut in half. Repeat for remaining sandwiches.

Serves 4.
Serving size: 1 sandwich

TIP: When buying an avocado for immediate use, select one that yields to gentle pressure. If planning to use days later, look for more firmness. To speed ripening, place avocado in paper bag with an apple slice.

One Serving

Calories: 322	Sodium: 566 mg
Calories from Fat: 247	Total Carbohy-drates: 41 g
Total Fat: 29 g	Dietary Fiber: 6 g
Saturated Fat: 4 g	Sugars: 2 g
Cholesterol: 0 mg	Protein: 11 g

Black Bean Burgers

Serve these burgers on whole wheat hamburger buns with all the fixins'.

1 (16 ounce) can black beans, drained, rinsed	455 g
2 tablespoons reduced-fat mayonnaise	30 g
½ teaspoon seasoning salt or lemon-pepper seasoning	2 ml
1 tablespoon plain breadcrumbs	15 ml
Small amount of flour	

Mash beans with mayonnaise in large bowl. Stir in seasoning and breadcrumbs. With lightly floured hands, form mixture into 4 (3 inch/8 cm) patties.

Add patties to sprayed non-stick 10-inch (25 cm) skillet over medium heat and cook about 3 minutes. Carefully turn patties and cook about 3 minutes.

Serves 4.
Serving size: 1 patty

One Serving

Calories: 188	Sodium: 1 mg
Calories from Fat: 56	Total Carbohydrates: 27 g
Total Fat: 6 g	Dietary Fiber: 5 g
Saturated Fat: 1 g	Sugars: 1 g
Cholesterol: 0 mg	Protein: 6 g

Hearty Cucumber Sandwich

Now this sandwich can whet the appetite of most anybody!

2 tablespoons part-skim ricotta cheese	35 g
2 slices dark rye or any whole grain bread	
5 - 6 slices seedless cucumber	
1 medium radish, sliced	
2 tablespoons alfalfa or broccoli sprouts	5 g
2 teaspoons reduced-fat mayonnaise	10 ml

Spread ricotta cheese on 1 slice bread. Top with cucumber and radish slices followed by sprouts. Spread mayonnaise on other slice bread. Cut in half.

Serves 1.
Serving size: 1 sandwich

One Serving

Calories: 409	Sodium: 759 mg
Calories from Fat: 232	Total Carbohydrates: 31 g
Total Fat: 26 g	Dietary Fiber: 2 g
Saturated Fat: 6 g	Sugars: 5 g
Cholesterol: 19 mg	Protein: 14 g

Classic Egg Salad Sandwich

Lots of us remember Mom's egg salad on good bread carried to school in a metal lunch box, which always had a special little treat inside.

⅓ cup reduced-fat mayonnaise	75 g
½ teaspoon dijon-style or yellow mustard	2 ml
4 eggs, hard-boiled, chopped	
⅓ cup diced celery	35 g
3 tablespoons thinly sliced green onions	20 g
8 slices whole wheat or whole grain bread	
Red or green leaf lettuce	

Stir mayonnaise and mustard in large bowl. Add eggs, celery and green onions and stir.

Make sandwich with 2 bread slices, one-fourth egg salad and lettuce leaves.

Serves 4.
Serving size: 1 sandwich

TIP: Kids and some adults may prefer this salad with chopped sweet pickles to replace the green onions.

One Serving

Calories: 116	Sodium: 235 mg
Calories from Fat: 59	Total Carbohydrates: 13 g
Total Fat: 7 g	Dietary Fiber: 1 g
Saturated Fat: 1 g	Sugars: 1 g
Cholesterol: 106 mg	Protein: 6 g

Mango Salsa Cheeseburgers

1 (10 ounce) package frozen meatless cheeseburgers	280 g
4 whole wheat hamburger buns, split	
¼ cup reduced-fat mayonnaise	60 g
¼ cup Mango Salsa (page 55)	60 ml

Cook frozen cheeseburgers according to package directions.

Lightly toast split buns. Spread each bun lightly with mayonnaise. Add cheeseburgers and top with 1 tablespoon (15 ml) Mango Salsa.

Serves 4.
Serving size: 1 cheeseburger

One Serving

Calories: 397	Sodium: 927 mg
Calories from Fat: 144	Total Carbohydrates: 38 g
Total Fat: 16 g	Dietary Fiber: 7 g
Saturated Fat: 2 g	Sugars: 3 g
Cholesterol: 0 mg	Protein: 21 g

Grilled Portobello Burgers

4 medium portobello mushrooms,
    stems removed
¼ cup reduced-sodium
    soy sauce   60 ml
4 whole wheat or whole
    grain buns
Dijon-style mustard
1 - 2 large tomatoes, thinly sliced
1 red onion, thinly sliced, separated
Red or green leaf lettuce

Marinate mushrooms in soy sauce for 30 minutes and turn occasionally.

Prepare outside grill. Over medium heat, grill mushrooms about 8 to 10 minutes per side and occasionally brush with soy sauce. Lightly toast buns on grill.

Serve hot mushrooms on warm buns with mustard, tomato slices, red onion rings and lettuce.

Serves 4.
Serving size: 1 burger

TIP: It also works well to broil mushrooms in oven.

One Serving

Calories: 162	Sodium: 268 mg
Calories from	Total Carbohy-
Fat: 17	drates: 30 g
Total Fat: 2 g	Dietary Fiber: 4 g
Saturated Fat: 0 g	Sugars: 4 g
Cholesterol: 0 mg	Protein: 8 g

Veggie Patty Melts

Hearty flavors combine for a delicious sandwich! Yum, yum!

1 (10 ounce) package frozen
    soy veggie patties   280 g
8 slices light or dark rye bread
4 - 5 teaspoons dijon-style
    mustard   20 - 25 ml
4 slices reduced-fat Swiss cheese
1 cup Tickled-Pink Pickled
    Onions (page 52)   250 ml

Cook patties according to package directions.

Spread rye bread slices with mustard. Add patty, cheese slice and ¼ cup (60 ml) Tickled-Pink Pickled Onions for each sandwich. Toast sandwiches on both sides in sprayed non-stick 10-inch (25 cm) skillet until cheese melts.

Serves 4.
Serving size: 1 sandwich

One Serving

Calories: 357	Sodium: 451 mg
Calories from	Total Carbohy-
Fat: 87	drates: 32 g
Total Fat: 11 g	Dietary Fiber: 8 g
Saturated Fat: 2 g	Sugars: 2 g
Cholesterol: 10 mg	Protein: 32 g

Veggie Sloppy Joes

6 ounces veggie protein crumbles	170 g
½ cup chopped onion	80 g
½ cup chopped green bell pepper	75 g
1 (8 ounce) can tomato sauce	230 g
1 - 1½ teaspoons chili powder or chili seasoning mix	5 ml
1 teaspoon Worcestershire sauce	5 ml
5 whole wheat hamburger buns, split	

🍞 Break apart crumbles in sprayed non-stick 12-inch (32 cm) skillet. Add onion and bell pepper, cook and stir until crumbles brown and vegetables are tender. Stir in tomato sauce, chili powder, Worcestershire sauce and 2 tablespoons (30 ml) water.

🍞 Bring to a boil, reduce heat and simmer uncovered for 5 minutes.

🍞 Lightly toast buns and spoon mixture generously over buns.

Serves 5.
Serving size: 1 sandwich

TIP: Three ounces veggie protein crumbles have 70 calories, 0 grams fat and 12 grams protein. Compare to 3 ounces of 80/20 lean ground beef with 231 calories, 15 grams fat and 23 grams protein.

One Serving

Calories: 167	Cholesterol: 0 mg	Dietary Fiber: 4 g
Calories from Fat: 19	Sodium: 329 mg	Sugars: 4 g
Total Fat: 2 g	Total Carbohydrates: 30 g	Protein: 8 g
Saturated Fat: 0 g		

Hearty Veggie Tostadas

*Tostadas are flat, crispy corn or flour tortillas and
have lots of uses. This is just one that is a tasty treat.*

2 teaspoons olive oil	10 ml
2 medium zucchini, cut in ½-inch cubes	1.2 cm
¼ cup frozen whole kernel corn, thawed	45 g
3 tablespoons chopped green chilies, drained	45 g
4 (5 inch) prepared tostada shells	4 (13 cm)
¼ cup thinly sliced green onions, divided	25 g
1 cup reduced-fat, finely shredded Monterey Jack cheese, divided	115 g

Preheat oven to 325° (160° C).

Heat oil in 10-inch (25 cm) skillet over medium-high heat. Add zucchini and corn, cook and stir until vegetables are tender. Stir in green chilies.

Arrange tostada shells on baking sheet and bake for 2 to 3 minutes. Remove tostadas and increase oven heat to 400° (205° C).

Spoon vegetable mixture evenly onto tostada shells and sprinkle with green onions and cheese. Return shells to baking sheet.

Bake for 2 to 3 minutes or until cheese melts.

Serves 4.
Serving size: 1 filled tostada shell

*TIP: Delicious garnishes for tostadas include chopped tomato, shredded lettuce, salsa, ripe
olives and sour cream.*

One Serving

Calories: 332
Calories from Fat: 176
Total Fat: 20 g
Saturated Fat: 8 g

Cholesterol: 29 mg
Sodium: 323 mg
Total Carbohydrates: 29 g

Dietary Fiber: 3 g
Sugars: 2 g
Protein: 12 g

Brown Bag White Bean Burritos

Pack for microwave lunch away from home.

1 (15 ounce) can cannellini beans, drained, rinsed	425 g
4 (10 inch) whole wheat or multigrain tortillas	4 (25 cm)
¼ cup Green Chile Sauce (page 238)	60 ml
¾ cup finely shredded Monterey Jack cheese	85 g

🌀 Mash beans and spread 2 to 3 tablespoons (30 - 45 ml) on each tortilla. Top with 1 tablespoon (15 ml) Green Chile Sauce and 3 tablespoons (45 ml) cheese. Fold one edge of tortilla over filling about 1 inch (2.5 cm). Roll each tortilla and wrap tightly in plastic wrap.

🌀 When ready for lunch, unwrap burrito and place seam-side down on microwave-safe plate. Cover loosely and microwave on HIGH for 45 seconds to 1 minute.

Serves 4.
Serving size: 1 burrito

TIP: Pack raw veggies and fruit to round out your brown bag lunch.

One Serving

Calories: 110	Sodium: 285 mg
Calories from Fat: 32	Total Carbohydrates: 15 g
Total Fat: 4 g	Dietary Fiber: 2 g
Saturated Fat: 1 g	Sugars: 0 g
Cholesterol: 7 mg	Protein: 5 g

Mashed Potato Burritos

This fun recipe will serve a crowd.

5 large russet potatoes, peeled, quartered	
¼ cup fat-free skim milk	60 ml
1 cup chopped green onions	100 g
1½ cups reduced-fat shredded cheddar cheese	170 g
12 (10 inch) vegetable-flavor flour tortillas	12 (25 cm)
1 cup ranch-style salad dressing	250 ml

🌀 Bring 3 to 4 quarts (3 - 4 L) water to a boil in large, heavy saucepan. Add potatoes, reduce heat and cook covered or uncovered until tender, about 20 to 30 minutes. Drain and transfer to large bowl. Add skim milk and mash potatoes until smooth. Stir in green onions and cheese and mix well.

🌀 Soften tortillas in microwave on HIGH for a few seconds. Spoon about 2 tablespoons (30 ml) potato mixture on each warmed tortilla. Fold 1 side of tortilla 1 inch (2.5 cm) around filling and roll.

🌀 Serve with ranch-style salad dressing for dipping.

Serves 12.
Serving size: 1 burrito

One Serving

Calories: 361	Sodium: 635 mg
Calories from Fat: 105	Total Carbohydrates: 51 g
Total Fat: 12 g	Dietary Fiber: 5 g
Saturated Fat: 3 g	Sugars: 2 g
Cholesterol: 7 mg	Protein: 12 g

Carrot-Zucchini-Sprouts Wraps

1 (3 ounce) package reduced-fat
   cream cheese, softened,
   divided   84 g
4 (7 inch) whole wheat or
   vegetable tortillas   4 (18 cm)
1 cup shredded carrots,
   divided   120 g
1 cup shredded zucchini,
   divided   120 g
1 cup alfalfa or broccoli
   sprouts, divided   40 g

Spread 1½ tablespoons (22 ml)
cream cheese on each tortilla.
Add ¼ cup (30 g) carrot, ¼ cup
(30 g) zucchini and ¼ cup (10 g)
sprouts on each tortilla and roll.

Serves 4.
Serving size: 1 wrap

One Serving

Calories: 212	Sodium: 311 mg
Calories from Fat: 61	Total Carbohydrates: 30 g
Total Fat: 7 g	Dietary Fiber: 2 g
Saturated Fat: 0 g	Sugars: 0 g
Cholesterol: 12 mg	Protein: 6 g

Hummus-Gorgonzola Wraps

*Hummus is a Middle Eastern
spread made with mashed
chick-peas (garbanzo beans).*

¾ cup All-Purpose Hummus
   (page 61) or prepared
   hummus   175 ml
4 (10 inch) whole wheat
   tortillas   4 (25 cm)
3 cups torn bite-size
   romaine leaves   130 g
2 medium tomatoes, diced
½ cup crumbled gorgonzola
   cheese   70 g
⅓ cup Basil Vinaigrette
   (page 102)   74 ml

Spread one-fourth of All-
Purposr Hummus on each
tortilla. Add about one-fourth
of romaine leaves, one-fourth
tomato and one-fourth of cheese.
Sprinkle with Basil Vinaigrette
and tightly roll tortilla.

Serves 4.
Serving size: 1 wrap

One Serving

Calories: 401	Sodium: 633 mg
Calories from Fat: 172	Total Carbohydrates: 46 g
Total Fat: 19 g	Dietary Fiber: 5 g
Saturated Fat: 5 g	Sugars: 3 g
Cholesterol: 14 mg	Protein: 11 g

Chorizo-Kidney Bean Wraps

This is so flavorful, you'll want to eat the chorizo bean mixture with a spoon!

2 teaspoons olive oil	10 ml
½ cup chopped onion	80 g
1 garlic clove, minced	
1 cup dark kidney beans, rinsed, drained	260 g
1 cup diced tomatoes with juice	180 g
¼ cup veggie protein chorizo sausage, cooked	60 ml
3 (10 inch) whole wheat, multigrain or vegetable tortillas	3 (25 cm)

Combine oil, onion and garlic in 10-inch (25 cm) skillet. Cook and stir until onion is tender.

Mash beans and add to skillet with tomatoes and cooked chorizo. Simmer about 5 minutes. Add water if needed.

Spread bean mixture on tortillas and roll.

Serves 3.
Serving size: 1 tortilla with filling

TIP: If you want to add cheese, sprinkle shredded mozzarella or Monterey Jack cheese on filling, roll and heat a few seconds in microwave oven on HIGH to warm cheese.

One Serving

Calories: 478	Cholesterol: 3 mg	Dietary Fiber: 14 g
Calories from Fat: 52	Sodium: 1344 mg	Sugars: 6 g
Total Fat: 6 g	Total Carbohydrates: 71 g	Protein: 18 g
Saturated Fat: 2 g		

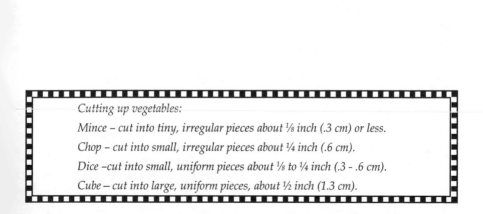

Cutting up vegetables:

Mince – cut into tiny, irregular pieces about ⅛ inch (.3 cm) or less.

Chop – cut into small, irregular pieces about ¼ inch (.6 cm).

Dice –cut into small, uniform pieces about ⅛ to ¼ inch (.3 - .6 cm).

Cube – cut into large, uniform pieces, about ½ inch (1.3 cm).

Tomatillo-Bean-Corn Wraps

1 (15 ounce) can black, pinto
  or kidney beans, drained,
  rinsed   425 g
½ cup Fresh Tomatillo Salsa
  (page 53) or bottled salsa
  verde   125 ml
1 cup frozen whole kernel
  corn, thawed, drained   165 g
4 (10 inch) whole wheat
  tortillas   4 (25 cm)
1 cup cheddar-flavor soy
  veggie shreds   110 g

Mash beans and combine with
Fresh Tomatillo Salsa and corn
in microwave-safe bowl. Cover
mixture loosely with plastic
wrap. Microwave on HIGH for
1 minute or until hot. Stir
mixture and spoon even
amounts onto tortillas. Sprinkle
each with one-fourth veggie
shreds and roll.

Serves 4.
Serving size: 1 wrap

One Serving

Calories: 400	Sodium: 799 mg
Calories from	Total Carbohy-
Fat: 71	drates: 70 g
Total Fat: 8 g	Dietary Fiber: 8 g
Saturated Fat: 2 g	Sugars: 2 g
Cholesterol: 0 mg	Protein: 14 g

Pepper-Olive Tortilla Rolls

*This is a great recipe for
those on-the-run days!*

1 (8 ounce) package reduced-fat
  cream cheese, softened   230 g
4 - 6 whole wheat or
  multigrain tortillas
1 cup diced red bell pepper   150 g
1 (4 ounce) can chopped ripe
  olives   115 g
2 - 3 cups shredded lettuce
  or alfalfa sprouts   85 - 130 g

Divide cream cheese evenly
and spread on each tortilla.
Sprinkle evenly with remaining
ingredients and roll tightly.

Makes 4 to 6 servings.
Serving size: 1 tortilla roll

*TIP: For a bit of zip, add 1 teaspoon (5 ml)
chopped drained green chilies to
each tortilla.*

One Serving

Calories: 314	Sodium: 686 mg
Calories from	Total Carbohy-
Fat: 113	drates: 34 g
Total Fat: 12 g	Dietary Fiber: 3 g
Saturated Fat: 6 g	Sugars: 3 g
Cholesterol: 26 mg	Protein: 10 g

Teriyaki-Vegetable Wraps

1 (16 ounce) package frozen seasoning blend (onion, celery, bell pepper)	455 g
1 clove garlic, minced	
1 cup chopped zucchini	125 g
1 cup chopped yellow squash	115 g
½ cup teriyaki sauce	125 ml
1 cup cooked brown rice	195 g
4 (10 inch) whole wheat tortillas	4 (25 cm)

Combine seasoning blend and garlic in sprayed non-stick 10-inch (25 cm) skillet over medium-high heat. Cook and stir until tender and moisture evaporates. Reduce heat to medium, add zucchini and yellow squash and cook about 5 minutes or until tender. Add sauce and rice and stir until hot.

Warm tortillas in microwave on HIGH just a few seconds. Spoon one-fourth mixture on each warmed tortilla and roll.

Serves 4.
Serving size: 1 wrap

TIP: Add 2 to 3 tablespoons (10 g) broccoli or alfalfa sprouts to wrap if you want more in your wrap. Serve with reduced-sodium soy sauce.

One Serving

Calories: 255	Cholesterol: 0 mg	Dietary Fiber: 5 g
Calories from Fat: 66	Sodium: 689 mg	Sugars: 3 g
Total Fat: 7 g	Total Carbohydrates: 38 g	Protein: 5 g
Saturated Fat: 2 g		

Vegetable Hash Burritos

2 teaspoons canola oil	10 ml
1 cup diced onion	160 g
1 clove garlic, minced	
2 cups shredded potatoes	300 g
2 cups shredded zucchini	250 g
1 (4 ounce) can chopped green chilies	115 g
4 (10 inch) whole wheat or multigrain tortillas	4 (25 cm)

Heat oil in non-stick 12-inch (32 cm) saucepan over medium-high heat. Add onion and garlic, cook and stir until onion is tender. Reduce heat to medium and add potatoes and zucchini. Cook uncovered until vegetables are tender. Stir occasionally.

Add green chilies and heat through. Spoon about one-fourth mixture on each tortilla. Fold one edge of tortilla about 1 inch (2.5 cm) over filling, then roll.

Serves 4.
Serving size: 1 burrito

TIP: If tortillas are stiff, put them in the microwave for about 15 seconds or until they are warm and more pliable.

One Serving

Calories: 346	Cholesterol: 0 mg	Dietary Fiber: 7 g
Calories from Fat: 74	Sodium: 669 mg	Sugars: 7 g
Total Fat: 8 g	Total Carbohydrates: 60 g	Protein: 10 g
Saturated Fat: 2 g		

Side Dishes

Contents

Skillet Fresh Artichokes

4 medium fresh artichokes	
1 tablespoon olive oil	15 ml
1 garlic clove, minced	
1 teaspoon crushed dried thyme	5 ml
1 cup vegetable broth	250 ml

Trim away tough outer leaves of artichoke. Cut off 1 inch (2.5 cm) from tops and snip off sharp leaf tips. Peel stems, cut into quarters and remove chokes with sharp knife.

Add oil and garlic to non-stick 12-inch (32 cm) skillet. Over medium heat; cook and stir garlic about 1 minute. Add artichoke quarters and cook, turning frequently, about 3 to 5 minutes. Add thyme, broth and ½ teaspoon (2 ml) salt and bring to a boil. Reduce heat, cover and simmer until artichokes are tender, about 15 to 30 minutes.

Use slotted spoon to transfer artichokes to serving dish. Increase heat under skillet and cook until remaining liquid thickens. Pour thickened liquid over artichokes.

Serves 4 to 6.
Serving size: ¾ cup (175 ml)

One Serving

Calories: 64	Sodium: 237 mg
Calories from Fat: 22	Total Carbohydrates: 10 g
Total Fat: 3 g	Dietary Fiber: 5 g
Saturated Fat: 0 g	Sugars: 0 g
Cholesterol: 0 mg	Protein: 3 g

Asparagus Stir-Fry

2 pounds (about 40 spears) asparagus	910 g
2 teaspoons sesame oil or canola oil	10 ml
2 garlic cloves, minced	
¼ cup vegetable broth	60 ml
1 tablespoon toasted sesame seeds	15 ml

Wash asparagus and carefully bend each stalk. The stalk will break at the natural breaking point, above the woody stem. Cut into 2-inch (5 cm) diagonal slices.

Heat oil in non-stick wok or 12-inch (32 cm) skillet over high heat and add asparagus. Stir-fry about 2 to 3 minutes. Add garlic and stir-fry 1 to 2 minutes. Add broth or ¼ cup (60 ml) water and reduce heat. Cover and cook until asparagus is tender, about 5 minutes. Sprinkle with sesame seeds.

Serves 8.
Serving size: 4 to 5 spears

One Serving

Calories: 49	Sodium: 9 mg
Calories from Fat: 21	Total Carbohydrates: 5 g
Total Fat: 3 g	Dietary Fiber: 2 g
Saturated Fat: 0 g	Sugars: 0 g
Cholesterol: 0 mg	Protein: 4 g

Beets with Apples

You'll enjoy this unlikely,
but delicious, combination.

2 (15 ounce) cans sliced beets, rinsed, drained	2 (425 g)
2 cups red delicious apples, cored, sliced	220 g
½ cup thinly sliced onion	60 g
1 tablespoon finely grated lemon peel	15 ml
2 tablespoons fresh lemon juice	30 ml
2 tablespoons brown sugar	25 g
2 tablespoons melted butter	30 g

Preheat oven to 350° (175° C).

Combine beets, apples and onion in large bowl. Sprinkle with grated lemon peel, lemon juice and sugar. Stir to coat. Arrange in sprayed 9 x 9-inch (23 x 23 cm) baking dish and drizzle with melted butter.

Cover, bake 45 minutes and stir occasionally.

Serves 4 to 6.
Serving size: ¾ cup (175 ml)

One Serving

Calories: 122	Sodium: 194 mg
Calories from Fat: 37	Total Carbohydrates: 22 g
Total Fat: 4 g	Dietary Fiber: 3 g
Saturated Fat: 2 g	Sugars: 18 g
Cholesterol: 10 mg	Protein: 1 g

Harvard Crimson Beets

As the story goes, the name Harvard
Beets was inspired by the crimson
uniforms of the Harvard
football team in the early 1930's.

½ cup sugar or sugar substitute	100 g
1½ teaspoons cornstarch	7 ml
¼ cup apple cider vinegar	60 ml
2 (14 ounce) cans sliced beets, drained	2 (400 g)
2 tablespoons butter	30 g

Combine sugar, cornstarch, vinegar and ¼ cup (60 ml) water in 2-quart (2 L) saucepan. Bring to a boil, whisking vigorously and cook for 3 to 4 minutes or until sauce thickens and turns from cloudy to clear. Add beets, toss well and let stand 30 minutes or more. Just before serving, add butter.

Serves 6.
Serving size: ¾ cup (175 ml)

One Serving
Nutrition facts are based on sugar substitute.

Calories: 67	Sodium: 191 mg
Calories from Fat: 37	Total Carbohydrates: 7 g
Total Fat: 4 g	Dietary Fiber: 2 g
Saturated Fat: 2 g	Sugars: 5 g
Cholesterol: 10 mg	Protein: 1 g

To slow down discoloration in slices of light-colored fruits, spritz with lemon juice or dip in a solution of 1 quart (1 L) water and 1 tablespoon (15 ml) lemon juice.

Red Cabbage and Apples

Rotkohl is the name for a German dish of cabbage, apples and bacon fat. Although similar in flavor and texture, this recipe does not use bacon fat.

1 small head red cabbage, quartered, cored, thinly sliced	
1/3 cup finely chopped onion	55 g
1 large Granny Smith apple, peeled, cored, sliced	
1/4 cup red wine vinegar	60 ml
3 tablespoons honey or brown sugar	65 g/40 g
1/4 teaspoon caraway seeds	1 ml

Rinse and drain sliced cabbage. Add onion to sprayed, large heavy pan. Cook and stir over medium-high heat until onion is tender.

Stir in cabbage, apple, vinegar, honey or brown sugar, caraway seeds, 1/2 teaspoon (2 ml) salt and 1/4 teaspoon (1 ml) pepper. Cover and cook over medium heat until cabbage wilts. Reduce heat and cook, stirring occasionally, about 1 to 1 hour 30 minutes or until cabbage is very tender. Add water during cooking, if needed.

Serves 6.
Serving size: 1/2 cup (125 ml)

One Serving

Calories: 117	Sodium: 35 mg
Calories from Fat: 2	Total Carbohydrates: 29 g
Total Fat: 0 g	Dietary Fiber: 4 g
Saturated Fat: 0 g	Sugars: 23 g
Cholesterol: 0 mg	Protein: 2 g

Dilled Cabbage and Carrots

Cabbage is an humble but amazingly versatile vegetable, raw or cooked.

1 cup vegetable broth	250 ml
1/2 pound (3 - 5) medium carrots, peeled, thinly sliced	230 g
2 pounds green cabbage, shredded	910 g
1 teaspoon dill seeds or 1 teaspoon dried dill weed	5 ml

Bring broth to a boil in large, heavy pan over medium-high heat. Add carrots and cook about 10 minutes or until carrots are tender.

Add cabbage, dill, 1/2 teaspoon (2 ml) salt and 1/8 teaspoon (.5 ml) pepper. Cover and cook over low heat about 10 minutes or until cabbage wilts. Uncover and cook until cabbage is tender.

Serves 4.
Serving size: 3/4 cup (175 ml)

One Serving

Calories: 52	Sodium: 203 mg
Calories from Fat: 2	Total Carbohydrates: 12 g
Total Fat: 0 g	Dietary Fiber: 5 g
Saturated Fat: 0 g	Sugars: 7 g
Cholesterol: 0 mg	Protein: 2 g

Sweet Dilled Carrots

1 pound carrots, peeled, sliced	455 g
2 tablespoons butter	30 g
1 tablespoon dried dill seeds	15 ml
¼ cup packed light brown sugar	55 g

Combine carrots and 2 cups (400 ml) water in 2-quart (2 L) saucepan. Bring to a boil, reduce heat, cover and cook until tender, about 10 minutes. Drain.

Melt butter in 10-inch (25 cm) skillet and add dill seeds and brown sugar. Cook and stir over medium heat until sugar melts. Stir in carrots and ½ teaspoon (2 ml) salt. Simmer, stirring frequently, about 5 minutes.

Serves 6.
Serving size: ½ cup (125 ml)

One Serving

Calories: 91	Sodium: 42 mg
Calories from Fat: 36	Total Carbohydrates: 14 g
Total Fat: 4 g	Dietary Fiber: 2 g
Saturated Fat: 2 g	Sugars: 12 g
Cholesterol: 10 mg	Protein: 0 g

Ginger-Orange Carrots

Nutritionally, carrots are chock full of vitamins A and C and have very few calories.

1 pound (4 - 6 large) carrots, peeled, sliced ¼ inch diagonally	455 g/.6 cm
1 tablespoon sugar	15 ml
1 teaspoon cornstarch	5 ml
½ teaspoon ground ginger	2 ml
¼ cup orange juice	60 ml
2 tablespoons grated orange peel	30 ml

Bring 2 cups (500 ml) water to a boil in 2-quart (2 L) saucepan and add carrots. Reduce heat to simmer, cover and cook until carrots are tender, about 10 minutes. Drain.

Combine sugar, cornstarch, ginger and ¼ teaspoon (1 ml) salt in 1-quart (1 L) saucepan and stir. Add orange juice and mix vigorously with whisk to dissolve cornstarch. Whisk constantly until mixture bubbles and turns from cloudy to clear.

Pour sauce over carrots and sprinkle with orange peel to serve.

Serves 6.
Serving size: ½ cup (125 ml)

One Serving

Calories: 43	Sodium: 38 mg
Calories from Fat: 0	Total Carbohydrates: 10 g
Total Fat: 0 g	Dietary Fiber: 2 g
Saturated Fat: 0 g	Sugars: 7 g
Cholesterol: 0 mg	Protein: 0 g

Parslied Carrots

Carrots are in a buttery sauce perked up with parsley and lemon juice.

1 pound carrots, sliced	455 g
1 tablespoon butter	15 ml
2 tablespoons finely chopped onion	20 g
½ teaspoon fresh lemon juice	2 ml
2 tablespoons chopped fresh parsley	10 g

Combine carrots and 2 cups (500 ml) water in 2-quart (2 L) saucepan and bring to a boil. Reduce heat to medium-low, cover and cook until tender, about 10 minutes. Drain.

Melt butter in 10-inch (25 cm) skillet over medium heat, add onion, cook and stir until tender. Add carrots, lemon juice and ½ teaspoon (2 ml) salt. Sprinkle with parsley.

Serves 6.
Serving size: ½ cup (125 ml)

One Serving

Calories: 40	Sodium: 38 mg
Calories from Fat: 18	Total Carbohydrates: 5 g
Total Fat: 2 g	Dietary Fiber: 2 g
Saturated Fat: 1 g	Sugars: 3 g
Cholesterol: 5 mg	Protein: 0 g

Roasted Garlic

2 large heads garlic	
2 teaspoons olive oil	10 ml

Preheat oven to 425° (220° C).

Peel away dry outer layers of garlic and leave skins and cloves intact. Cut ¼ inch (.6 cm) off pointed tops.

Set garlic heads on small squares of foil and drizzle oil on them. Wrap and roast for 45 minutes or until soft when pressed. Cool and squeeze out garlic paste from individual cloves. Use as is or in recipes.

Serves 4.
Serving size: 1 tablespoon (15 ml)

One Serving

Calories: 20	Sodium: 0 mg
Calories from Fat: 20	Total Carbohydrates: 0 g
Total Fat: 2 g	Dietary Fiber: 0 g
Saturated Fat: 0 g	Sugars: 0 g
Cholesterol: 0 mg	Protein: 0 g

Oven-Crisped Cauliflower

This recipe is a delicious reduced-fat alternative to breading and frying cauliflower in oil.

1 large head cauliflower
2 fresh lemons, divided
½ cup egg substitute or 2 beaten eggs   **125 g**
30 - 40 whole wheat saltine crackers, coarsely crushed, divided

Preheat oven to 400° (205° C).

Trim leaves from cauliflower and remove core. (You will have about 1 pound/455 g trimmed florets.) Cut or pull apart large florets into 1-inch (2.5 cm) pieces.

Bring 2 to 3 quarts (2 - 3 L) water, juice from 1 lemon and 1 teaspoon (5 ml) salt to a boil in large, heavy pan. Add florets and boil uncovered for about 3 to 5 minutes or until florets are slightly tender. Remove and drain.

Add eggs, ½ teaspoon (2 ml) salt and ⅛ teaspoon (.5 ml) pepper to shallow bowl. In separate shallow dish, add one-half cracker crumbs. Dip florets in egg mixture and roll in cracker crumbs. If crumbs become too moist, discard and use remaining crumbs.

Arrange florets on sprayed non-stick baking sheet. Lightly spray tops of florets. Bake about 10 minutes. Turn and bake additional 4 to 5 minutes or until crispy and golden brown on both sides. Serve with lemon wedges.

Serves 4 to 6.
Serving size: 3 to 4 florets

One Serving
Nutrition facts are based on egg substitute.

Calories: 141	Cholesterol: 0 mg	Dietary Fiber: 6 g
Calories from Fat: 38	Sodium: 211 mg	Sugars: 4 g
Total Fat: 4 g	Total Carbohydrates: 21 g	Protein: 7 g
Saturated Fat: 1 g		

Scalloped Corn

There is no end to the versatility of corn!

3 tablespoons butter	45 g
1 (16 ounce) package frozen seasoning blend (onion, celery, bell peppers)	455 g
3 tablespoons unbleached white flour	25 g
1 cup fat-free skim milk	250 ml
2 cups frozen whole kernel corn, thawed	330 g
1 egg yolk, slightly beaten	
⅔ cup soft breadcrumbs	40 g

Preheat oven to 400° (205° C).

Melt butter in 10-inch (25 cm) skillet over medium heat and add seasoning blend. Cook and stir until vegetables are tender. Whisk in flour and cook until bubbles form. Add skim milk and bring mixture to a boil.

Reduce heat and cook until thick. Add 1 teaspoon (5 ml) salt and ¼ teaspoon (1 ml) pepper. Remove from heat and stir in corn and egg yolk.

Spoon mixture into sprayed 1½-quart (1.5 L) baking dish and sprinkle with crumbs. Bake for 25 minutes or until it bubbles and crumbs brown.

Serves 6.
Serving size: ¾ cup (175 ml)

One Serving

Calories: 221	Sodium: 113 mg
Calories from Fat: 70	Total Carbohydrates: 32 g
Total Fat: 8 g	Dietary Fiber: 4 g
Saturated Fat: 4 g	Sugars: 4 g
Cholesterol: 51 mg	Protein: 6 g

Corn and Bell Peppers

It's hard to beat the combination of corn and bell peppers.

2 tablespoons olive oil	30 ml
1 large onion, chopped	
1 medium green bell pepper, seeded, chopped	
1 medium red bell pepper, seeded, chopped	
2 cups frozen whole kernel corn, thawed	330 g
½ cup vegetable broth	125 ml
2 tablespoons chopped fresh cilantro	30 ml

Combine oil, onion and bell peppers in 12-inch (32 cm) skillet over medium-high heat. Cook and stir until tender. Add corn, broth, ½ teaspoon (2 ml) salt and ⅛ teaspoon (.5 ml) pepper. Bring to a boil. Reduce heat, cover and simmer until corn is tender. Sprinkle with cilantro.

Serves 8.
Serving size: ¾ cup (175 ml)

One Serving

Calories: 83	Sodium: 60 mg
Calories from Fat: 34	Total Carbohydrates: 12 g
Total Fat: 4 g	Dietary Fiber: 2 g
Saturated Fat: 0 g	Sugars: 1 g
Cholesterol: 0 mg	Protein: 1 g

Down South Mustard Greens

The traditional Southern approach to mustard greens was to cook them with bacon fat. This recipe is an updated version using olive oil.

1 pound fresh mustard greens	455 g
1 tablespoon olive oil	15 ml
1 (16 ounce) package frozen seasoning blend (onions, celery, peppers)	455 g
3 garlic cloves, minced	
1 cup canned diced tomatoes with liquid	255 g
¾ teaspoon Creole seasoning or ¼ teaspoon crushed red pepper	4 ml/1 ml

Soak mustard greens in large pan with water. Pour off water and repeat. Trim center ribs from greens and discard. Chop greens with large, heavy knife.

Heat oil in large, heavy pan over medium-high heat. Add seasoning blend and garlic. Cook and stir about 5 minutes or until vegetables are tender.

Add chopped greens and cook covered until it wilts, about 5 minutes. Stir in ¼ cup (60 ml) water and bring to a boil. Reduce heat to simmer and add tomatoes, Creole seasoning and ½ teaspoon (2 ml) salt.

Cook, stirring occasionally, until greens are tender, about 15 to 20 minutes.

Serves 4.

Serving size: ¾ cup (175 ml)

TIP: Make fresh seasoning blend with 1 cup (160 g) chopped onion, ½ cup (50 g) chopped celery and ½ cup (75 g) chopped red, yellow or green bell pepper.

One Serving

Calories: 102	Cholesterol: 0 mg	Dietary Fiber: 7 g
Calories from Fat: 33	Sodium: 32 mg	Sugars: 5 g
Total Fat: 4 g	Total Carbohydrates: 13 g	Protein: 4 g
Saturated Fat: 0 g		

Corn and Summer Squash

*This is such a colorful melange
of favorite vegetables.*

2 teaspoons canola or olive oil	10 ml
1 pound small crookneck yellow squash, trimmed, sliced	455 g
½ cup chopped onion	80 g
1 cup diced green bell pepper	150 g
4 medium roma or pear tomatoes, seeded, diced	
1½ cups frozen whole kernel corn, thawed	250 g

 Heat oil in non-stick 12-inch (32 cm) skillet and stir in squash, onion, bell pepper and ½ cup (125 ml) water. Cover and cook over medium-high heat for about 6 minutes.

Add tomatoes, corn, ½ teaspoon (2 ml) salt and ⅛ teaspoon (.5 ml) pepper. Cover and cook about 8 minutes or until vegetables are tender. Add water if needed.

Serves 6 to 8.
Serving size: ½ cup (125 ml)

TIP: Also known as sweet bell peppers, green bell peppers are less costly than the riper yellow and red peppers, which have a milder, mellow flavor.

One Serving

Calories: 70	Sodium: 4 mg
Calories from Fat: 14	Total Carbohydrates: 13 g
Total Fat: 2 g	Dietary Fiber: 3 g
Saturated Fat: 0 g	Sugars: 1 g
Cholesterol: 0 mg	Protein: 2 g

Green Beans Amandine

It's so easy and so delicious!

¼ cup slivered almonds	45 g
1 tablespoon butter	15 ml
1 (16 ounce) package frozen whole green beans, cooked, drained	455 g
2 teaspoons fresh lemon juice	10 ml

Toast almonds in dry 10-inch (25 cm) skillet over medium heat, stirring constantly, until almonds are golden brown. Add butter, green beans, ½ teaspoon (2 ml) salt and ⅛ teaspoon (.5 ml) pepper. Cook and stir until butter melts and coats beans. Sprinkle with lemon juice.

Serves 4.
Serving size: ½ cup (125 ml)

One Serving

Calories: 148	Sodium: 1 mg
Calories from Fat: 95	Total Carbohydrates: 9 g
Total Fat: 11 g	Dietary Fiber: 4 g
Saturated Fat: 2 g	Sugars: 3 g
Cholesterol: 8 mg	Protein: 4 g

Herbed Green Beans

Fresh parsley, dried basil and rosemary are the herbs in this recipe. You can vary the flavor by choosing fresh herbs or your favorite dried herb blend.

1 (16 ounce) package frozen cut green beans	455 g
1 tablespoon butter	15 ml
½ cup finely chopped onion	80 g
1 garlic clove, minced	
¼ cup chopped parsley	15 g
¼ teaspoon crushed dried basil leaves	1 ml
¼ teaspoon crushed dried rosemary	1 ml

Prepare green beans according to package directions. Drain and keep warm.

Melt butter in 10-inch (25 cm) skillet, add onion and garlic and cook over medium heat until tender. Stir in parsley, basil and rosemary. Pour over green beans.

Serves 4.
Serving size: ½ cup (125 ml)

One Serving

Calories: 63	Sodium: 1 mg
Calories from Fat: 27	Total Carbohydrates: 6 g
Total Fat: 3 g	Dietary Fiber: 3 g
Saturated Fat: 2 g	Sugars: 3 g
Cholesterol: 8 mg	Protein: 1 g

Green Beans and Mushrooms

You'll love this recipe because it is simple to make and a delicious combination of vegetables.

1 (16 ounce) package frozen whole or cut green beans	455 g
1 tablespoon olive oil	15 ml
1 tablespoon finely chopped onion	15 ml
1 (8 ounce) package fresh sliced mushrooms	230 g

Prepare green beans according to package directions. Drain and set aside.

Heat oil in 10-inch (25 cm) skillet over medium heat and add onion and mushrooms. Cook and stir until mushrooms are tender, about 3 to 5 minutes. Add cooked beans, ½ teaspoon (2 ml) salt and ⅛ teaspoon (.5 ml) pepper.

Serves about 5.
Serving size: ½ cup (125 ml)

One Serving

Calories: 65	Sodium: 2 mg
Calories from Fat: 27	Total Carbohydrates: 7 g
Total Fat: 3 g	Dietary Fiber: 3 g
Saturated Fat: 0 g	Sugars: 3 g
Cholesterol: 0 mg	Protein: 2 g

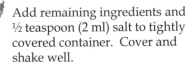

Green Beans with Tarragon Vinaigrette

Tarragon is commonly used in herb blends or dried form. Tarragon vinegar may be found in gourmet food shops or in large supermarkets.

1 (16 ounce) package frozen whole or cut green beans	455 g
½ teaspoon garlic powder	2 ml
2 teaspoons finely chopped green onion	10 ml
1 teaspoon dijon-style mustard	5 ml
2 tablespoons tarragon vinegar	30 ml
¼ cup olive oil	60 ml

Prepare green beans according to package directions. Drain and keep warm.

Add remaining ingredients and ½ teaspoon (2 ml) salt to tightly covered container. Cover and shake well.

Pour vinaigrette over hot green beans and serve warm or cold.

Serves 4.
Serving size: ¾ cup (175 ml)

One Serving

Calories: 45	Sodium: 2 mg
Calories from Fat: 0	Total Carbohydrates: 8 g
Total Fat: 0 g	Dietary Fiber: 3 g
Saturated Fat: 0 g	Sugars: 4 g
Cholesterol: 0 mg	Protein: 1 g

Oven-Fried Okra

1 (16 ounce) package fresh okra or cut frozen okra, thawed, drained	455 g
2 tablespoons canola oil	30 ml
½ cup plain breadcrumbs or Italian seasoned breadcrumbs	60 g
½ teaspoon dried thyme, crushed	2 ml
Small amount cayenne pepper	

Preheat oven to 425° (220° C).

For fresh okra, trim stems and slice pods ½-inch (1.2 cm) thick.

Pour oil on baking sheet and spread evenly.

Combine breadcrumbs, thyme, cayenne pepper, ½ teaspoon (2 ml) salt and ⅛ teaspoon (.5 ml) pepper in bowl. Add okra and toss until evenly coated. Shake off excess crumbs with slotted spoon and transfer okra to baking sheet.

Bake for about 10 minutes and turn with spatula. Continue baking for 10 minutes or until okra is tender and crispy brown.

Serves 4.
Serving size: ¾ cup (175 ml)

TIP: Finely ground cornbread stuffing mix works as well as breadcrumbs.

One Serving

Calories: 138	Sodium: 103 mg
Calories from Fat: 63	Total Carbohydrates: 17 g
Total Fat: 9 g	Dietary Fiber: 3 g
Saturated Fat: 4 g	Sugars: 4 g
Cholesterol: 16 mg	Protein: 4 g

Okra, Tomatoes and Corn

The convenience of frozen okra allows you to enjoy this recipe year-round.

1 (16 ounce) package fresh okra or 1 (16 ounce) package frozen cut okra, thawed, drained	**455 g**
1 tablespoon canola oil	**15 ml**
1 medium onion, halved, sliced	
2 garlic cloves, minced	
1 (14 ounce) can diced tomatoes with liquid	**400 g**
1 cup frozen whole kernel corn	**165 g**
¼ cup chopped fresh basil or 1 teaspoon dried basil, crushed	**10 g/5 ml**

If using fresh okra, trim stems and cut okra into ½-inch (1.2 cm) slices.

Combine oil, okra, onion and garlic in large, heavy pan over medium-high heat. Cook and stir about 10 minutes.

Reduce heat to medium and cook, stirring frequently, about 15 minutes or until stringing of okra liquid ceases.

Add tomatoes, corn, basil, ½ teaspoon (2 ml) salt and ⅛ teaspoon (.5 ml) pepper. Bring to a boil, reduce heat to simmer and cover. Cook, stirring frequently, until corn is tender.

Serves 6 to 8.
Serving size: ¾ cup (175 ml)

TIP: The secret to selecting excellent cooking and eating okra is to choose non-blemished small pods. The younger the pods are when picked, the less slippery the liquid inside.

One Serving

Calories: 65	Cholesterol: 0 mg	Dietary Fiber: 2 g
Calories from Fat: 18	Sodium: 99 mg	Sugars: 3 g
Total Fat: 3 g	Total Carbohydrates: 11 g	Protein: 2 g
Saturated Fat: 0 g		

Caramelized Onions

This fragrant, delicious side dish or topping for a burger is very easy.

2 tablespoons butter or canola oil	30 g/30 ml
3 large Vidalia or Texas 1015 onions, thinly sliced	
1 tablespoon brown sugar	15 ml

Melt butter (or heat oil) in non-stick 12-inch (32 cm) skillet over medium heat. Stir in onions and cook uncovered 10 minutes, stirring occasionally. Reduce heat to low and sprinkle brown sugar and ¼ teaspoon (1 ml) salt over onions.

Cook onions additional 30 to 40 minutes or until onions brown and stir occasionally. Add water if needed.

Serves 3 to 4.
Serving size: ¼ cup (60 ml)

One Serving

Calories: 122	Sodium: 4 mg
Calories from Fat: 54	Total Carbohydrates: 17 g
Total Fat: 6 g	Dietary Fiber: 3 g
Saturated Fat: 4 g	Sugars: 11 g
Cholesterol: 16 mg	Protein: 2 g

Maple Syrup-Glazed Parsnips

Parsnips look like large, creamy carrots and have a sweet and slightly nippy taste.

1½ pounds parsnips, peeled	680 g
2 tablespoons butter	30 g
2 teaspoons light brown sugar	10 ml
3 tablespoons pure maple syrup	45 ml
¼ teaspoon ground cinnamon	1 ml

Cut parsnips into large pieces. Cook them immediately to prevent discoloration.

Bring 2 cups (500 ml) water, parsnips, butter, brown sugar and ½ teaspoon (2 ml) salt to a boil in non-stick 12-inch (32 cm) skillet over medium-high heat. Reduce heat, cover and cook for 10 to 12 minutes or until parsnips are tender.

Remove cover and increase heat to reduce liquid. Stir constantly until liquid is syrupy. (Be careful not to scorch the parsnips.) Add maple syrup and cinnamon and serve.

Serves 4 to 6.
Serving size: ¾ cup (175 ml)

One Serving

Calories: 159	Sodium: 14 mg
Calories from Fat: 39	Total Carbohydrates: 31 g
Total Fat: 4 g	Dietary Fiber: 6 g
Saturated Fat: 2 g	Sugars: 15 g
Cholesterol: 10 mg	Protein: 1 g

Roasted Parsnips and Carrots

1 pound (3 cups) parsnips, peeled, sliced	455 g
1 pound (3 cups) carrots, peeled, sliced	455 g
1 tablespoon olive oil	15 ml
1 teaspoon dried thyme or basil	5 ml

Preheat oven to 425° (220° C).

Toss parsnips, carrots, oil, thyme or basil, ½ teaspoon (2 ml) salt and ⅛ teaspoon (.5 ml) pepper in bowl. Transfer to sprayed baking sheet and arrange in single layer. Lightly spray again.

Roast for 20 minutes and shake pan every 5 minutes until parsnips and carrots are brown and tender.

Serves 4 to 6.
Serving size: ¾ cup (175 ml)

One Serving

Calories: 101	Sodium: 46 mg
Calories from Fat: 23	Total Carbohydrates: 19 g
Total Fat: 3 g	Dietary Fiber: 5 g
Saturated Fat: 0 g	Sugars: 6 g
Cholesterol: 0 mg	Protein: 1 g

Petite Peas Amandine

In this simple dish, almonds and peas cook in butter for a tantalizing flavor.

2 tablespoons butter	30 g
¼ cup sliced almonds	50 g
1 (16 ounce) bag frozen petite peas, thawed, drained	455 g
2 teaspoons lemon juice	10 ml

Melt butter in 10-inch (25 cm) skillet over medium heat. Add almonds; cook and stir 1 to 2 minutes or until light brown. Stir in peas, lemon juice and ½ teaspoon (2 ml) salt. Cook and stir about 5 to 6 minutes or until peas are tender. Do not overcook peas.

Serves 6.
Serving size: ½ cup (125 ml)

One Serving

Calories: 149	Sodium: 86 mg
Calories from Fat: 81	Total Carbohydrates: 12 g
Total Fat: 9 g	Dietary Fiber: 4 g
Saturated Fat: 3 g	Sugars: 5 g
Cholesterol: 10 mg	Protein: 6 g

Petite Peas and Pearl Onions

This makes a pretty dish to serve at family gatherings and buffet meals.

1 pound small white boiling
    pearl onions   455 g
1 (16 ounce) package frozen
    petite peas   455 g
2 tablespoons butter   30 g
1 teaspoon dried basil, crushed 5 ml

Combine onions and water to cover in 2-quart (2 L) saucepan. Bring to a boil and reduce heat to medium. Cook onions for 15 to 20 minutes and drain. When onions are cool enough to handle, use sharp knife to cut off stem end and squeeze opposite end. The onions will pop out of outside layers.

Prepare peas according to package directions. Drain.

Melt butter in large, heavy pan over medium heat. Add onions, peas, basil, ½ teaspoon (2 ml) salt and ⅛ teaspoon (.5 ml) pepper. Cook and stir until peas and onions coat with butter and are thoroughly hot.

Serves 8.
Serving size: ¾ cup (175 ml)

TIP: Add ½ cup (125 ml) fat-free half-and-half cream for creamed peas and onions.

One Serving

Calories: 93	Sodium: 67 mg
Calories from Fat: 27	Total Carbohydrates: 13 g
Total Fat: 3 g	Dietary Fiber: 3 g
Saturated Fat: 2 g	Sugars: 6 g
Cholesterol: 8 mg	Protein: 1 g

Skillet Pepper Medley

2 tablespoons olive oil   30 ml
2 medium green bell peppers,
    seeded, cut in ¼-inch
    strips   .6 cm
2 medium red bell peppers,
    seeded, cut in ¼-inch
    strips   .6 cm
2 medium yellow bell peppers,
    seeded, cut in ¼-inch
    strips   .6 cm
2 tablespoons chopped fresh
    parsley   10 g

Heat oil in non-stick 12-inch (32 cm) skillet over medium-high heat. Add bell peppers, ½ teaspoon (2 ml) salt and ⅛ teaspoon (.5 ml) pepper; cook and stir 8 to 10 minutes or until peppers are tender. Sprinkle with parsley.

Serves 6.
Serving size: ½ cup (125 ml)

One Serving

Calories: 64	Sodium: 3 mg
Calories from Fat: 36	Total Carbohydrates: 5 g
Total Fat: 4 g	Dietary Fiber: 3 g
Saturated Fat: 2 g	Sugars: 0 g
Cholesterol: 10 mg	Protein: 0 g

Side Dishes

Garlic Mashed Potatoes

1½ pounds russet potatoes,
    peeled, cut in large chunks 680 g
6 garlic cloves, peeled
6 tablespoons light plain
    soymilk   90 ml
1 tablespoon butter   15 ml
1 tablespoon finely chopped
    parsley   15 ml

Combine potatoes, garlic, 1 teaspoon (5 ml) salt and enough water to cover in large, heavy pan. Bring to a boil and reduce heat to simmer. Cover and cook until potatoes are tender, about 25 minutes. Drain and return to pan. Shake over medium heat until potatoes are mealy and dry.

Stir in soymilk, butter, 1 teaspoon (5 ml) salt and ¼ teaspoon (1 ml) pepper and mash potatoes with potato ricer or masher. Remove to serving dish and sprinkle parsley on top.

Serves 4 to 6.
Serving size: ½ cup (125 ml)

TIP: *It takes about 4 medium russet potatoes to equal 1½ pounds (680 g).*

One Serving

Calories: 145	Sodium: 24 mg
Calories from Fat: 25	Total Carbohydrates: 27 g
Total Fat: 3 g	Dietary Fiber: 2 g
Saturated Fat: 1 g	Sugars: 1 g
Cholesterol: 5 mg	Protein: 6 g

Home Fries

Here's a way to use leftover baked potatoes and satisfy that craving for french fries.

2 large russet potatoes with peels,
    baked, cold
1 tablespoon canola or olive oil 15 ml
2 medium onions, halved,
    thinly sliced
1 garlic clove, minced

Cut potatoes into ½-inch (1.2 cm) cubes and set aside.

Combine oil, onions and garlic in non-stick 12-inch (32 cm) skillet over medium heat and cook about 10 minutes.

Turn heat to medium-low and add potatoes, ½ teaspoon (2 ml) salt and ¼ teaspoon (1 ml) pepper to skillet. Cook without stirring for 15 minutes or until golden crust forms on bottom. Turn with wide spatula and cook without stirring for additional 15 minutes.

Serves 4 to 6.
Serving size: ½ cup (125 ml)

One Serving

Calories: 128	Sodium: 6 mg
Calories from Fat: 21	Total Carbohydrates: 25 g
Total Fat: 3 g	Dietary Fiber: 2 g
Saturated Fat: 0 g	Sugars: 2 g
Cholesterol: 0 mg	Protein: 3 g

Mashed Potatoes and Turnips

*This combination will surprise you with the pleasing
mild turnip flavor in the mashed potatoes.*

½ pound russet potatoes, peeled, cubed	230 g
1½ pounds turnips, peeled, cubed	680 g
1 cup vegetable broth	250 ml
1 tablespoon butter	15 ml
1 tablespoon chopped fresh parsley	15 ml
6 tablespoons fat-free half-and-half cream, divided	90 ml

Combine potatoes, 1 teaspoon (5 ml) salt and enough water to cover in large, heavy pan. Bring to a boil and reduce heat to medium-low. Cover and cook until potatoes are tender, about 25 minutes. Drain and return to pan. Shake potatoes over medium heat until they are mealy and dry. Mash and cover pan with foil to keep warm.

Combine turnips and broth in 2-quart (2 L) saucepan. Bring to a boil and reduce heat to medium. Cook uncovered until turnips are tender, about 8 to 10 minutes. Mash turnips in broth.

Transfer turnip mixture to pan with potatoes. Add butter, 1 teaspoon (5 ml) salt, ¼ teaspoon (1 ml) pepper and parsley. Fold in half-and-half cream 2 tablespoons (30 ml) at a time until mixture is fluffy.

Serves 4 to 6.
Serving size: ¾ cup (175 ml)

TIP: Mashing the potatoes and turnips by hand results in a fluffy texture.

One Serving

Calories: 125	Cholesterol: 6 mg	Dietary Fiber: 3 g
Calories from Fat: 24	Sodium: 279 mg	Sugars: 6 g
Total Fat: 2 g	Total Carbohydrates: 24 g	Protein: 3 g
Saturated Fat: 1 g		

Mashed Rutabagas and Walnuts

*If you didn't grow up eating rutabagas, you may be reluctant to try this recipe.
Go ahead and try it — you will find the rustic texture and flavor delicious.*

2 - 3 rutabagas	
2 tablespoons butter	30 g
2 tablespoons fat-free half-and-half cream	30 ml
1 tablespoon pure maple syrup	15 ml
½ cup walnut pieces, toasted	65 g
Nutmeg	

Peel rutabagas and cut away any green flesh. Cut into 2-inch (5 cm) cubes and place in steamer basket in large, heavy pan. Add 2 to 3 inches (5 cm) water to pan and bring to a boil. Cover and steam about 30 minutes or until rutabagas are tender. Add water if needed. Remove from heat.

Use potato masher or ricer to mash rutabagas until fairly smooth. Over medium heat, cook 2 to 3 minutes or until rutabagas are slightly dry. Stir in butter, half-and-half cream, syrup, walnut pieces, ½ teaspoon (2 ml) salt and ⅛ teaspoon (.5 ml) pepper. Sprinkle nutmeg on top.

Serves 4.
Serving size: ¾ cup (175 ml)

TIP: If you don't have maple syrup or don't want to buy it, replace it with 1 tablespoon (15 ml) light or dark brown sugar. Stir into rutabaga mixture until sugar dissolves.

TIP: If you use an electric steamer, steam rutabagas about 30 minutes or until tender.

One Serving

Calories: 273	Cholesterol: 16 mg	Dietary Fiber: 8 g
Calories from Fat: 142	Sodium: 80 mg	Sugars: 20 g
Total Fat: 15 g	Total Carbohydrates: 30 g	Protein: 8 g
Saturated Fat: 4 g		

Ratatouille

Ratatouille [rat-uh-TOO-ee] is a Mediterranean dish that's delicious served hot or cold.

1 tablespoon olive oil	15 ml
1 medium onion, chopped	
2 cloves garlic, minced	
3 cups cubed, peeled eggplant	455 g
1 medium green bell pepper, chopped	
2 medium zucchini, cubed	
1 (14 ounce) can Italian seasoned tomatoes	400 g

Heat oil in large, heavy pan over medium heat. Add onion and garlic and cook until onion is tender.

Add eggplant, bell pepper, zucchini and tomatoes and bring to a boil. Reduce heat, cover and simmer over medium-low heat for 10 to 15 minutes or until vegetables are tender. Uncover and cook about 5 minutes or until liquid evaporates.

Serves 6.
Serving size: ¾ cup (175 ml)

One Serving

Calories: 62	Sodium: 134 mg
Calories from Fat: 21	Total Carbohydrates: 8 g
Total Fat: 2 g	Dietary Fiber: 4 g
Saturated Fat: 0 g	Sugars: 4 g
Cholesterol: 0 mg	Protein: 2 g

Creamy Spinach

1 (10 ounce) package frozen leaf spinach	280 g
2 tablespoons reduced-fat cream cheese, softened	30 g
3 tablespoons fat-free half-and-half cream	45 ml
¼ teaspoon ground nutmeg	1 ml

Prepare spinach according to package instructions and drain. Squeeze spinach between paper towels to completely remove excess moisture.

Combine cream cheese, half-and-half cream, nutmeg, ½ teaspoon salt (2 ml) and ⅛ teaspoon (.5 ml) pepper in medium bowl. Stir into hot spinach until it blends and is smooth.

Serves 4 to 6.
Serving size: ½ cup (125 ml)

One Serving

Calories: 46	Sodium: 85 mg
Calories from Fat: 22	Total Carbohydrates: 4 g
Total Fat: 2 g	Dietary Fiber: 2 g
Saturated Fat: 1 g	Sugars: 1 g
Cholesterol: 6 mg	Protein: 3 g

Squash and Apples

1 pound butternut squash	455 g
1 tablespoon butter	15 ml
1 medium apple, peeled, cored, cut in ½-inch cubes	1.2 cm
2 teaspoons fresh lemon juice	10 ml
¼ cup packed light brown sugar	55 g
¼ teaspoon cinnamon	1 ml

Preheat oven to 350° (175° C).

Cut squash in half with heavy knife and remove seeds. Add 1 inch (2.5 cm) water to roasting pan. Add squash to pan, cut sides down. Bake for 45 to 90 minutes or until tender. Drain, cool and scrape out strings with melon baller. Cut into ½-inch (1.2 cm) cubes.

Melt butter in 12-inch (32 cm) skillet over medium-high heat. Add squash, apple, lemon juice and ¼ cup (60 ml) water. Cover and cook, stirring occasionally, about 4 to 5 minutes or until apples are tender and liquid is absorbed. Stir in brown sugar, cinnamon and ¼ (1 ml) teaspoon salt.

Serves 6.
Serving size: ½ cup (125 ml)

TIP: Garnish with toasted pecans, if you like.

One Serving

Calories: 87	Cholesterol: 5 mg	Dietary Fiber: 2 g
Calories from Fat: 21	Sodium: 7 mg	Sugars: 11 g
Total Fat: 2 g	Total Carbohydrates: 17 g	Protein: 1 g
Saturated Fat: 1 g		

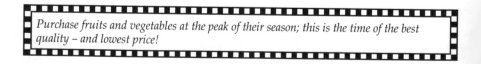

Purchase fruits and vegetables at the peak of their season; this is the time of the best quality – and lowest price!

Tomatoes Provencal

A delicious and different way to serve tomatoes.

1 garlic clove, minced
1 tablespoon finely chopped parsley   15 ml
1 tablespoon fresh whole wheat breadcrumbs   15 ml
4 medium tomatoes
1 tablespoon olive oil   15 ml

Preheat oven to 400° (205° C).

Combine garlic, parsley, breadcrumbs and ¼ teaspoon (1 ml) salt in small bowl.

Cut tomatoes in half, remove stem and gently squeeze to remove juice and seeds. Arrange on sprayed baking sheet and drizzle with oil.

Bake uncovered for 10 minutes. Remove and sprinkle with crumb mixture and bake an additional 15 minutes or until tomatoes are soft throughout and crumbs are brown.

Serves 8.
Serving size: One tomato half

TIP: Keep whole wheat bread crumbs ready for use. Add torn pieces of stale bread to food processor or blender container. Cover and process until fine. Freeze in zippered bags.

One Serving

Calories: 21	Cholesterol: 0 mg	Dietary Fiber: 0 g
Calories from Fat: 16	Sodium: 2 mg	Sugars: 1 g
Total Fat: 2 g	Total Carbohydrates: 1 g	Protein: 0 g
Saturated Fat: 0 g		

Zucchini-Bell Pepper Stir-Fry

Colorful, flavorful and quick to fix!

2 teaspoons olive oil	10 ml
1 medium onion, halved, sliced	
2 garlic cloves, minced	
1 medium red bell pepper, cut in thin strips	
1 pound small zucchini, thinly sliced	455 g
1 teaspoon dried basil, crushed	5 ml

Heat oil in large, heavy pan over medium-high heat. Cook and stir onion, garlic and red bell pepper strips until tender. Reduce heat to medium.

Add zucchini, basil, ½ teaspoon (2 ml) salt and ⅛ teaspoon (.5 ml) pepper. Cook uncovered, stirring frequently, until zucchini is tender.

Serves 6.
Serving size: ½ cup (125 ml)

TIP: Select zucchini about 6 inches (15 cm) in length and 1½ inches (3 cm) in diameter for the best texture and flavor.

One Serving

Calories: 36	Sodium: 8 mg
Calories from Fat: 14	Total Carbohydrates: 5 g
Total Fat: 2 g	Dietary Fiber: 2 g
Saturated Fat: 0 g	Sugars: 2 g
Cholesterol: 0 mg	Protein: 1 g

Best Deviled Eggs

You may want to double this recipe because these won't last long!

6 eggs, hard-boiled	
3 tablespoons reduced-fat mayonnaise	45 g
2 teaspoons dijon-style or yellow mustard	10 ml
¼ teaspoon Creole or Cajun seasoning	1 ml
Paprika	

Slice eggs in half lengthwise. Carefully remove egg yolks with fork and thoroughly mash in bowl. Add mayonnaise, mustard and seasoning. Beat with fork until mixture is creamy and smooth. Mound egg yolk mixture evenly onto egg white halves. Sprinkle with paprika.

Serves 6.
Serving size: 2 halves

One Serving

Calories: 126	Sodium: 168 mg
Calories from Fat: 84	Total Carbohydrates: 2 g
Total Fat: 9 g	Dietary Fiber: 0 g
Saturated Fat: 3 g	Sugars: 1 g
Cholesterol: 212 mg	Protein: 6 g

Main
Dishes

Contents

Contents

Island Baked Beans

Here's a great dish for potluck suppers.

1 (8 ounce) can crushed pineapple, drained	230 g
2 tablespoons brown sugar	25 g
1 teaspoon onion powder	5 ml
1 tablespoon reduced-sodium soy sauce	15 ml
1 tablespoon dijon-style mustard	15 ml
2 (16 ounce) cans vegetarian baked beans in tomato sauce	2 (455 g)

🫘 Preheat oven to 350° (175° C).

🫘 Combine pineapple, brown sugar, onion powder, soy sauce and mustard in 1½-quart (1.5 L) baking dish.

🫘 Combine beans with pineapple mixture in dish and bake uncovered for 1 hour 30 minutes. Remove and stir. Let stand 5 to 10 minutes before serving.

Serves 7.
Serving size: 1 cup (250 ml)

TIP: Soy bacon bits make a nice garnish if you want to get fancy.

One Serving

Calories: 193	Sodium: 453 mg
Calories from Fat: 13	Total Carbohydrates: 40 g
Total Fat: 1 g	Dietary Fiber: 6 g
Saturated Fat: 0 g	Sugars: 12 g
Cholesterol: 0 mg	Protein: 6 g

Zesty Butter Beans

Lima beans are perked up with flavorful vegetables and green chilies.

1 (16 ounce) package frozen butter beans	455 g
2 teaspoons olive oil	10 ml
1 cup chopped onion	160 g
1 garlic clove, minced	
½ cup chopped celery	50 g
½ cup chopped red or green bell pepper	75 g
⅓ cup canned tomatoes and green chilies with liquid	80 g

🫘 Prepare butter beans according to package directions. Drain.

🫘 Combine oil, onion, garlic, celery and bell pepper in large, heavy pan over medium-high heat. Cook and stir until vegetables are tender.

🫘 Stir in cooked beans, tomatoes and green chilies, and ½ teaspoon (2 ml) salt.

🫘 Reduce heat and simmer about 5 minutes.

Serves 4.
Serving size: ¾ cup (175 ml)

One Serving

Calories: 52	Sodium: 96 mg
Calories from Fat: 21	Total Carbohydrates: 7 g
Total Fat: 2 g	Dietary Fiber: 2 g
Saturated Fat: 0 g	Sugars: 3 g
Cholesterol: 0 mg	Protein: 1 g

Fava Bean Pasta Salad

Fava beans are tan, flat beans similar to large lima beans and are usually found canned rather than fresh in supermarkets.

1 (19 ounce) can fava beans, drained, rinsed	540 g
1½ cups whole wheat penne or rotini pasta, cooked	210 g
1 cup diagonally sliced celery	105 g
1 cup red or yellow bell pepper narrow strips	95 g
1 cup red onion rings	115 g
1 cup Feta Cheese Dressing (page 105)	250 ml

Combine fava beans, pasta, celery, bell pepper strips and red onion rings in large bowl. Drizzle with Feta Cheese Dressing and toss.

Serves 8.
Serving size: 1 cup (250 ml)

One Serving

Calories: 279	Sodium: 346 mg
Calories from Fat: 131	Total Carbohydrates: 29 g
Total Fat: 14 g	Dietary Fiber: 6 g
Saturated Fat: 3 g	Sugars: 3 g
Cholesterol: 11 mg	Protein: 8 g

Cannellini Bean Cakes

Cannellini beans are generally interchangeable with great northern and navy beans, but you may prefer cannellini beans once you try them.

2 (15 ounce) cans cannellini, great northern or navy beans, drained, rinsed	2 (425 g)
2 garlic cloves, minced	
1 cup Italian seasoned breadcrumbs, divided	120 g
Small amount of flour	
2 tablespoons olive oil, divided	30 ml

Mash beans and add garlic, ½ teaspoon (2 ml) salt and ¼ teaspoon (1 ml) pepper in mixing bowl. Sprinkle beans with ½ cup (60 g) breadcrumbs. Form into 4 patties with lightly floured hands and add more breadcrumbs if needed.

Heat 1 tablespoon olive oil in non-stick 12-inch (32 cm) skillet over medium-high heat. Add bean patties and cook until brown on bottom side. Carefully turn each patty and cook other side until brown. Add more oil if needed.

Serves 4.
Serving size: 1 cake

TIP: Top with Roma Tomato Sauce (page 242).

One Serving

Calories: 136	Sodium: 233 mg
Calories from Fat: 77	Total Carbohydrates: 10 g
Total Fat: 9 g	Dietary Fiber: 3 g
Saturated Fat: 1 g	Sugars: 0 g
Cholesterol: 0 mg	Protein: 3 g

Kale and Cannellini Beans

This dish of hearty greens and white beans in a spicy sauce with cheese makes a great entree.

1 pound kale	455 g
2 tablespoons olive oil	30 ml
3 garlic cloves, minced	
¼ teaspoon crushed red pepper flakes	1 ml
1 (15 ounce) can cannellini beans, drained, rinsed	425 g
½ cup freshly grated parmesan or romano cheese	100 g

Remove stems and thick ribs of kale and shred leaves. Combine oil, garlic and red pepper in 12-inch (32 cm) skillet over medium heat. Cook and stir 1 to 2 minutes. Do not burn garlic. Stir in kale, ½ teaspoon (2 ml) salt, ¼ teaspoon (1 ml) pepper and ½ cup (125 ml) water.

Cover and simmer until kale wilts and is tender, about 8 to 10 minutes. Add water as needed. Add cannellini beans and stir. Transfer to serving dish and sprinkle with cheese.

Serves 4.
Serving size: 1 cup (250 ml)

TIP: Kale has frilly, dark green, thick leaves and is sold in bunches. Kale is most abundant, flavorful and tender during winter months; however, it is generally available most of the year.

One Serving

Calories: 270	Cholesterol: 11 mg	Dietary Fiber: 8 g
Calories from Fat: 109	Sodium: 558 mg	Sugars: 1 g
Total Fat: 12 g	Total Carbohydrates: 28 g	Protein: 13 g
Saturated Fat: 3 g		

Italian Bean Bake

Italian beans are flat in shape and are marketed frozen or canned.

1 (16 ounce) package frozen Italian green beans	455 g
1 (8 ounce) can no-salt tomato sauce	230 g
1 teaspoon dry mustard	5 ml
⅛ teaspoon onion salt	.5 ml
⅛ teaspoon garlic salt	.5 ml
½ cup shredded mozzarella or provolone cheese	60 g

Prepare beans according to package directions. Drain.

Combine tomato sauce, dry mustard, onion salt, garlic salt and ¼ teaspoon (1 ml) pepper in small bowl.

Combine beans and tomato sauce mixture in 1-quart (1 L) microwave-safe baking dish.

Microwave covered on HIGH for 3 to 4 minutes, stirring once. Sprinkle with cheese and microwave uncovered on HIGH for 30 seconds or just until cheese melts.

Serves 5.
Serving size: ¾ cup (175 ml)

TIP: If you are reducing sodium in your diet, replace onion salt with onion powder and garlic salt with garlic powder.

One Serving

Calories: 87	Cholesterol: 9 mg	Dietary Fiber: 3 g
Calories from Fat: 25	Sodium: 248 mg	Sugars: 3 g
Total Fat: 3 g	Total Carbohydrates: 8 g	Protein: 6 g
Saturated Fat: 2 g		

Curried Garbanzo Beans

Garbanzo beans (chick-peas) are in the legume family, which is the main source of protein for many people throughout the world.

2 (15 ounce) cans garbanzo beans, rinsed, drained	2 (425 g)
1 (14 ounce) can crushed tomatoes	400 g
2 teaspoons curry powder	10 ml
1 teaspoon garlic powder	5 ml
2 tablespoons pine nuts, toasted	20 g

Combine beans, tomatoes, curry powder and garlic powder in 2-quart (2 L) microwave-safe dish. Cook on HIGH for about 5 minutes or until hot. Sprinkle with pine nuts.

Servings 4.
Serving size: 1 cup (250 ml)

TIP: Toasting brings out the flavors of nuts and seeds. Place nuts or seeds on baking sheet and bake at 225° (110° C) for 10 minutes. Be careful not to burn them.

One Serving

Calories: 332	Sodium: 821 mg
Calories from Fat: 74	Total Carbohy- drates: 53 g
Total Fat: 8 g	Dietary Fiber: 11 g
Saturated Fat: 0 g	Sugars: 3 g
Cholesterol: 0 mg	Protein: 13 g

Vegetarian Chili

Just raid your pantry to make this delicious, reduced-sodium meatless chili.

1 (14 ounce) can diced tomatoes	400 g
1 (12 ounce) can beer or 1 (14 ounce) can vegetable broth	355 ml/400 g
1 (8 ounce) can no-salt tomato sauce	230 g
2 tablespoons reduced-sodium chili seasoning mix	30 ml
2 (15 ounce) cans pinto or red kidney beans, rinsed, drained	2 (425 g)

Combine all ingredients and 1 cup (250 ml) water in large, heavy pan. Bring to a boil, reduce heat and simmer uncovered 15 to 20 minutes. Add water if needed.

Serves 4 to 6.
Serving size: 1 cup (250 ml)

TIP: Make your own reduced-sodium chili seasoning mix with 1 tablespoon (15 ml) plus 2 teaspoons (10 ml) chili powder, ½ teaspoon (2 ml) cumin and 1 teaspoon (5 ml) garlic powder. Makes about 2 tablespoons (30 ml).

One Serving

Calories: 192	Sodium: 940 mg
Calories from Fat: 0	Total Carbohy- drates: 33 g
Total Fat: 0 g	Dietary Fiber: 10 g
Saturated Fat: 0 g	Sugars: 4 g
Cholesterol: 0 mg	Protein: 10 g

Creamy Succotash

Here are wholesome lima beans and corn baked in cheese sauce.

1 (10 ounce) package frozen lima beans	280 g
2 tablespoons butter	30 g
2 tablespoons unbleached white flour	15 g
1½ cups fat-free skim milk	360 ml
1 (10 ounce) package frozen whole kernel corn	280 g
1 (7 ounce) package cheddar-flavor soy veggie shreds	200 g

Preheat oven to 350° (175° C).

Cook lima beans and corn according to package directions. Drain.

Melt butter in 1-quart (1 L) saucepan. Stir in flour, ¼ teaspoon (1 ml) salt and pinch of black pepper. Cook and stir over medium heat until it bubbles. Add milk; cook and stir until it thickens. Stir in veggie shreds.

Combine lima beans and corn in 2-quart (2 L) baking dish. Pour sauce over beans and corn.

Bake 15 to 20 minutes or until it bubbles.

Serves 4.
Serving size: 1 cup (250 ml)

One Serving

Calories: 485	Cholesterol: 18 mg	Dietary Fiber: 7 g
Calories from Fat: 80	Sodium: 635 mg	Sugars: 5 g
Total Fat: 9 g	Total Carbohydrates: 55 g	Protein: 17 g
Saturated Fat: 4 g		

Refried Bean Enchiladas

½ cup chopped onion	80 g
2 garlic cloves, minced	
1 (15 ounce) can vegetarian refried beans	425 g
6 (10 inch) whole wheat tortillas	6 (25 cm)
1 (4 ounce) can sliced ripe olives, divided	115 g
2 cups reduced-fat shredded cheddar cheese, divided	230 g
2 cups Red Chile Sauce (page 238), divided	500 ml

Preheat oven to 350° (175° C).

Combine onion and garlic in sprayed non-stick 10-inch (25 cm) skillet over medium-high heat; cook and stir until onion is tender. Stir in refried beans.

Soften tortillas a few seconds on HIGH in microwave oven. Spoon about 2 tablespoons (30 ml) bean mixture on each warmed tortilla. Sprinkle with 2 teaspoons (10 ml) olives and 2 to 3 tablespoons (30 - 45 ml) cheese. Roll tightly.

Spread ½ cup (125 ml) Red Chile Sauce in sprayed 9 x 9-inch (23 x 23 cm) baking dish. Arrange rolled enchiladas on sauce. Pour remaining sauce on enchiladas and top with remaining cheese and ripe olives.

Bake for about 15 to 20 minutes or until bubbly.

Serves 6.
Serving size: 1 enchilada

TIP: If you don't want to make Red Chile Sauce, use 2 (10 ounce/280 g) cans mild red enchilada sauce instead.

One Serving

Calories: 423	Cholesterol: 20 mg	Dietary Fiber: 6 g
Calories from Fat: 97	Sodium: 936 mg	Sugars: 3 g
Total Fat: 11 g	Total Carbohydrates: 56 g	Protein: 14 g
Saturated Fat: 5 g		

Sugar Snap Peas and Rice

Sugar snap peas are a cross between snow peas and green peas. Sugar snaps are thin and crisp and should be eaten raw or cooked only briefly, as in this recipe.

1 teaspoon canola oil	5 ml
1 garlic clove, minced	
½ cup diced red bell pepper	75 g
2 cups sugar-snap peas or snow peas, sliced diagonally	200 g
2 cups cooked brown rice	390 g
¼ cup All-Purpose Stir-Fry Sauce (page 242) or bottled stir-fry sauce	60 ml

Heat oil in non-stick wok or 12-inch (32 cm) skillet over high heat. Add garlic and bell pepper and stir-fry about 2 minutes.

Add sugar-snap peas, rice and All-Purpose Stir-Fry Sauce and stir to mix.

Serves 5.
Serving size: 1 cup (250 ml)

TIP: Sugar snap peas are available in supermarkets in both fresh and frozen forms.

One Serving

Calories: 138	Cholesterol: 0 mg	Dietary Fiber: 3 g
Calories from Fat: 24	Sodium: 234 mg	Sugars: 2 g
Total Fat: 3 g	Total Carbohydrates: 24 g	Protein: 3 g
Saturated Fat: 0 g		

Fruited Lentil Pilaf Salad

Wait until you taste the terrific flavors of this hearty salad!

1 (7 ounce) box lentil pilaf mix	200 g
2 medium navel oranges	
¾ cup Craisins®	90 g
½ cup slivered almonds or coarsely chopped walnuts, toasted	85 g

Prepare lentil pilaf mix according to package directions. Transfer to large bowl and cool.

Peel and slice oranges. Cut orange slices into 1-inch (2.5 cm) pieces. Add orange pieces, Craisins® and toasted nuts to cooled lentil pilaf. Stir gently to mix.

Servings 4.
Serving size: 1 cup (250 ml)

TIP: If desired, toss with a simple oil and vinegar dressing or Balsamic Vinaigrette (page 101).

One Serving

Calories: 444	Sodium: 615 mg
Calories from Fat: 135	Total Carbohydrates: 54 g
Total Fat: 15 g	Dietary Fiber: 13 g
Saturated Fat: 1 g	Sugars: 15 g
Cholesterol: 0 mg	Protein: 17 g

Lemony Lentil Pilaf

Lentils and rice combine with the fresh flavors of green onion, bell pepper and tomatoes for a special pilaf.

1 (7 ounce box) lentil pilaf mix	200 g
¼ cup chopped green onions	25 g
⅓ cup chopped green or yellow bell pepper	50 g
1½ cups cherry tomato halves	225 g
⅓ cup pine nuts, toasted or sunflower seeds, toasted	45 g
½ cup Lemony Vinaigrette (page 108)	125 ml

Prepare pilaf according to package directions. Cool.

Add green onion, bell pepper, tomatoes and nuts or seeds to cooled pilaf.

Drizzle with Lemony Vinaigrette and toss gently.

Serves 4.
Serving size: 1 cup (250 ml)

TIP: Lentil rice pilaf mixes are easy to use and take the guesswork out of which spices to use.

One Serving

Calories: 365	Sodium: 573 mg
Calories from Fat: 191	Total Carbohydrates: 35 g
Total Fat: 21 g	Dietary Fiber: 8 g
Saturated Fat: 3 g	Sugars: 5 g
Cholesterol: 0 mg	Protein: 12 g

Artichoke-Bowtie Salad

This pasta salad is great to pack up and carry to potluck suppers or picnics.

6 ounces (2 cups) bowtie pasta (farfalle)	170 g
1 (6 ounce) jar marinated artichoke heart quarters	170 g
1 large red or green bell pepper, chopped	
1 garlic clove, minced	
½ cup freshly grated parmesan cheese	50 g
½ cup reduced-fat sour cream	120 g
¼ cup sliced green onions	25 g

Prepare pasta according to package directions. Drain and cool.

Drain marinade from artichokes and set aside. Cut artichoke quarters in half and set aside. Add marinade to 10-inch (25 cm) skillet and bring to a boil. Stir in bell pepper and garlic. Reduce heat and simmer about 5 minutes or until bell pepper is tender. Stir in artichoke pieces, remove from heat and cool.

Combine parmesan cheese, sour cream and green onions in large bowl. Add cooked pasta and artichoke mixture and toss gently. Cover and refrigerate until ready to serve.

Serves 6 to 8.
Serving size: 1 cup (250 ml)

TIP: Six ounces or 2 cups (170 g) uncooked small to medium pasta equals 3 cups (420 g) cooked.

One Serving

Calories: 175	Cholesterol: 16 mg	Dietary Fiber: 3 g
Calories from Fat: 54	Sodium: 279 mg	Sugars: 1 g
Total Fat: 6 g	Total Carbohydrates: 21 g	Protein: 9 g
Saturated Fat: 3 g		

Broccoli-Carrot Pasta Salad

A simple, wholesome combination of pasta and
colorful vegetables makes this a repeat recipe.

2 tablespoons sesame seeds	20 g
8 ounces rotini or mini penne pasta	230 g
4 cups fresh broccoli florets	285 g
1 cup fresh baby carrots	140 g
2 tablespoons rice vinegar	30 ml
¼ cup canola oil	60 ml

Preheat oven to 350° (175° C).

Spread sesame seeds in shallow baking pan and bake for 5 to 10 minutes or until seeds are light brown. Stir once or twice during baking.

Prepare pasta according to package directions. Drain and cool.

Cook broccoli and carrots in covered saucepan with small amount of boiling salted water for 8 to 10 minutes or until tender. Drain.

Combine pasta, broccoli, carrots, vinegar and canola oil in large bowl. Cover and refrigerate. At serving time, sprinkle with sesame seeds.

Serves 6 to 8
Serving size: 1 cup (250 ml)

TIP: Check Asian food section for toasted sesame seeds. They are generally cheaper than sesame seeds in spice sections.

One Serving

Calories: 205	Cholesterol: 0 mg	Dietary Fiber: 3 g
Calories from Fat: 85	Sodium: 1 mg	Sugars: 1 g
Total Fat: 10 g	Total Carbohydrates: 25 g	Protein: 5 g
Saturated Fat: 1 g		

Broccoli Linguine

Broccoli crowns are generally 3½ to 5 inches (8.5 - 13 cm) in diameter and have stems while florets are smaller, usually 1½ to 3 inches (3 - 8 cm) across.

1 (13 ounce) package whole wheat linguine	370 g
2 pounds broccoli crowns	910 g
1 tablespoon olive oil	15 ml
2 garlic cloves, minced	
¼ teaspoon red pepper flakes	1 ml

Prepare linguine according to package directions. Drain and cover to keep warm.

Wash broccoli crowns and remove florets. Peel and coarsely chop stems. Bring 2 cups (500 ml) water to a boil in large, heavy pan. Add broccoli and cook uncovered until tender. Drain.

Heat oil in 12-inch (32 cm) over medium heat. Add garlic and red pepper flakes; cook and stir about 1 to 2 minutes. Stir in broccoli and remove from heat.

Toss broccoli with linguine. Serve immediately.

Serves about 7 to 8.
Serving size: 1 cup (250 ml)

TIP: Pass extra red pepper flakes and grated parmesan cheese at the table.

One Serving

Calories: 218	
Calories from Fat: 37	Sodium: 37 mg
Total Fat: 4 g	Total Carbohydrates: 39 g
Saturated Fat: 0 g	Dietary Fiber: 5 g
Cholesterol: 0 mg	Sugars: 3 g
	Protein: 9 g

Broccoli Lo Mein

Lo mein [loh MAYN] is a Chinese dish of boiled noodles combined with stir-fry ingredients.

8 ounces whole wheat spaghetti or linguine	230 g
1 tablespoon canola oil, divided	15 ml
¾ pound broccoli, cut into bite-size pieces	340 g
2 garlic cloves, minced	
1½ teaspoons minced fresh ginger	7 ml
¾ cup Lo Mein Sauce (page 239)	175 ml

Prepare spaghetti according to package directions. Drain and keep warm.

Heat 1½ teaspoons (7 ml) oil in large, heavy pan over high heat. Add broccoli and stir-fry about 1 minute. Stir in garlic and ginger and stir-fry 1 minute. Transfer to plate and keep warm. Add remaining oil to pan and heat. Add cooked spaghetti and stir-fry about 2 minutes or until thoroughly hot. Toss spaghetti and Lo Mein Sauce.

Serves 4.
Serving size: 1 cup (250 ml)

TIP: Eight ounces spaghetti is equal to a 1½-inch (3 cm) diameter bunch.

One Serving

Calories: 300	Sodium: 387 mg
Calories from Fat: 65	Total Carbohydrates: 49 g
Total Fat: 8 g	Dietary Fiber: 8 g
Saturated Fat: 1 g	Sugars: 5 g
Cholesterol: 0 mg	Protein: 10 g

Linguine Primavera

The Italian term primavera means spring style and
indicates the addition of fresh vegetables to a dish.

6 ounces whole wheat linguine	170 g
1½ cups canned vegetable broth	375 ml
1 cup fresh baby carrots	140 g
1 cup frozen or fresh sugar snap peas	100 g
1 cup (about 6) fresh asparagus spears, cut in 1-inch diagonal pieces	135 g/2.5 cm
1 cup grated parmesan cheese	100 g
1 (8 ounce) carton fat-free half-and-half cream	230 g

Prepare linguine according to package directions and drain.

Bring broth to a boil in large skillet. Lower heat, add carrots and peas and cook about 10 minutes. Add asparagus and cook about 5 minutes.

Add linguine and parmesan cheese and cook on low until hot. Remove from heat and stir in half-and-half cream. Serve immediately.

Serves 6 to 8.
Serving size: 1 cup (250 ml)

TIP: To speed preparation, use frozen vegetable blend.

One Serving

Calories: 222	Cholesterol: 23 mg	Dietary Fiber: 3 g
Calories from Fat: 73	Sodium: 598 mg	Sugars: 3 g
Total Fat: 8 g	Total Carbohydrates: 23 g	Protein: 14 g
Saturated Fat: 4 g		

Couscous Stuffed Bell Peppers

This is the healthy way to have stuffed peppers.

¾ cup couscous	130 g
4 medium green, yellow or red bell peppers	
2 teaspoons olive oil	10 ml
1 cup chopped onion	160 g
2 garlic cloves, minced	
1 cup coarsely chopped mushrooms	75 g
1 cup reduced-fat shredded Monterey Jack cheese	115 g

Preheat oven to 350° (175° C).

Cook couscous according to package directions. Remove from heat and set aside.

Cut tops off bell peppers, seed and trim membrane. Bring 3 quarts (3 L) water to a boil in large, heavy pan. Add pepper shells and boil for about 3 minutes. Remove and drain.

Combine oil, onion, garlic, mushrooms, ½ teaspoon (2 ml) salt and ¼ teaspoon (1 ml) pepper in non-stick 12-inch (32 cm) skillet. Cook and stir over medium heat until vegetables are tender. Stir in cooked couscous.

Arrange bell pepper shells in sprayed 9 x 9-inch (23 x 23 cm) baking dish. Spoon couscous mixture evenly into shells. Sprinkle each pepper with one-fourth cheese. Bake about 30 minutes or until peppers are tender.

Serves 4.
Serving size: 1 stuffed pepper

TIP: You can replace mushrooms with shredded carrots or shredded zucchini, if you like.

One Serving

Calories: 288	Cholesterol: 29 mg	Dietary Fiber: 4 g
Calories from Fat: 105	Sodium: 179 mg	Sugars: 2 g
Total Fat: 12 g	Total Carbohydrates: 32 g	Protein: 12 g
Saturated Fat: 6 g		

Couscous-Vegetable Salad

Couscous [KOOS koos] is coarsely ground semolina or durum wheat.

¾ cup couscous	130 g
½ cup shredded carrot	55 g
½ cup diced red bell pepper	75 g
½ cup canned whole kernel gold and white corn, drained	85 g
2 tablespoons chopped red onion	20 g
1 tablespoon chopped cilantro	15 ml
½ cup Feta Cheese Dressing (page 105)	125 ml

⋈ Cook couscous according to package directions. Cool.

⋈ Combine couscous, carrot, bell pepper, corn, red onion and cilantro in large bowl. Drizzle with Feta Cheese Dressing and toss.

Serves 4.
Serving size: 1 cup (250 ml)

TIP: Packaged precooked couscous is available in large supermarkets and specialty markets carrying Middle Eastern foods. Use 2 cups (315 g) cooked couscous.

One Serving

Calories: 300	Sodium: 134 mg
Calories from Fat: 127	Total Carbohydrates: 35 g
Total Fat: 14 g	Dietary Fiber: 3 g
Saturated Fat: 3 g	Sugars: 1 g
Cholesterol: 11 mg	Protein: 7 g

Three-Cheese Baked Rigatoni

Rigatoni is large, grooved macaroni about 2 inches (5 cm) wide.

8 ounces rigatoni pasta	230 g
1 (16 ounce) carton part-skim ricotta cheese	455 g
1 cup reduced-fat shredded mozzarella cheese	115 g
2 cups Roma Tomato Sauce (page 242) or tomato pasta sauce	500 ml
¼ cup finely grated parmesan or romano cheese	25 g

⋈ Preheat oven to 350° (175° C).

⋈ Prepare rigatoni according to package directions. Drain and transfer to sprayed 9 x 13-inch (23 x 33 cm) baking dish.

⋈ Combine ricotta and mozzarella cheeses, ½ teaspoon (2 ml) salt and ¼ teaspoon (1 ml) pepper in medium bowl and spread over pasta. Pour Roma Tomato Sauce over combined cheeses. Bake 45 minutes. Sprinkle with parmesan cheese.

Serves 6.
Serving size: 1 cup (250 ml)

One Serving

Calories: 372	Sodium: 615 mg
Calories from Fat: 133	Total Carbohydrates: 37 g
Total Fat: 15 g	Dietary Fiber: 5 g
Saturated Fat: 9 g	Sugars: 4 g
Cholesterol: 49 mg	Protein: 22 g

Eggplant-Mushroom Lasagna

9 whole wheat lasagna noodles	
1 medium (about 1 pound) eggplant, peeled, cubed	455 g
3 - 4 cups sliced mushrooms	220 - 290 g
4 cups Roma Tomato Sauce (page 242) or tomato pasta sauce, divided	950 ml
2 cups part-skim ricotta cheese	495 g
2 cups reduced-fat shredded mozzarella cheese	230 g
1½ cups finely grated romano cheese, divided	150 g

Prepare lasagna noodles according to package directions. Drain and set aside.

Combine eggplant, mushrooms and ¼ cup (60 ml) water in sprayed, large heavy pan over medium heat. Stir occasionally and cook until vegetables are tender, about 15 minutes. Add 1¼ cups (310 ml) sauce and heat about 5 minutes.

Preheat oven to 350° (175° C).

Stir ricotta cheese, mozzarella cheese, 1 cup (100 g) romano cheese and ¼ teaspoon (1 ml) black pepper in large bowl.

Spread ¾ cup (175 ml) Roma Tomato Sauce, 3 noodles, ¾ cup (175 ml) cheese mixture and one-third of eggplant-mushroom mixture in sprayed 9 x 13-inch (23 x 33 cm) baking dish for first layer. Repeat for second and third layers. Spoon remaining sauce and romano cheese over top layer.

Bake uncovered for 40 to 50 minutes. Let stand 10 minutes before serving.

Serves 10.
Serving size: 3-inch (8 cm) square

One Serving

Calories: 469	Cholesterol: 62 mg	Dietary Fiber: 9 g
Calories from Fat: 196	Sodium: 484 mg	Sugars: 2 g
Total Fat: 23 g	Total Carbohydrates: 36 g	Protein: 23 g
Saturated Fat: 11 g		

Fettuccine Gorgonzola

1 (8 ounce) package refrigerated fresh fettuccine	230 g
1 (10 ounce) package frozen petite peas or mixed vegetables	280 g
1 cup (about 6 ounces) crumbled gorgonzola cheese	170 g

 Prepare fettuccine according to package directions. During last minute of cooking, stir in peas. Remove from heat and drain.

 Return pasta and peas to pan, add cheese and 2 tablespoons (30 ml) hot water. Mix lightly over low heat until pasta coats well with melted cheese, about 2 to 3 minutes. Add ¼ teaspoon (1 ml) pepper.

Serves 4.
Serving size: 1 cup (250 ml)

One Serving

Calories: 507	Sodium: 842 mg
Calories from Fat: 141	Total Carbohy-drates: 58 g
Total Fat: 16 g	Dietary Fiber: 8 g
Saturated Fat: 8 g	Sugars: 7 g
Cholesterol: 44 mg	Protein: 30 g

Cheese Tortellini and Olives

These small, stuffed twists of pasta are really good with kalamata olives.

2 (9 ounce) packages refrigerated cheese-filled tortellini	2 (255 g)
3 cups Marinara Sauce (page 239) or tomato pasta sauce	750 ml
½ cup sliced kalamata olives	65 g
3 tablespoons coarsely chopped parsley	15 g

 Cook tortellini according to package directions. Drain and keep warm.

 Heat Marinara Sauce in 2-quart (2 L) saucepan over medium heat.

 Pour sauce over cooked tortellini and sprinkle with olives and parsley.

Serves 6.
Serving size: 1 cup (250 ml)

TIP: You can replace refrigerated tortellini with dried cheese-filled tortellini if you like. Look for 9-ounce (255 g) packages in various flavors.

One Serving

Calories: 330	Sodium: 759 mg
Calories from Fat: 73	Total Carbohy-drates: 48 g
Total Fat: 8 g	Dietary Fiber: 5 g
Saturated Fat: 3 g	Sugars: 4 g
Cholesterol: 36 mg	Protein: 14 g

Lasagna-Ricotta Rolls

What a neat way to prepare and serve lasagna — no messy squares to cut.

10 whole wheat lasagna noodles	
1 (10 ounce) package frozen chopped spinach, thawed	280 g
1 cup mozzarella-flavor veggie shreds	110 g
1 cup finely grated parmesan cheese, divided	100 g
1½ cups part-skim ricotta cheese	370 g
4 cups Roma Tomato Sauce (page 242) or tomato pasta sauce	1 L

Preheat oven to 350° (175° C).

Cook lasagna noodles according to package directions. Drain and spread on non-stick baking sheet.

Squeeze spinach between paper towels to completely remove excess moisture. Combine spinach, veggie shreds, ½ cup (50 g) parmesan cheese, ricotta cheese, 1 teaspoon (5 ml) salt and ½ teaspoon (2 ml) pepper in large bowl. Spread ¼ cup (60 ml) mixture down length of each noodle and roll.

Arrange rolled noodles in sprayed 9 x 13-inch (23 x 33 cm) baking dish. Pour Roma Tomato Sauce over noodle rolls.

Bake for 15 to 20 minutes or until sauce bubbles and rolls are hot. Remove from oven and sprinkle tops with remaining parmesan cheese.

Serves 10.
Serving size: 1 stuffed noodle

TIP: For a different flavor, replace spinach with 1 (10 ounce/280 g) package frozen chopped broccoli.

One Serving

Calories: 413	Cholesterol: 32 mg	Dietary Fiber: 8 g
Calories from Fat: 102	Sodium: 551 mg	Sugars: 2 g
Total Fat: 11 g	Total Carbohydrates: 41 g	Protein: 20 g
Saturated Fat: 3 g		

Mushroom Stroganoff

¼ cup (½ stick) butter, divided 60 g
1 (16 ounce) package fresh
   mushrooms, sliced 455 g
2 medium onions, cut in wedges
2 garlic cloves, minced
2 tablespoons unbleached
   white flour 15 g
1 cup vegetable broth 250 ml
1 (8 ounce) carton reduced-fat
   sour cream 230 g

Melt 2 tablespoons (30 g) butter in non-stick 12-inch (32 cm) skillet and add mushrooms, onions and garlic. Cook and stir over medium heat until vegetables are tender. Remove vegetables and keep warm.

Add remaining butter and stir in flour. Cook over medium-high heat until mixture bubbles. Pour in broth and stir continuously until sauce thickens. Remove from heat and stir in mushroom mixture and sour cream.

Serves 4 to 6.
Serving size: 1 cup (250 ml)

TIP: *Serve over whole wheat noodles or brown rice.*

One Serving

Calories: 165	Sodium: 190 mg
Calories from	Total Carbohy-
Fat: 126	drates: 7 g
Total Fat: 14 g	Dietary Fiber: 1 g
Saturated Fat: 8 g	Sugars: 2 g
Cholesterol: 35 mg	Protein: 5 g

Bell Pepper- Mushroom Orzo

Orzo pasta (rice-shaped pasta) cooks quickly and makes dinner a snap.

8 ounces orzo pasta 230 g
1 tablespoon olive oil 15 ml
2 tablespoons thinly sliced
   green onions 15 g
1 garlic clove, minced
½ cup diced red bell pepper 75 g
½ cup chopped fresh
   mushrooms 40 g
¼ - ½ teaspoon ground
   cumin 1 - 2 ml

Bring 2 quarts (2 L) water to a boil in large, heavy pan. Add orzo and ½ teaspoon (2 ml) salt. Bring back to a boil and reduce heat to medium. Cook, stirring frequently, about 5 to 6 minutes.

Combine oil, remaining ingredients, ½ teaspoon salt (2 ml) and ¼ teaspoon (1 ml) pepper in non-stick 12-inch (32 cm) skillet over medium-high heat. Cook and stir until vegetables are tender. Add cooked orzo and cook until hot.

Serves 6.
Serving size: 1 cup (250 ml)

One Serving

Calories: 170	Sodium: 1 mg
Calories from	Total Carbohy-
Fat: 31	drates: 29 g
Total Fat: 3 g	Dietary Fiber: 4 g
Saturated Fat: 0 g	Sugars: 2 g
Cholesterol: 0 mg	Protein: 5 g

Baby Portobellos with Pasta

Naming and marketing mushrooms today seems to be based mainly on consumer appeal. Baby portobellos are also marketed as cremini and baby bellas.

7 ounces whole wheat spaghetti	200 g
1 (6 ounce) package baby portobello mushrooms	170 g
2 tablespoons olive oil, divided	30 ml
1 medium red or green bell pepper, chopped	
2 garlic cloves, minced	
¼ teaspoon crushed red pepper	1 ml
1 (15 ounce) can crushed tomatoes in puree	425 g

⋈ Prepare spaghetti according to package directions. Drain, return to pan and cover to keep warm.

⋈ Wash mushrooms, trim stems and cut into quarters. Combine 1 tablespoon (15 ml) oil and quartered mushrooms in non-stick 12-inch (32 cm) skillet over medium-high heat. Add ½ teaspoon (2 ml) salt and ¼ teaspoon (1 ml) pepper. Cook and stir about 2 minutes. Remove mushrooms and keep warm.

⋈ Add remaining oil, bell pepper, garlic and crushed red pepper to skillet. Cook and stir over medium heat until bell pepper is tender. Add tomatoes and mushrooms and simmer about 10 minutes. Add water if needed. Serve over cooked spaghetti.

Serves 7.
Serving size: 1 cup (250 ml) pasta and sauce
Makes 7 cups (1.7 L).

One Serving

Calories: 277	Cholesterol: 0 mg	Dietary Fiber: 6 g
Calories from Fat: 71	Sodium: 196 mg	Sugars: 6 g
Total Fat: 8 g	Total Carbohydrates: 42 g	Protein: 8 g
Saturated Fat: 1 g		

Creamy Peas and Fettucine

This is a delicious pasta dish, even without the peas.

1 (16 ounce) package spinach or whole wheat fettucine	455 g
2 tablespoons butter	30 g
2 tablespoons unbleached white flour	15 g
1½ cups fat-free skim milk	375 ml
1 (10 ounce) package frozen petite peas, slightly thawed	280 g
¾ cup freshly grated parmesan or romano cheese	75 g

📭 Prepare fettucine according to package directions. Drain and keep warm.

📭 Melt butter in non-stick 12-inch (32 cm) skillet over medium heat. Stir in flour; cook and stir until mixture bubbles. Stir in milk all at once and cook until it thickens.

📭 Reduce heat and add peas, cheese, ½ teaspoon (2 ml) salt and ¼ teaspoon (1 ml) pepper and cook until hot. Remove and toss with fettucine.

Serves 4 to 6.
Serving size: ¾ cup (175 ml)

One Serving

Calories: 515	Sodium: 339 mg
Calories from Fat: 119	Total Carbohydrates: 72 g
Total Fat: 13 g	Dietary Fiber: 9 g
Saturated Fat: 6 g	Sugars: 9 g
Cholesterol: 34 mg	Protein: 21 g

Mini-Penne Tomato Bake

8 ounces mini-penne whole wheat pasta	230 g
2 tablespoons olive oil	30 ml
1 medium green bell pepper, diced	
2 tablespoons unbleached white flour	15 g
1 (15 ounce) can tomato sauce	425 g
1½ cups reduced-fat shredded sharp cheddar cheese, divided	170 g

📭 Preheat oven to 350° (175° C).

📭 Prepare pasta according to package directions.

📭 Heat oil in non-stick 12-inch (32 cm) skillet over medium-high heat. Add bell pepper and cook and stir until tender. Stir in flour and simmer 1 to 2 minutes Gradually add tomato sauce; cook and stir until it thickens. Add 1 cup (115 g) cheese, ½ teaspoon (2 ml) salt and ¼ teaspoon (1 ml) pepper.

📭 Layer half pasta and half tomato sauce mixture in sprayed 2-quart (2 L) baking dish. Layer remaining pasta and remaining sauce mixture. Top with remaining cheese. Bake for 50 to 60 minutes.

Serves 4 to 6.
Serving size: 1 cup (250 ml)

One Serving

Calories: 316	Sodium: 177 mg
Calories from Fat: 141	Total Carbohydrates: 31 g
Total Fat: 16 g	Dietary Fiber: 5 g
Saturated Fat: 6 g	Sugars: 2 g
Cholesterol: 29 mg	Protein: 12 g

Penne with Creamy Tomato Sauce

8 ounces whole wheat penne
  pasta   230 g
2 cups Roma Tomato Sauce (page 242)
  or tomato pasta sauce   500 ml
½ cup fat-free half-and-half
  cream   125 ml
1 (8 ounce) package sliced
  mushrooms   230 g

▱ Cook pasta according to package directions. Drain and keep warm.

▱ While pasta cooks, heat Roma Tomato Sauce in 2-quart (2 L) saucepan over medium heat. Remove from heat and stir in half-and-half cream. Keep warm.

▱ Combine mushrooms, ½ teaspoon (2 ml) salt and ¼ teaspoon (1 ml) pepper in sprayed non-stick 10-inch (25 cm) skillet over medium-high heat. Cook and stir until mushrooms are tender.

▱ Lightly toss cooked pasta, sauce and mushrooms in large bowl.

Serves 4.
Serving size: 1 cup (250 ml)

TIP: Pass freshly grated parmesan or romano cheese at the table.

One Serving
Calories: 265
Calories from
  Fat: 32
Total Fat: 3 g
Saturated Fat: 0 g
Cholesterol: 1 mg
Sodium: 48 mg
Total Carbohy-
  drates: 49 g
Dietary Fiber: 7 g
Sugars: 4 g
Protein: 10 g

Poppy Seed Pasta Bake

4 ounces whole wheat noodles
  or linguine   115 g
2 teaspoons butter   10 ml
½ cup finely chopped onion   80 g
1 clove garlic, minced
1½ cups reduced-fat small
  curd cottage cheese   340 g
1 cup reduced-fat sour cream
  or nonfat plain yogurt 240 g/230 g
2 teaspoons poppy seeds   10 ml

▱ Preheat oven to 350° (175° C).

▱ Prepare noodles according to package directions and drain.

▱ Melt butter in non-stick 12-inch (32 cm) skillet over medium heat and add onion and garlic. Cook and stir until onion is tender. Combine with cooked noodles in large bowl.

▱ Stir in cottage cheese, sour cream, poppy seeds, ½ teaspoon (2 ml) salt and ¼ teaspoon (1 ml) pepper. Transfer to sprayed 9 x 9-inch (23 x 23 cm) baking dish. Bake for 30 minutes.

Serves 4 to 6.
Serving size: 1 cup (250 ml)

One Serving
Calories: 204
Calories from
  Fat: 76
Total Fat: 8 g
Saturated Fat: 4 g
Cholesterol: 17 mg
Sodium: 248 mg
Total Carbohy-
  drates: 19 g
Dietary Fiber: 2 g
Sugars: 3 g
Protein: 12 g

Spinach and Noodles

2 cups whole wheat noodles	480 ml
1 (10 ounce) package frozen cut leaf spinach, thawed	280 g
3 beaten eggs or ¾ cup egg substitute	185 g
1½ cups light plain soymilk	375 ml
1 cup shredded Monterey Jack cheese	115 g
2 cups part-skim ricotta cheese	495 g

Preheat oven to 375° (190° C).

Prepare noodles according to package directions and drain.

Squeeze spinach between paper towels to completely remove excess moisture. Spread in sprayed 7 x 11-inch (18 x 28 cm) baking dish. Cover spinach with noodles.

Combine remaining ingredients in medium bowl. Add ½ teaspoon (2 ml) salt and ¼ teaspoon (1 ml) pepper. Mix thoroughly and pour over noodles.

Bake for 35 to 45 minutes or until knife inserted in center comes out clean.

Serves 6.
Serving size: 1 cup (250 ml)

One Serving
Nutrition facts are based on egg substitute.

Calories: 401	Sodium: 342 mg
Calories from Fat: 146	Total Carbohydrates: 37 g
Total Fat: 16 g	Dietary Fiber: 6 g
Saturated Fat: 8 g	Sugars: 3 g
Cholesterol: 45 mg	Protein: 27 g

Pepperoni-Focaccia Pizza

1 (12.5 ounce) package focaccia bread	70 g
1½ cups Marinara Sauce (page 239) or 1 (15 ounce) can pizza sauce	375 ml
2 teaspoons dried crushed Italian herbs	10 ml
1 (4 ounce) package pepperoni-style veggie protein slices	115 g
3 cups mozzarella-flavor veggie shreds	335 g

Preheat oven to 400° (205° C).

Add focaccia bread to baking sheet and spoon on Marinara Sauce. Sprinkle with herbs and arrange pepperoni slices on top. Sprinkle with veggie shreds.

Bake for 10 to 15 minutes until shreds melt and sauce is hot.

Serves 4.
Serving size: ¼ pizza

One Serving

Calories: 240	Sodium: 665 mg
Calories from Fat: 83	Total Carbohydrates: 28 g
Total Fat: 10 g	Dietary Fiber: 3 g
Saturated Fat: 2 g	Sugars: 4 g
Cholesterol: 0 mg	Protein: 12 g

Vegetable-Goat Cheese Pizza

A freshly prepared pizza crust and fresh vegetables make this recipe a winner!

1 (12 inch) prepared pizza crust	32 cm
Small amount of olive oil	
1 medium tomato, seeded, cubed	
1 cup grated zucchini	125 g
¼ cup chopped red onion	40 g
2 tablespoons chopped sun-dried tomatoes	10 g
1 cup crumbled goat cheese	130 g

🍕 Preheat oven according to pizza crust directions.

🍕 Place pizza crust on baking sheet. Brush lightly with olive oil. Sprinkle evenly with tomato, zucchini, red onion and sun-dried tomatoes. Top with cheese.

🍕 Bake pizza for time given in package directions.

Serves 4.
Serving size: ¼ pizza

One Serving

Calories: 238	Sodium: 202 mg
Calories from Fat: 54	Total Carbohydrates: 37 g
Total Fat: 6 g	Dietary Fiber: 2 g
Saturated Fat: 4 g	Sugars: 2 g
Cholesterol: 15 mg	Protein: 10 g

Whole Wheat Pita Pizzas

Pita breads are a quick and easy substitute for pizza crust.

4 large whole wheat pita breads, split	
2 tablespoons olive oil, divided	30 ml
¾ cup Marinara Sauce (page 239) or tomato pasta sauce	175 ml
1 (7 ounce) package mozzarella-flavor veggie shreds	200 g
½ cup chopped red onion	80 g
½ cup chopped green bell pepper	75 g
2 tablespoons fresh oregano leaves or 1 teaspoon crushed dried oregano	30 ml/5 ml

🍕 Preheat oven to 375° (190° C).

🍕 Brush each pita lightly with olive oil and add 2 tablespoons (30 ml) Marinara Sauce. Add one-fourth of shreds, red onion and bell pepper. Drizzle with ½ teaspoon (2 ml) oil and sprinkle with oregano. Transfer to baking sheet and bake until shreds melt, about 10 minutes.

Serves 4.
Serving size: 1 pita pizza

One Serving

Calories: 281	Sodium: 495 mg
Calories from Fat: 89	Total Carbohydrates: 41 g
Total Fat: 11 g	Dietary Fiber: 7 g
Saturated Fat: 1 g	Sugars: 4 g
Cholesterol: 0 mg	Protein: 8 g

Almond-Raisin Curried Rice

Bottled curry powder is actually a pulverized blend of up to 20 spices, herbs and seeds. The characteristic yellow-orange color of curried dishes comes from the turmeric in curry powder. Use this potent spice sparingly.

1 cup brown rice	185 g
2¾ cups vegetable broth	675 g
1 tablespoon butter	15 ml
1 tablespoon finely chopped onion	15 ml
½ - 1 teaspoon curry powder	2 - 5 ml
⅓ cup slivered almonds, toasted	60 g
⅓ cup golden raisins	50 g

🥣 Combine brown rice and broth in 2-quart (2 L) saucepan and bring to a boil. Reduce heat to low. Cover and simmer 45 to 50 minutes. Fluff with fork and let stand in saucepan.

🥣 Add butter and onion to non-stick 12-inch (32 cm) skillet over medium heat. Cook and stir about 2 minutes. Add curry powder, ¼ teaspoon (1 ml) salt and ¼ teaspoon (1 ml) pepper and stir. Transfer onion mixture to hot brown rice and stir to mix.

🥣 Sprinkle almonds and raisins on top.

Serves 4.
Serving size: 1 cup (250 ml)

TIP: Turmeric also gives yellow mustard its bright yellow color.

One Serving

Calories: 239	Cholesterol: 8 mg	Dietary Fiber: 4 g
Calories from Fat: 122	Sodium: 651 mg	Sugars: 10 g
Total Fat: 14 g	Total Carbohydrates: 27 g	Protein: 6 g
Saturated Fat: 3 g		

Curried Rice with Almonds

This is a simple rice dish with the exotic flavor of curry and the toasted goodness of almonds.

1 cup brown rice	185 g
2¾ cups vegetable broth	650 ml
1 tablespoon butter	15 ml
1 tablespoon finely chopped onion	15 ml
½ - 1 teaspoon curry powder	2 - 5 ml
⅓ cup slivered almonds, toasted	60 g

◉ Combine brown rice and broth in 2-quart (2 L) saucepan and bring to a boil. Reduce heat to low, cover and simmer 45 to 50 minutes. Fluff with fork and let stand in saucepan.

◉ Combine butter and onion in non-stick 12-inch (32 cm) skillet over medium heat. Cook and stir about 2 minutes. Add curry powder, ¼ teaspoon (1 ml) each of salt and pepper and stir. Transfer onion mixture to hot brown rice and stir to mix. Sprinkle with almonds.

Serves 4.
Serving size: ¾ cup (175 ml)

One Serving

Calories: 203	Sodium: 650 mg
Calories from Fat: 122	Total Carbohy-drates: 17 g
Total Fat: 14 g	Dietary Fiber: 3 g
Saturated Fat: 3 g	Sugars: 3 g
Cholesterol: 8 mg	Protein: 6 g

Oven-Baked Rice

Your family will love this light-as-a-feather rice dish.

2 tablespoons butter	30 g
1 cup long grain white rice	185 g
2 cups vegetable broth	500 ml

◉ Preheat oven to 350° (175° C).

◉ Melt butter in 10-inch (25 cm) skillet over medium heat. Add rice; cook and stir until rice browns.

◉ Add rice and broth to 1½-quart (1.5 L) baking dish. Cover and bake about 35 minutes or until rice is tender and absorbs broth. Fluff with fork before serving.

Serves 4.
Serving size: ¾ cup (175 ml)

TIP: Rice Math: 1 cup (185 g) regular rice = 3 cups (475 g) cooked rice; 1 cup (185 g) brown rice = 3½ to 4 cups (680 to 780 g) cooked brown rice.

One Serving

Calories: 99	Sodium: 236 mg
Calories from Fat: 54	Total Carbohy-drates: 10 g
Total Fat: 6 g	Dietary Fiber: 0 g
Saturated Fat: 4 g	Sugars: 0 g
Cholesterol: 16 mg	Protein: 1 g

Rice and Garden Vegetables

Carrots, peas, onion and garlic combine with brown rice for a colorful, wholesome dish.

1 tablespoon olive oil	15 ml
1 cup brown rice	185 g
1 garlic clove, minced	
1 cup chopped onion	160 g
3 cups vegetable broth	750 ml
1 cup shredded carrots	110 g
½ cup frozen petite green peas	75 g

Heat oil in large heavy pan over medium-high heat. Add brown rice; cook and stir until it browns. (Be careful not to burn rice.) Add garlic and onion, cook and stir until onion is tender.

Add broth and bring to a boil. Reduce heat to low, cover and simmer about 45 to 50 minutes or until rice is tender and absorbs broth.

Stir in carrots, peas, ½ teaspoon (2 ml) salt and ¼ teaspoon (1 ml) pepper. Simmer covered about 5 minutes or until carrots and peas are tender. Add small amount of water, if needed.

Serves 6 to 8.
Serving size: 1 cup (250 ml)

TIP: You can use frozen black-eyed peas instead of frozen peas, if you like.

One Serving

Calories: 77	Cholesterol: 0 mg	Dietary Fiber: 2 g
Calories from Fat: 20	Sodium: 437 mg	Sugars: 3 g
Total Fat: 2 g	Total Carbohydrates: 12 g	Protein: 2 g
Saturated Fat: 0 g		

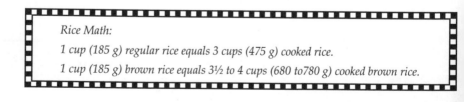

Rice Math:

1 cup (185 g) regular rice equals 3 cups (475 g) cooked rice.

1 cup (185 g) brown rice equals 3½ to 4 cups (680 to 780 g) cooked brown rice.

Brown Rice and Vegetables

Choose from the wide variety of frozen vegetable blends to make this a different dish every time you make it.

1 tablespoon oil	15 ml
1 cup brown rice	185 g
½ cup (2 - 3) sliced green onions	50 g
2¾ cups canned vegetable broth	675 ml
1 (16 - 20 ounce) package frozen vegetable blend	455 - 570 g
¼ cup chopped sun-dried tomatoes	15 g

Heat oil in large saucepan over medium heat. Add rice and green onions and cook, stirring constantly, until rice lightly browns. Add vegetable broth and simmer covered 45 to 50 minutes.

Cook vegetable blend according to package directions.

Combine cooked rice, vegetables and sun-dried tomatoes.

Serves 6.
Serving size: 1 cup (250 ml)

TIP: To speed preparation, use the handy microwave precooked brown rice pouches with about 2 cups (390 g) in one pouch.

One Serving

Calories: 94	Sodium: 463 mg
Calories from Fat: 24	Total Carbohydrates: 14 g
Total Fat: 3 g	Dietary Fiber: 3 g
Saturated Fat: 0 g	Sugars: 4 g
Cholesterol: 0 mg	Protein: 2 g

Classic Brown Rice Pilaf

Brown rice is the entire grain with only the inedible outer husk removed. The nutritious and high fiber bran coating gives brown rice the tan color, nut-like flavor and chewy texture.

1 cup brown rice	185 g
½ cup (1 medium) chopped onion	80 g
1 garlic clove, minced	
1 tablespoon butter	15 ml
2¾ cups vegetable broth	650 ml
¼ cup finely chopped parsley	20 g

Combine rice, onion, garlic and butter in 2-quart (2 L) saucepan over medium heat. Cook until onion is tender and rice browns.

Stir in broth, ½ teaspoon (2 ml) salt and ⅛ teaspoon (.5 ml) pepper. Bring to a boil, reduce heat to low and simmer tightly covered 40 to 50 minutes.

Remove from heat and let stand covered for about 5 minutes. Fluff with fork and stir in parsley.

Serves 4.
Serving size: 1 cup (250 ml)

One Serving

Calories: 214	Sodium: 650 mg
Calories from Fat: 38	Total Carbohydrates: 40 g
Total Fat: 4 g	Dietary Fiber: 2 g
Saturated Fat: 2 g	Sugars: 3 g
Cholesterol: 8 mg	Protein: 4 g

Black-Eyed Pea Jambalaya

These flavors are very similar to a true New Orleans jambalaya.

2 teaspoons olive oil	10 ml
1 cup chopped onions	160 g
2 garlic cloves, minced	
½ cup chopped celery	50 g
½ cup chopped red or green bell pepper	75 g
1 (6 ounce) box jambalaya brown rice mix	170 g
1 (16 ounce) can black-eyed peas, rinsed, drained	455 g

Combine oil, onions, garlic, celery and bell pepper in large, heavy pan over medium heat. Cook and stir until vegetables are tender.

Stir in jambalaya brown rice mix and add water according to package directions. Bring to a boil, reduce heat and simmer until rice is tender. Add black-eyed peas and simmer until hot. Add water if needed.

Serves 4 to 6.
Serving size: 1 cup (250 ml)

TIP: Bell pepper, celery, onions and ground red pepper are essential ingredients in most Creole and Cajun dishes.

One Serving

Calories: 264	Sodium: 904 mg
Calories from Fat: 17	Total Carbohydrates: 53 g
Total Fat: 2 g	Dietary Fiber: 4 g
Saturated Fat: 0 g	Sugars: 2 g
Cholesterol: 0 mg	Protein: 8 g

Carrot-Pine Nut Pilaf

Carrots give this simple rice dish a pleasing sweetness and a warm orange color.

2 tablespoons butter	30 g
1 cup finely chopped onion	160 g
1 cup shredded carrots	110 g
¼ cup pine nuts	35 g
1 cup brown rice	185 g
2½ cups vegetable broth	625 ml
½ cup chopped parsley	35 g

Melt butter in large, heavy pan over medium-high heat and add onion, carrots and pine nuts. Reduce heat to medium; cook and stir until vegetables are tender, about 5 minutes.

Over medium heat, add rice; continue to cook and stir until rice browns. Add vegetable broth, ½ teaspoon (2 ml) salt and ¼ teaspoon (1 ml) pepper and bring to a boil.

Reduce heat, cover and simmer, stirring occasionally, until rice is tender and absorbs liquid, about 45 minutes. Fluff with fork and stir in parsley.

Serves 6.
Serving size: 1 cup (250 ml)

TIP: Replace pine nuts with chopped pecans, walnuts or almonds.

One Serving

Calories: 212	Sodium: 407 mg
Calories from Fat: 78	Total Carbohydrates: 31 g
Total Fat: 9 g	Dietary Fiber: 3 g
Saturated Fat: 3 g	Sugars: 3 g
Cholesterol: 10 mg	Protein: 4 g

Cashew-Fruit Rice Pilaf

*This simple brown rice dish becomes company best
with the added sweetness of dried fruits and cashews.*

1 cup brown rice	185 g
2¾ cups vegetable broth	650 ml
1 tablespoon butter	15 ml
¼ cup cashews	30 g
¼ cup sweetened dried cherries or cranberries	30 g
¼ cup chopped dried apricots	40 g
¼ cup chopped pitted dates	40 g

- Combine rice, broth and ½ teaspoon (2 ml) salt in 3-quart (3 L) saucepan and bring to a boil. Reduce heat, cover and simmer about 45 minutes or until rice is tender and absorbs liquid.

- Melt butter in 8-inch (20 cm) skillet over medium-low heat and add cashews. Cook and stir until cashews brown. Remove cashews and set aside.

- Fluff rice mixture with fork, add dried fruit and sprinkle browned cashews on top.

Serves 6.
Serving size: 1 cup (250 ml)

TIP: Dried mango, mixed fruit bits, chopped figs or prunes are other good fruit choices.

One Serving

Calories: 240	Cholesterol: 5 mg	Dietary Fiber: 3 g
Calories from Fat: 47	Sodium: 440 mg	Sugars: 15 g
Total Fat: 6 g	Total Carbohydrates: 45 g	Protein: 4 g
Saturated Fat: 2 g		

Chile-Cheese Rice

2¾ cups vegetable broth	650 ml
1 cup brown rice	185 g
1 (4 ounce) can chopped green chilies	115 g
1 cup reduced-fat shredded cheddar cheese	115 g
½ cup reduced-fat sour cream	120 g

🥣 Pour vegetable broth into saucepan. Cook over medium-high heat, bring to a boil and stir in rice. Reduce heat to low, cover and simmer 40 to 60 minutes or until rice is tender and absorbs broth.

🥣 Stir in chilies and cheese. Remove from heat and stir in sour cream. Cover and let stand about 5 minutes.

Serves 4.
Serving size: 1 cup (250 ml)

One Serving

Calories: 226	Sodium: 347 mg
Calories from Fat: 166	Total Carbohydrates: 1 g
Total Fat: 18 g	Dietary Fiber: 0 g
Saturated Fat: 12 g	Sugars: 0 g
Cholesterol: 59 mg	Protein: 14 g

Coconut Basmati Rice

Cool down a spicy main dish with this delicious rice. Basmati, Jasmine and Texmati are aromatic rice varieties that have a fragrant, nut-like flavor.

1¾ cups basmati rice or long grain white rice	185 g
1 (15 ounce) can reduced-fat coconut milk	425 g

🥣 Combine rice, coconut milk, 2 cups (500 ml) water and ½ teaspoon (2 ml) salt in sprayed 2-quart (2 L) saucepan over medium-high heat.

🥣 Cook and stir until rice mixture boils. Reduce heat to medium-low, cover and cook about 15 to 20 minutes or until rice absorbs most of liquid. Turn off heat and let stand covered about 5 to 10 minutes. Fluff with fork.

Serves 4 to 6.
Serving size: ¾ cup (175 ml)

TIP: Garnish with 2 tablespoons (30 ml) toasted shredded coconut. To toast coconut, add to 8-inch (20 cm) dry skillet and cook, stirring constantly, over medium heat.

One Serving

Calories: 127	Sodium: 18 mg
Calories from Fat: 53	Total Carbohydrates: 15 g
Total Fat: 6 g	Dietary Fiber: 0 g
Saturated Fat: 5 g	Sugars: 2 g
Cholesterol: 0 mg	Protein: 1 g

Corn-Red Pepper Risotto

Italian arborio rice, used to make creamy risottos, is short grain rice. Short grain rice has a high starch content, which makes it moist and sticky when cooked.

2⅓ cups vegetable broth, divided	575 ml
1 cup arborio rice	200 g
2 garlic cloves, minced	
¼ teaspoon ground cumin	1 ml
2 cups frozen whole kernel corn	330 g
2 tablespoons roasted red pepper, diced	20 g
1 tablespoon chopped cilantro	15 ml

Bring 2 cups (500 ml) broth to a boil in large, heavy pan and stir in rice. Reduce heat to low and cook covered for 20 to 25 minutes or until rice absorbs liquid. Remove from heat, fluff with fork and set aside.

Pour ⅓ cup (75 ml) broth in non-stick 10-inch (25 cm) skillet. Cook over medium-high heat and bring to a boil. Add garlic, cook and stir 1 minute. Add cumin and frozen corn; cook and stir until corn is tender.

Gently stir corn mixture, red pepper and cilantro into cooked rice.

Serves 6 to 8.
Serving size: ¾ cup (175 ml)

One Serving

Calories: 115	Cholesterol: 0 mg	Dietary Fiber: 1 g
Calories from Fat: 3	Sodium: 314 mg	Sugars: 1 g
Total Fat: 0 g	Total Carbohydrates: 24 g	Protein: 3 g
Saturated Fat: 0 g		

Louisiana Red Beans and Rice

Here's a famously simple, hearty and spicy dish. Don't forget to pass around Louisiana hot sauce for those who like it hot and hotter.

2 teaspoons olive oil	10 ml
1 (16 ounce) package frozen seasoning blend (onion, celery, bell pepper)	455 g
2 garlic cloves, minced	
1 (16 ounce) can dark kidney beans, rinsed, drained	455 g
1 (14 ounce) can diced tomatoes seasoned with basil	400 g
1 teaspoon Creole or Cajun seasoning	5 ml
2 cups cooked brown rice	390 g

◉ Combine oil, seasoning blend and garlic in non-stick 12-inch (32 cm) skillet over medium-high heat. Cook and stir until vegetables are tender. Reduce heat to medium and add beans, tomatoes and seasoning. Simmer covered for about 10 minutes and stir occasionally.

◉ Serve over brown rice.

Serves 4 to 6.
Serving size: 1 cup (250 ml)

TIP: French bread slices toasted with butter and garlic make this dish complete.

One Serving

Calories: 246	Sodium: 409 mg
Calories from Fat: 33	Total Carbohydrates: 44 g
Total Fat: 4 g	Dietary Fiber: 8 g
Saturated Fat: 0 g	Sugars: 3 g
Cholesterol: 0 mg	Protein: 7 g

Spanish Rice with Corn

Onion, cumin, cilantro and lime juice give a great flavor boost to brown rice and corn. Remember to use cumin sparingly as it can make a dish bitter if too much is used. Use the smaller amount in the recipe and taste before adding more cumin.

¼ cup finely chopped onion	40 g
¼ cup frozen whole kernel corn, thawed, drained	45 g
¼ - ½ teaspoon ground cumin	1 - 2 ml
1 (8 ounce) can Mexican tomato sauce	230 g
2 cups cooked brown rice	390 g
¼ cup chopped cilantro	5 g
1 tablespoon lime juice	15 ml

◉ Cook and stir onion, corn and cumin in sprayed non-stick 10-inch (25 cm) skillet over medium heat about 2 to 3 minutes. Reduce heat to low, add tomato sauce and simmer 5 minutes. Stir in rice, cilantro and lime juice. Simmer until hot.

Serves 4 to 6.
Serving size: 1 cup (250 ml)

TIP: Replace tomato sauce with 1 cup (125 g) diced or stewed tomatoes, if you like.

One Serving

Calories: 108	Sodium: 186 mg
Calories from Fat: 8	Total Carbohydrates: 23 g
Total Fat: 1 g	Dietary Fiber: 2 g
Saturated Fat: 0 g	Sugars: 3 g
Cholesterol: 0 mg	Protein: 3 g

Mushroom-Brown Rice Stir-Fry

This hearty, flavorful dish is similar to Oriental stir-fried rice.

1 medium onion, halved, sliced	
1 (8 ounce) package fresh mushrooms, sliced	230 g
3 teaspoons canola oil	15 ml
2 cups cooked brown rice	390 g
½ cup egg substitute	125 g
3 tablespoons reduced-sodium soy sauce	45 ml
¼ cup chopped green onions	25 g

Place onion in sprayed non-stick wok or 12-inch (32 cm) skillet over high heat and stir-fry for about 1 minute. Add mushrooms and stir-fry for about 1 minute. Remove onions and mushrooms from pan and set aside.

Add oil and cooked brown rice and cook over medium-high heat. Stir-fry until hot, about 2 minutes. Push rice to sides of skillet and add egg. Lightly stir egg until softly scrambled. Return onions and mushrooms to skillet. Add soy sauce and green onions and toss lightly.

Serves 4 to 6.
Serving size: 1 cup (250 ml)

One Serving

Calories: 155	Cholesterol: 0 mg	Dietary Fiber: 2 g
Calories from Fat: 41	Sodium: 274 mg	Sugars: 2 g
Total Fat: 5 g	Total Carbohydrates: 22 g	Protein: 6 g
Saturated Fat: 1 g		

Chick'n Fajitas

The seasoned veggie strip product in this recipe is just
one of the amazing soy solutions now available.

1 tablespoon canola oil	15 ml
1 medium red or green bell pepper, cut in strips	
1 medium onion, halved, sliced	
2 (6 ounce) cartons seasoned veggie chicken strips	2 (170 g)
6 (7 inch) whole wheat or multigrain tortillas	6 (18 cm)
Fresh Tomatillo Salsa (page 53)	
Reduced-fat sour cream	

☞ Preheat oil in non-stick 12-inch (32 cm) skillet over medium-high heat. Add bell pepper strips and onion slices. Cook and stir until vegetables are tender. Reduce heat to medium and add veggie strips. Cook and stir 3 minutes or until strips are hot.

☞ Place tortillas between 2 plates or use tortilla warmer. Heat tortillas in microwave on HIGH for about 10 to 15 seconds.

☞ Spoon fajita mixture onto each tortilla and add Fresh Tomatillo Salsa. Garnish with sour cream.

Serves 6.
Serving size: 1 fajita

TIP: Fajitas, which originated in Texas, are traditionally prepared with skirt steak marinated in lime juice and garlic and grilled over mesquite.

One Serving

Calories: 227	Cholesterol: 0 mg	Dietary Fiber: 4 g
Calories from Fat: 57	Sodium: 637 mg	Sugars: 2 g
Total Fat: 6 g	Total Carbohydrates: 35 g	Protein: 15 g
Saturated Fat: 1 g		

Stuffed Bell Peppers

A healthy update of a traditional family favorite.

5 large green bell peppers	
2 teaspoons olive oil	10 ml
2 tablespoons chopped onion	20 g
1 clove garlic, minced	
6 ounces veggie protein crumbles	170 g
1 cup cooked brown rice	195 g
1 (15 ounce) can tomato sauce, divided	425 g

☝ Preheat oven to 350° (175° C).

☝ Cut thin slice from stem end of each bell pepper and remove top, seeds and membrane. Cook peppers in 3 to 4 quarts (3 - 4 L) boiling water for about 5 minutes. Remove and drain.

☝ Combine oil, onion and garlic in non-stick 12-inch (32 cm) skillet. Stir in veggie protein and cook about 6 minutes over medium heat. Stir in cooked rice and 1 cup (245 g) tomato sauce and heat through.

☝ Stuff peppers with rice mixture. Stand peppers upright in sprayed 9 x 9-inch (23 x 23 cm) baking dish. Pour remaining tomato sauce over peppers.

☝ Cover and bake for 45 minutes. Uncover and bake about 15 minutes or until peppers are tender and stuffing is hot.

Serves 5.
Serving size: 1 stuffed bell pepper

TIP: Replace green bell papers with sweeter, although more expensive, red or yellow bell peppers, if you like.

One Serving

Calories: 145	Cholesterol: 0 mg	Dietary Fiber: 7 g
Calories from Fat: 21	Sodium: 437 mg	Sugars: 7 g
Total Fat: 2 g	Total Carbohydrates: 25 g	Protein: 8 g
Saturated Fat: 0 g		

Veggie Crumble Chili

This bean and soy protein chili will please the fussiest of chili lovers.

2 teaspoons canola oil	10 ml
1 (16 ounce) package frozen seasoning blend (onions, celery, peppers)	455 g
1 (12 ounce) package refrigerated veggie protein crumbles	340 g
1 (14 ounce) can diced tomatoes with liquid	400 g
1 (16 ounce) can dark kidney beans, rinsed, drained	455 g
1 (16 ounce) can black beans, rinsed, drained	455 g
1 (1 ounce) packet low-sodium chili seasoning mix	30 g

Combine oil and seasoning blend in large, heavy pan over medium heat. Cook and stir until vegetables are tender. Add veggie protein crumbles; cook and stir until crumbles brown.

Add tomatoes, kidney beans, black beans and chili seasoning mix. Bring to a boil, reduce heat, cover and simmer about 10 minutes.

Serves 10.
Serving size: 1 cup (250 ml)

TIP: Serve with shredded cheddar cheese, sour cream and Chop Chop (page 51). Also use with Chili Dogs (page 215).

One Serving

Calories: 272	Cholesterol: 0 mg	Dietary Fiber: 7 g
Calories from Fat: 20	Sodium: 47 mg	Sugars: 2 g
Total Fat: 3 g	Total Carbohydrates: 26 g	Protein: 12 g
Saturated Fat: 0 g		

Chili Dogs

Bring out these chili dogs for a healthier Fourth of July picnic.

1 (12 ounce) package veggie hot dogs	340 g
Veggie Crumble Chili (page 214) or 1 (15 ounce) can vegetarian chili	425 g
8 whole wheat hot dog buns	
1 (7 ounce) package cheddar-flavor veggie soy shreds	200 g
1 cup chopped onion	160 g
½ cup sweet pickle relish with mustard	125 g

☗ Bring 1 quart (1 L) water in 2-quart (2 L) saucepan to a boil. Turn off heat, add hot dogs and let stand for 2 minutes.

☗ Heat Veggie Crumble Chili in microwave 1 minute on HIGH. Stir and microwave on HIGH just until hot.

☗ Use oven or toaster oven to lightly toast buns. Layer hot dog, chili, veggie soy shreds, onion and relish on toasted buns.

Serves 8.
Serving size: 1 hot dog and fixins'

One Serving

Calories: 450	Cholesterol: 1 mg	Dietary Fiber: 8 g
Calories from Fat: 60	Sodium: 1129 mg	Sugars: 9 g
Total Fat: 8 g	Total Carbohydrates: 42 g	Protein: 19 g
Saturated Fat: 0 g		

Veggie Chorizo Frittata

Regular chorizo [chor EE zoh] is a high-calorie pork sausage
flavored with garlic, chili powder and other spices. Soy chorizo
has all the flavors without the fat of pork sausage. It's great.

½ cup diced green bell pepper	75 g
½ cup sliced onion	80 g
⅔ cup cooked veggie protein chorizo	490 g
¼ cup reduced-fat shredded mozzarella cheese	30 g

☞ Preheat oven on broil.

☞ Combine bell pepper, onion and ½ teaspoon (2 ml) salt in sprayed ovenproof 10-inch (25 cm) skillet over medium heat. Cook and stir until bell pepper and onion are tender. Spray skillet again if needed.

☞ Stir in chorizo and spread mixture in single layer in skillet. Pour egg substitute on top and turn heat to low. Cover and cook 7 to 10 minutes without stirring.

☞ Top with cheese and place 4 inches (10 cm) from broiler for 2 to 3 minutes or until eggs are set on top and cheese browns. Cut into 4 to 6 wedges to serve.

Serves 4 to 6.
Serving size: 1 wedge

One Serving

Calories: 104	Cholesterol: 7 mg	Dietary Fiber: 8 g
Calories from Fat: 116	Sodium: 210 mg	Sugars: 2 g
Total Fat: 8 g	Total Carbohydrates: 245 g	Protein: 14 g
Saturated Fat: 2 g		

Veggie Crumble Stroganoff

*Ingredients in this recipe are similar to the original
19th century Russian recipe, except for the sliced beef.*

6 ounces veggie protein crumbles	170 g
2 tablespoons butter	30 g
1 cup thinly sliced mushrooms	75 g
1 tablespoon unbleached white flour	15 ml
½ cup fat-free skim milk	125 ml
1 cup reduced-fat plain yogurt	230 g
2 (9 ounce) pouches precooked microwave rice pilaf	2 (255 g)

☕ Cook crumbles according to package directions.

☕ Melt butter in non-stick 10-inch (25 cm) skillet over medium heat and add mushrooms. Cook and stir until mushrooms are tender. Stir in flour, ½ teaspoon (2 ml) salt and ¼ teaspoon (1 ml) pepper and cook and stir until mixture bubbles. Add skim milk; cook and stir until mixture thickens. Remove from heat and stir in yogurt and cooked crumbles.

☕ Prepare rice pilaf according to package directions. Serve stroganoff over rice pilaf.

Serves 6 to 8.
Serving size: 1 cup (250 ml)

One Serving

Calories: 72	Cholesterol: 9 mg	Dietary Fiber: 1 g
Calories from Fat: 30	Sodium: 70 mg	Sugars: 5 g
Total Fat: 3 g	Total Carbohydrates: 6 g	Protein: 5g
Saturated Fat: 2 g		

Veggie Crumble Tacos

Veggie protein crumbles are typically sold as a block in 12-ounce cartons. Half of the block, crumbled, is about equal in volume to one pound ground beef.

6 ounces veggie protein crumbles	170 g
1 (1 ounce) packet low-sodium taco seasoning mix	30 g
1 (5 ounce) package standing yellow corn taco shells	145 g
1 (7 ounce) package cheddar-flavor veggie soy shreds	200 g
2 cups shredded iceberg lettuce	145 g
Pico de Gallo (page 54) or mild salsa	
1 cup reduced-fat sour cream	240 g

☗ Lightly brown veggie protein crumbles in sprayed non-stick 10-inch (25 cm) skillet and stir in taco seasoning mix according to package directions.

☗ Heat taco shells according to package directions.

☗ To assemble tacos, arrange taco shells on baking sheet. Spoon 2 to 3 tablespoons (30 - 45 ml) hot taco mixture into shells and sprinkle with 1 to 2 tablespoons (15 - 30 ml) veggie soy shreds. Add shredded lettuce, Pico de Gallo and dollop of sour cream.

Serves 5.
Serving size: 1 taco

TIP: Look for reduced-sodium taco seasoning mixes. One package of mix indicates sodium was reduced from 560 mg to 330 mg per serving.

One Serving

Calories: 416	Cholesterol: 19 mg	Dietary Fiber: 3 g
Calories from Fat: 129	Sodium: 541 mg	Sugars: 2 g
Total Fat: 15 g	Total Carbohydrates: 33 g	Protein: 14 g
Saturated Fat: 5 g		

Rotini and Veggie Crumbles

Your family will go for this hearty, wholesome dish.

4 ounces whole wheat rotini (spirals)	115 g
½ cup chopped onion	80 g
6 ounces veggie protein crumbles	170 g
1 (14 ounce) can diced tomatoes	400 g
1 (8 ounce) can tomato sauce	230 g
1 teaspoon Worcestershire sauce	5 ml
½ cup sliced green olives or 1 (4 ounce) can sliced ripe olives, drained	115 g

☞ Cook rotini according to package directions. Drain and set aside.

☞ Place onion in sprayed, non-stick large, heavy pan over medium heat. Cook and stir until tender. Add crumbles and cook, stirring constantly, about 2 minutes.

☞ Add tomatoes, tomato sauce, Worcestershire sauce, 1 teaspoon (5 ml) salt and ¼ teaspoon (1 ml) pepper and bring to a boil. Reduce heat and simmer covered about 15 minutes. Stir in cooked rotini. Sprinkle olives on top.

Serves 6 to 8.
Serving size: 1 cup (250 ml)

TIP: Veggie protein crumbles come in refrigerated 12-ounce (340 g) packages.

One Serving

Calories: 105	Cholesterol: 0 mg	Dietary Fiber: 3 g
Calories from Fat: 16	Sodium: 384 mg	Sugars: 2 g
Total Fat: 2 g	Total Carbohydrates: 17 g	Protein: 5 g
Saturated Fat: 0 g		

Golden Sesame Tofu

These browned tofu slices are especially good with Peanut Sauce (page 240).

1 (16 ounce) carton extra firm tofu	455 g
3 tablespoons toasted sesame seeds	25 g
1 tablespoon sesame oil	15 ml

Blot tofu with paper towels to remove excess moisture. Cut into 8 slices. Spread sesame seeds in pie pan. Add tofu slices and lightly coat with sesame seeds.

Heat sesame oil in non-stick 12-inch (32 cm) skillet over medium heat. Add tofu slices and cook until golden brown on both sides, about 5 minutes on each side.

Serves 4 to 6.
Serving size: 1 slice

TIP: *Canola or olive oil can replace sesame oil in this recipe.*

One Serving

Calories: 107	Sodium: 49 mg
Calories from Fat: 69	Total Carbohydrates: 2 g
Total Fat: 9 g	Dietary Fiber: 1 g
Saturated Fat: 1 g	Sugars: 0 g
Cholesterol: 0 mg	Protein: 7 g

Tex-Mex Tofu and Rice

Here's a unique recipe for Tex-Mex aficionados.

1 (14 ounce) package extra-firm tofu	400 g
2 (9 ounce) pouches precooked microwave brown rice	2 (255 g)
1 (15 ounce) can diced tomatoes	425 g
1 (4 ounce) can chopped green chilies, drained	115 g
1/4 cup sliced green onions	25 g
1/4 cup chopped cilantro	5 g

Blot tofu with paper towels to remove excess moisture. Cut into 1/2-inch (1.2 cm) cubes. Heat rice in microwave according to package directions.

Bring tomatoes and green chilies to a boil in non-stick 12-inch (32 cm) skillet over medium-high heat. Hear rice in microwave according to package directions. Stir in rice and tofu. Reduce heat to low, cover and simmer for 10 minutes. Stir in green onions and cilantro.

Serves 8.
Serving size: 1 cup (250 ml)

TIP: *Serve with baked tortilla chips and your favorite salsa.*

One Serving

Calories: 273	Sodium: 165 mg
Calories from Fat: 25	Total Carbohydrates: 52 g
Total Fat: 4 g	Dietary Fiber: 3 g
Saturated Fat: 0 g	Sugars: 1 g
Cholesterol: 0 mg	Protein: 9 g

Sesame Tofu and Brown Rice

*Tofu is also known as soybean curd. Silken tofu is named for
its silky smooth texture and comes in soft, regular and firm styles.*

1 (16 ounce) carton silken tofu	**455 g**
¾ cup reduced-sodium soy sauce, divided	**175 ml**
2 teaspoons sesame oil	**10 ml**
2 (9 ounce) pouches pre-cooked microwave brown rice	**2 (255 g)**
1 tablespoon toasted sesame seeds	**15 ml**

Blot tofu with paper towels to remove excess moisture. Cut into
6 to 8 slices.

Pour ¼ cup (60 ml) soy sauce into shallow dish. Add tofu and pour
¼ cup (60 ml) soy sauce over tofu. Let stand at least 1 hour. Drain when
ready to cook.

Add sesame oil to non-stick 10-inch (25 cm) skillet over medium-high
heat. Add tofu and cook until firm and light brown. Turn carefully to
other side and cook until light brown. Heat rice in microwave according
to package directions.

Serve tofu over brown rice and sprinkle with sesame seeds. Drizzle
remaining soy sauce over individual servings.

Serves 6 to 8.
Serving size: 1 cup (250 ml)

*TIP: Save money by preparing brown rice and freezing in 2-cup (390 g) portions. The small
portions can easily be heated in microwave oven.*

One Serving

Calories: 473	Cholesterol: 0 mg	Dietary Fiber: 3 g
Calories from Fat: 82	Sodium: 626 mg	Sugars: 0 g
Total Fat: 11 g	Total Carbohydrates: 67 g	Protein: 12 g
Saturated Fat: 1 g		

Tofu Fried Rice

This is a hearty dish for hungry folks.

1 (14 ounce) carton firm tofu	400 g
2 teaspoons sesame oil	10 ml
1 (9 ounce) pouch precooked microwave brown rice	255 g
½ cup egg substitute	125 g
½ cup frozen peas and carrots, thawed	70 g
⅓ cup All-Purpose Stir-Fry Sauce (page 242) or bottled stir-fry sauce	75 ml

☗ Blot tofu with paper towels to remove excess moisture. Cut into 1-inch (2.5 cm) cubes.

☗ Heat oil in non-stick 12-inch (32 cm) skillet over medium heat until hot. Add tofu and cook, stirring gently, about 5 minutes. Heat rice in microwave according to package directions. Add rice to skillet, cook and stir for 2 to 3 minutes.

☗ With spatula, push tofu mixture to edges of skillet and leave space in center. Add eggs to center of skillet. Cook and stir until scrambled, about 1 minute. Add carrots, peas and All-Purpose Stir-Fry Sauce. Stir and cook until hot.

Serves 6 to 8.
Serving size: 1 cup (250 ml)

One Serving

Calories: 371	Cholesterol: 0 mg	Dietary Fiber: 3
Calories from Fat: 84	Sodium: 422 mg	Sugars: 0 g
Total Fat: 12 g	Total Carbohydrates: 52 g	Protein: 16 g
Saturated Fat: 1 g		

Tofu Tabbouleh

This is a Middle Eastern dish of bulghur wheat
(wheat kernels that are steamed, dried and crushed).

1 (8 ounce) carton cubed super-firm tofu	230 g
¾ cup bulghur wheat	120 g
1 small cucumber, peeled, seeded, chopped	
3 tablespoons finely chopped parsley	15 g
2 tablespoons chopped red onion	20 g
½ cup Lemony Vinaigrette (page 108)	125 ml
1 small tomato, seeded, chopped	

☕ Blot tofu with paper towels to remove excess moisture.

☕ Place bulghur wheat in colander, rinse with cold water and drain.

☕ Combine bulghur wheat, cucumber, parsley, onion and tofu in large bowl.

☕ Drizzle Lemony Vinaigrette over bulghur wheat and toss lightly to coat. Cover and refrigerate for 4 to 24 hours. Bring to room temperature and stir in tomato before serving.

Serves 5.
Serving size: 1 cup (250 ml)
Makes 5 cups (1.2 L).

TIP: Add 2 teaspoons (10 ml) chopped mint leaves or 1 teaspoon (5 ml) dried mint, crushed.

One Serving

Calories: 124	Cholesterol: 0 mg	Dietary Fiber: 1 g
Calories from Fat: 88	Sodium: 26 mg	Sugars: 0 g
Total Fat: 10 g	Total Carbohydrates: 4 g	Protein: 4 g
Saturated Fat: 1 g		

Bok Choy Stir-Fry

Bok choy is a mild vegetable with crunchy white stalks and tender dark-green leaves.

1 (3 pound) head bok choy	1.4 kg
1 tablespoon canola oil	15 ml
1 medium onion, sliced	
1 teaspoon minced fresh ginger	5 ml
¼ cup packed light brown sugar	50 g
2½ tablespoons All-Purpose Stir-Fry Sauce (page 242) or bottled	
stir-fry sauce	40 ml

Separate bok choy leaves, wash thoroughly and cut stalks away from leaves. Cut stalks into ½-inch (1.2 cm) diagonal pieces. Roll leaves and shred finely, about ¼-inch (.6 cm) wide.

Heat oil in non-stick wok or 12-inch (32 cm) skillet over high heat. Add diagonal bok choy stem pieces, sliced onion and ginger and stir-fry about 5 minutes. Stir in brown sugar, shredded bok choy leaves and 2 tablespoons (30 ml) water.

Cover and steam about 2 minutes or until leaves wilt. Uncover and toss with All-Purpose Stir-Fry sauce.

Serves 4.
Serving size: 1 cup (250 ml)

TIP: Serve over thin noodles or brown rice and sprinkle with chopped peanuts or cashews. Trimmed 3 pound (1.4 kg) bok choy is about 8 cups (560 g) shredded leaves.

One Serving

Calories: 130	Cholesterol: 0 mg	Dietary Fiber: 2 g
Calories from Fat: 42	Sodium: 293 mg	Sugars: 15 g
Total Fat: 5 g	Total Carbohydrates: 19 g	Protein: 3 g
Saturated Fat: 0 g		

Mushroom-Bok Choy Stir-Fry

The Chinese term bok choy is translated as white (bok) vegetable (choy).

1 (3 pound) head bok choy	1.4 kg
1 tablespoon canola oil	15 ml
1 (8 ounce) package mushrooms, sliced	230 g
½ cup vegetable broth	125 ml
2 tablespoons All-Purpose Stir-Fry Sauce (page 242) or bottled	
stir-fry sauce	30 ml

Separate bok choy leaves, wash thoroughly and cut stalks away from leaves. Cut stalks in ½-inch (1.2 cm) diagonal pieces. Roll leaves and shred finely to about ¼ inch (6 cm) wide.

Preheat non-stick wok or 12-inch (32 cm) skillet over high heat and add oil. Add diagonal bok choy stalk pieces and mushrooms, cook and stir for 3 to 5 minutes. Add shredded bok choy leaves, broth, ½ teaspoon (2 ml) salt and ⅛ teaspoon (.5 ml) pepper. Cover and cook about 2 minutes or until leaves wilt. Uncover and add All-Purpose Stir-Fry Sauce. Do not overcook bok choy.

Serves 4 to 6.
Serving size: 1 cup (250 ml)

TIP: Mature bok choy measures about 16 inches (40 cm) compared to baby bok choy, which measures 6 to 8 inches (15 cm). Baby bok choy is generally available only in specialty stores.

One Serving

Calories: 58	Cholesterol: 0 mg	Dietary Fiber: 2 g
Calories from Fat: 30	Sodium: 272 mg	Sugars: 2 g
Total Fat: 3 g	Total Carbohydrates: 5 g	Protein: 3 g
Saturated Fat: 0 g		

Stir-frying is a technique for quickly cooking small pieces of food at a very high heat. To replace the oil typically used in stir-frying, spray non-stick wok or wide skillet before preheating and stir the foods constantly while cooking.

Broccoli-Cheese Bake

All the good flavors of cheese and broccoli are in this easy baked dish.

2 tablespoons butter	30 g
2 tablespoons flour	15 g
1¼ cups fat-free skim milk	310 ml
½ teaspoon ground nutmeg	2 ml
1 cup shredded sharp cheddar cheese	115 g
2 pounds broccoli florets and stalks	910 g
¼ cup fresh breadcrumbs	15 g

Preheat oven to 425° (220° C).

Melt butter in 1-quart (1 L) saucepan, add flour, cook and stir until mixture bubbles. Add skim milk, reduce heat and simmer until it thickens. Add nutmeg, cheese, ½ teaspoon (2 ml) salt and ¼ teaspoon (1 ml) pepper. Set aside.

Wash broccoli and trim leaves. Separate florets into bite size-pieces. Trim stalks and cut into 1-inch (2.5 cm) pieces.

Bring 2 cups (500 ml) water to a boil in 3-quart (3 L) saucepan. Add broccoli florets and stalks and boil uncovered until tender. Drain and transfer to sprayed 3-quart (3 L) baking dish.

Pour cheese sauce over broccoli and sprinkle with breadcrumbs. Bake for about 20 minutes or until hot.

Serves 4 to 6.
Serving size: 1 cup (250 ml)

One Serving

Calories: 202	Cholesterol: 31 mg	Dietary Fiber: 5 g
Calories from Fat: 94	Sodium: 199 mg	Sugars: 6 g
Total Fat: 10 g	Total Carbohydrates: 18 g	Protein: 11 g
Saturated Fat: 6 g		

Napa Cabbage Stir-Fry

According to Chinese literature, Chinese cabbage, which includes
napa cabbage, was cultivated as early as the fifth century A.D.

1 (2 pound) head napa cabbage	910 g
1 tablespoon olive oil	15 ml
2 garlic cloves, minced	
1 tablespoon peeled fresh ginger, minced	15 ml
1 cup shredded carrots	110 g
2 tablespoons plus 1 teaspoon All-Purpose Stir-Fry Sauce (page 242)	
or bottled stir-fry sauce	35 ml
Sliced green onions	

Wash, core and quarter cabbage. Thinly slice quarters.

Preheat non-stick wok or non-stick 12-inch (32 cm) skillet on high heat and stir-fry oil, garlic and ginger only a few seconds. Do not burn garlic. Add carrots and stir-fry about 2 to 3 minutes. Add cabbage slices and stir-fry about 3 more minutes or until cabbage is tender. Add All-Purpose Stir-Fry Sauce and toss to mix. Garnish with green onions.

Serves 4 to 6.
Serving size: 1 cup (250 ml)

TIP: Serve over rice or chow mein stir-fry noodles.

One Serving

Calories: 49	Cholesterol: 0 mg	Dietary Fiber: 1 g
Calories from Fat: 28	Sodium: 212 mg	Sugars: 1 g
Total Fat: 3 g	Total Carbohydrates: 4 g	Protein: 0 g
Saturated Fat: 0 g		

Easy Baked Polenta

Polenta originated in Italy and is a versatile, all-purpose corn dish.

1 cup yellow cornmeal **160 g**

Pour 2¼ cups (560 ml) water in non-stick large, heavy pan. Heat to a boil over medium-high heat. Combine cornmeal, 1 cup (250 ml) cold water and 1 teaspoon (5 ml) salt in small bowl.

Slowly add cornmeal mixture to boiling water and stir constantly. Return to a boil, cover, reduce heat to low and cook 10 to 15 minutes. Mixture will be very thick. Pour evenly into sprayed 9-inch (23 cm) pie pan. Cool and refrigerate about 30 minutes or overnight.

When ready to bake, preheat oven to 350° (175° C).

Bake polenta uncovered about 20 minutes or until hot. Cut into wedges to serve.

Serves 6.
Serving size: 1 (2 inch/5 cm) wedge

TIP: Here's another way to prepare polenta. Pour cornmeal into non-stick 8 x 4-inch (20 x 10 cm) loaf pan instead of pie pan. After it is chilled, cut in slices and fry in small amount of oil or butter until it browns. Serve with honey or maple syrup.

One Serving

Calories: 74	Cholesterol: 0 mg	Dietary Fiber: 2 g
Calories from Fat: 6	Sodium: 7 mg	Sugars: 0 g
Total Fat: 1 g	Total Carbohydrates: 16 g	Protein: 2 g
Saturated Fat: 0 g		

Corn-Green Chile Bake

This is like a cheese souffle with corn and green chilies.

1 (10 ounce) package frozen whole kernel corn	280 g
1 cup diced onion	160 g
1 garlic clove, minced	
1 cup egg substitute	245 g
1 (4 ounce) can chopped green chilies, drained	115 g
¾ cup finely shredded Monterey Jack or cheddar cheese, divided	85 g

 Preheat oven to 350° (175° C).

Cook corn according to package directions and drain. Cook and stir onion and garlic in sprayed 10-inch (25 cm) skillet over medium heat until tender.

Combine corn, onion-garlic mixture, eggs, green chilies and ½ cup (55 g) cheese in large bowl. Pour into sprayed 9 x 9-inch (23 x 23 cm) baking dish.

Bake uncovered for about 30 minutes or until puffy and golden. Add remaining cheese and return to oven until cheese melts.

Serves 6.
Serving size: 1 cup (250 ml)

TIP: Great dish to serve with Vegetarian Chili (page 182) and a salad of mixed greens.

One Serving

Calories: 152	Cholesterol: 15 mg	Dietary Fiber: 2 g
Calories from Fat: 58	Sodium: 208 mg	Sugars: 1 g
Total Fat: 6 g	Total Carbohydrates: 15 g	Protein: 10 g
Saturated Fat: 3 g		

Hominy-Cheese Casserole

Hominy and cheese definitely have an affinity for green chilies in this dish.

1 (16 ounce) package frozen seasoning blend (onion, celery, bell pepper)	455 g
2 (14 ounce) cans white or yellow hominy, rinsed, drained	2 (400 g)
3 tablespoons butter	45 g
3 tablespoons unbleached white flour	25 g
1½ cups light plain soymilk or fat-free skim milk	375 ml
1 (4 ounce) can chopped green chilies with liquid	115 g
1 cup reduced-fat shredded cheddar cheese	115 g

Preheat oven to 350° (175° C).

Add seasoning blend to sprayed, large heavy pan, cook and stir over medium heat until vegetables are tender. Stir in hominy and heat 1 or 2 minutes. Remove from heat and set aside.

In same pan, melt butter over medium heat and stir in flour. Cook and stir until mixture bubbles. Add soymilk; cook and stir until sauce thickens. Stir in green chilies, ½ teaspoon (2 ml) salt and ⅛ teaspoon (.5 ml) pepper.

Spread hominy mixture in sprayed 9 x 13-inch (23 x 33 cm) baking dish. Pour green chile sauce over hominy and sprinkle cheese on top.

Bake for about 30 minutes or until hot.

Serves 6 to 8.
Serving size: ¾ cup (175 ml)

TIP: Replace canned green chilies with ½ cup (125 ml) Mild Green Chile Salsa (page 54).

One Serving

Calories: 229	Cholesterol: 26 mg	Dietary Fiber: 6 g
Calories from Fat: 98	Sodium: 354 mg	Sugars: 1 g
Total Fat: 11 g	Total Carbohydrates: 24 g	Protein: 6 g
Saturated Fat: 6 g		

Potatoes au Gratin

This cheesy potato bake has withstood the test of time as a family favorite.

2 tablespoons butter	30 g
¼ cup finely chopped onion	40 g
2½ teaspoons whole wheat flour	12 ml
2 cups fat-free skim milk	500 ml

2 cups (8 ounces) reduced-fat
    shredded sharp cheddar
    cheese, divided
	230 g

6 cups peeled, thinly sliced red potatoes	900 g

Preheat oven to 375° (190° C).

Melt butter in 2-quart (2 L) saucepan over medium heat, add onion and cook until tender. Stir in flour, ½ teaspoon (2 ml) salt and ¼ teaspoon (1 ml) pepper and cook until mixture bubbles. Add skim milk; cook and stir until mixture thickens. Remove from heat and stir in 1½ cups (170 g) cheese.

Spread potatoes in sprayed 1½-quart (1.5 L) baking dish and cover with cheese sauce. Bake uncovered for 1 hour. Sprinkle remaining cheese on top and bake for 15 to 20 minutes.

Serves 6 to 8.
Serving size: 1 cup (250 ml)

One Serving

Calories: 261	Sodium: 213 mg

Calories from
    Fat: 112
	Total Carbohy-
	    drates: 26 g

Total Fat: 12 g	Dietary Fiber: 2 g
Saturated Fat: 8 g	Sugars: 5 g
Cholesterol: 38 mg	Protein: 11 g

Potato-Veggie Chorizo

Veggie chorizo has a similar texture and flavor as the original chorizo which is a highly seasoned sausage.

½ pound (8 inches in casing) veggie soy chorizo	230 g/20 cm
1 large onion, chopped	
2 large potatoes, peeled, sliced in ¼-inch slices	2 (.6 cm)

Remove chorizo from casing. Crumble chorizo in non-stick 12-inch (32 cm) skillet on medium-high heat and cook until brown and crisp. Remove from skillet and set aside.

Add onion and potatoes to skillet and cook over medium-high heat about 2 to 3 minutes. Reduce heat, cover and simmer until potatoes are tender, stirring occasionally. Add water if needed. Stir in cooked chorizo.

Serves 4 to 6.
Serving size: ¾ cup (175 ml)

One Serving

Calories: 211	Sodium: 374 mg

Calories from
    Fat: 8
	Total Carbohy-
	    drates: 32 g

Total Fat: 0 g	Dietary Fiber: 3 g
Saturated Fat: 0 g	Sugars: 5 g
Cholesterol: 7 mg	Protein: 9 g

Ranch Skillet Potatoes

The popular ranch salad dressing mixes and dips are great timesavers for adding seasonings and flavors to recipes.

4 - 5 medium russet potatoes, peeled, cubed	
2 teaspoons olive oil	10 ml
⅓ cup finely chopped onion	55 g
3 tablespoons ranch salad dressing mix	45 ml
⅓ cup reduced-fat sour cream	80 g
2 cups fat-free skim milk	500 ml
1 tablespoon finely chopped fresh parsley	15 ml

Add potatoes and water to cover in large, heavy pan. Bring to a boil, reduce heat to medium and cook until potatoes are tender. Drain.

Combine potatoes, oil and onion in 12-inch (32 cm) skillet over medium-high heat and cook, stirring frequently, until potatoes and onion brown. Add dressing mix, sour cream, skim milk and parsley. Reduce heat and simmer until sauce thickens.

Serves 4 to 6.
Serving size: 1 cup (250 ml)

One Serving

Calories: 155	Sodium: 128 mg
Calories from Fat: 43	Total Carbohy-drates: 23 g
Total Fat: 4 g	Dietary Fiber: 1 g
Saturated Fat: 1 g	Sugars: 6 g
Cholesterol: 8 mg	Protein: 5 g

Scalloped Red Potatoes

3 tablespoons butter	45 g
¼ cup finely chopped onion	40 g
3 tablespoons unbleached white flour	25 g
2½ cups soymilk	625 ml
6 cups new (red) potatoes with peels, thinly sliced	900 g

Preheat oven to 350° (175° C).

Melt butter in 2-quart (2 L) saucepan over medium heat and cook onion in butter until tender. Stir in flour, 1 teaspoon (5 ml) salt and ¼ teaspoon (1 ml) pepper. Cook and stir until it bubbles. Add soymilk, cook and stir until sauce thickens.

Spread potatoes evenly in layers in sprayed 2-quart (2 L) baking dish and pour sauce over potatoes. Cover and bake for 30 minutes. Uncover and bake for 1 hour or until potatoes are tender.

Serves 5.
Serving size: ¾ cup (175 ml)

TIP: Sprinkle with ¼ cup (30 g) shredded cheddar cheese toward end of cooking, if you like.

One Serving

Calories: 287	Sodium: 78 mg
Calories from Fat: 91	Total Carbohy-drates: 43 g
Total Fat: 10 g	Dietary Fiber: 4 g
Saturated Fat: 4 g	Sugars: 4 g
Cholesterol: 19 mg	Protein: 9 g

Buttered Spaghetti Squash

This simple, delicious recipe will encourage you to prepare spaghetti squash whenever it is available.

1 (3 pound) spaghetti squash	1.4 kg
3 tablespoons melted butter	45 g

Halve squash lengthwise. With spoon, remove seeds and discard with loose strings.

Add squash halves to large, heavy pan, cover with water and add 1 teaspoon (5 ml) salt. Bring water to a boil. Slowly boil squash until tender, about 12 to 15 minutes.

Remove squash with tongs and drain on paper towels. When squash is cool enough to handle, pull out strands of squash with fork. Mash slightly with fork.

Transfer to serving dish and drizzle with melted butter. Sprinkle with ½ teaspoon (2 ml) salt and ¼ teaspoon (1 ml) pepper. Toss to mix.

Serves 6.
Serving size: ¾ cup (175 ml)

TIP: For a change you can sprinkle freshly grated parmesan cheese on each serving or serve spaghetti squash with Marinara Sauce (page 239) instead of butter.

One Serving

Calories: 123	Cholesterol: 16 mg	Dietary Fiber: 0 g
Calories from Fat: 62	Sodium: 41 mg	Sugars: 0 g
Total Fat: 6 g	Total Carbohydrates: 16 g	Protein: 0 g
Saturated Fat: 4 g		

Cheesy Squash Casserole

You get all the taste without all the calories!

6 cups (1½ pounds) sliced yellow crookneck squash	680 g
1 tablespoon butter	15 ml
½ cup chopped onion	80 g
¾ cup whole wheat or multigrain cracker crumbs, divided	45 g
¼ cup reduced-fat mayonnaise	60 g
½ cup reduced-fat shredded cheddar cheese	60 g

Preheat oven to 350° (175° C).

Bring 2 cups (500 ml) water to a boil in large, heavy pan. Cook squash in boiling water for 15 minutes or until tender. Drain, mash squash and transfer to large bowl.

Melt butter in 8-inch (20 cm) skillet over medium heat. Add onion and cook until tender. Add onion, ½ cup (30 g) cracker crumbs, mayonnaise and cheese to squash. Add ½ teaspoon (2 ml) salt and ⅛ teaspoon (.5 ml) pepper and mix lightly.

Pour mixture into sprayed 2-quart (2 L) baking dish. Sprinkle remaining cracker crumbs on top. Bake uncovered for 40 minutes or until hot.

Serves 6 to 8.
Serving size: 1 cup (250 ml)

TIP: You can replace mayonnaise with either 2 slightly beaten eggs or ½ cup (120 g) reduced-fat sour cream, if you like.

One Serving

Calories: 128	Cholesterol: 11 mg	Dietary Fiber: 2 g
Calories from Fat: 57	Sodium: 101 mg	Sugars: 0 g
Total Fat: 6 g	Total Carbohydrates: 14 g	Protein: 4 g
Saturated Fat: 3 g		

Ricotta Stuffed Squash

Colorful, attractive and delicious, this dish makes a hit with dinner guests.

4 crookneck yellow squash, about same size and shape, ends trimmed	
1 (10 ounce) package frozen chopped spinach, thawed, drained	280 g
1 egg, slightly beaten or ¼ cup egg substitute	60 g
1 cup part-skim ricotta cheese	250 g
2 tablespoons grated parmesan cheese	15 g
2 tablespoons chopped green onions	15 g
¾ teaspoon dried Italian herbs, crushed	4 ml

Cut squash in half lengthwise. With teaspoon, scoop out seeds and part of flesh, leaving shells ½-inch (1.2 cm) thick. Steam squash shells in electric steamer or steamer basket in large heavy pan until tender, about 15 minutes. Plunge in cold water and drain upside down on paper towels. Squeeze spinach between paper towels to completely remove excess moisture..

Preheat oven to 350° (175° C).

Combine spinach, egg, ricotta cheese, parmesan cheese, green onions and herbs in medium bowl. Mix well and mound about 3 tablespoons (45 ml) filling inside each squash shell. Arrange filled shells in sprayed 9 x 13-inch (23 x 33 cm) baking dish and lightly spray tops. Bake for about 20 minutes or until filling is hot.

Serves 8.
Serving size: 1 squash half

TIP: Heated Marinara Sauce (page 239) poured over stuffed squash before serving is really good, too.

One Serving
Nutrition facts are based on egg substitute.

Calories: 92	Cholesterol: 12 mg	Dietary Fiber: 3 g
Calories from Fat: 36	Sodium: 129 mg	Sugars: 0 g
Total Fat: 4 g	Total Carbohydrates: 7 g	Protein: 8 g
Saturated Fat: 2 g		

Pilaf Stuffed Zucchini

Pilaf originated in the Near East. Basic preparation of rice pilaf always begins with browning the rice in butter or oil before cooking it in broth.

3 (6 inch) zucchini, halved	3 (15 cm)
2 cups Classic Brown Rice Pilaf (page 205)	500 ml
1 (7 ounce) package mozzarella-flavor veggie soy shreds	200 g

Preheat oven to 375° (190° C).

Spoon out zucchini seeds and flesh, leaving about ½-inch (1.2 cm) thick shell. Mound 3 to 4 tablespoons (45 - 60 ml) Classic Brown Rice Pilaf into zucchini shells.

Pour about ¼ inch (.6 cm) water into 9 x 13-inch (23 x 33 cm) baking dish and arrange zucchini shells in dish. Bake uncovered for 20 minutes. Arrange soy shreds on top of pilaf. Continue baking for 20 minutes or until zucchini is tender and pilaf is hot.

Serves 6.
Serving size: 1 zucchini shell

TIP: Use microwave pouches of rice pilaf to save lots of time!

One Serving

Calories: 227	Cholesterol: 2 mg	Dietary Fiber: 3 g
Calories from Fat: 19	Sodium: 284 mg	Sugars: 3 g
Total Fat: 2 g	Total Carbohydrates: 25 g	Protein: 7 g
Saturated Fat: 0 g		

Baked Zucchini and Mushrooms

Just add a green salad and whole wheat rolls and you have a delicious meal.

2 teaspoons olive oil	10 ml
1 medium onion, finely chopped	
1 (16 ounce) package fresh mushrooms, thinly sliced	455 g
4 large zucchini (2 pounds), shredded	910 g
3 beaten eggs or ¾ cup egg substitute	185 g
½ cup Italian seasoned breadcrumbs	60 g
¼ cup freshly grated parmesan or romano cheese	25 g

 Preheat oven to 325° (160° C).

 Combine oil, onion and mushrooms in non-stick 10-inch (25 cm) skillet over medium-high heat. Cook and stir until onions and mushrooms are tender. Add water as needed.

 Squeeze zucchini between paper towels to completely remove excess moisture. Combine onion mixture, zucchini, eggs, breadcrumbs, cheese, ½ teaspoon (2 ml) salt and ⅛ teaspoon (.5 ml) pepper in large bowl and mix well.

 Pour into sprayed shallow 3-quart (3 L) baking dish. Bake for about 45 minutes or until knife inserted in center comes out clean.

Serves about 6 to 8.
Serving size: 1 cup (250 ml)

TIP: For more variety, decrease zucchini to 1 pound (455 g) and add 1 pound (455 g) shredded carrots.

One Serving
Nutrition facts are based on egg substitute.

Calories: 73	Cholesterol: 3 mg	Dietary Fiber: 2 g
Calories from Fat: 31	Sodium: 108 mg	Sugars: 2 g
Total Fat: 3 g	Total Carbohydrates: 4 g	Protein: 7 g
Saturated Fat: 1 g		

Green Chile Sauce

1 tablespoon butter	15 ml
1½ tablespoons flour	22 ml
1½ cups vegetable broth	375 ml
1 (4 ounce) can chopped green chilies with liquid	114 g

 Melt butter in 1-quart (1 L) saucepan over medium heat. Add flour and whisk until mixture bubbles. Continue to cook and whisk for 1 minute.

Stir in broth all at once, cook and whisk until mixture boils and thickens. Add green chilies and simmer 10 to 15 minutes.

Serves 8.
Serving size: ¼ cup (60 ml)
Makes 2 cups (500 ml).

One Serving

Calories: 17	Sodium: 211 mg
Calories from Fat: 14	Total Carbohydrates: 1 g
Total Fat: 2 g	Dietary Fiber: 0 g
Saturated Fat: 1 g	Sugars: 0 g
Cholesterol: 4 mg	Protein: 0 g

Red Chile Sauce

This is a simple, basic recipe that can be used for various kinds of enchiladas and Tex-Mex dishes.

1 medium onion, finely chopped	
2 garlic cloves, minced	
3½ cups no-salt tomato sauce	825 ml
2 tablespoons chili powder	30 ml

 Stir onion and garlic in sprayed 2-quart (2 L) saucepan over medium heat until tender. Add tomato sauce and bring to a boil. Gradually stir in chili powder.

Serves 8.
Serving size: ½ cup (125 ml)
Makes 4 cups (1 L).

TIP: Use with Ranch-Style Eggs (page 30) and Refried Bean Enchiladas (page 184).

One Serving

Calories: 43	Sodium: 12 mg
Calories from Fat: 2	Total Carbohydrates: 9 g
Total Fat: 0 g	Dietary Fiber: 2 g
Saturated Fat: 0 g	Sugars: 4 g
Cholesterol: 0 mg	Protein: 1 g

Lo Mein Sauce

¼ cup vegetable broth   60 ml
¼ cup reduced-sodium
    soy sauce   60 ml
2 teaspoons rice wine vinegar
    or white wine vinegar   10 ml
2 teaspoons sesame oil   10 ml
1 teaspoon red pepper flakes,
    crushed   5 ml
1 teaspoon sugar or sugar
    substitute   5 ml

Combine ingredients in airtight container. Shake.

Serves 6.
Serving size: 2 tablespoons (30 ml)
Makes ¾ cup (175 ml).

TIP: Use with Broccoli Lo Mein (page 189).

One Serving
Nutrition facts are based on sugar substitute.

Calories: 40	Sodium: 478 mg
Calories from	Total Carbohy-
Fat: 27	drates: 3 g
Total Fat: 3 g	Dietary Fiber: 0 g
Saturated Fat: 1 g	Sugars: 2 g
Cholesterol: 0 mg	Protein: 1 g

Marinara Sauce

2 tablespoons olive oil   30 ml
4 medium cloves garlic, minced
2 medium onions, chopped
4 (14 ounce) cans diced
    tomatoes   4 (400 g)
2 teaspoons dried basil,
    crushed   10 ml
½ teaspoon dried oregano,
    crushed   2 ml

Heat olive oil in large, heavy pan over medium heat. Add garlic and onions; cook and stir until tender but not brown, about 7 to 8 minutes.

Add tomatoes, basil, oregano and 1 teaspoon (5 ml) salt. Bring to a boil, reduce heat and simmer uncovered, stirring occasionally, until mixture thickens, about 1 hour.

Serve hot or refrigerate until ready to use.

Serves 5.
Serving size: 1 cup (250 ml)
Makes 5 cups (1.2 L).

TIP: Add ½ cup (75 g) diced green or red bell pepper and cook with garlic and onions. Use with Cheese Tortellini and Olives (page 194), Three-Cheese Crepes (page 35), Buttered Spaghetti Squash (page 233), Ricotta Stuffed Squash, (page 235), Pepperoni-Focaccia Pizza (page 200) and Whole Wheat Pita Pizzas (page 201).

One Serving

Calories: 108	Sodium: 616 mg
Calories from	Total Carbohy-
Fat: 33	drates: 17 g
Total Fat: 4 g	Dietary Fiber: 4 g
Saturated Fat: 0 g	Sugars: 9 g
Cholesterol: 0 mg	Protein: 3 g

Peanut Sauce

Here's a nice all-purpose sauce for baked or grilled tofu or vegetables.

½ cup peanut butter	145 g
2 tablespoons lime juice	30 ml
½ teaspoon ground coriander	2 ml
¼ teaspoon ground cumin	1 ml
2 garlic cloves, minced	

 Add ½ cup (125 ml) water and all ingredients in 2-quart (2 L) saucepan. Whisk to combine and cook over medium heat until smooth.

Serves 16.
Serving size: 1 tablespoon (15 ml)
Makes 1 cup (250 ml).

TIP: Use with Golden Sesame Tofu (page 220).

One Serving

Calories: 95	Sodium: 3 mg
Calories from Fat: 68	Total Carbohydrates: 3 g
Total Fat: 8 g	Dietary Fiber: 1 g
Saturated Fat: 2 g	Sugars: 2 g
Cholesterol: 0 mg	Protein: 4 g

Homemade Basil Pesto

2 cups firmly packed fresh basil leaves	80 g
¾ cup grated parmesan or romano cheese	75 g
¼ cup pine nuts	35 g
½ cup olive oil	125 ml
3 garlic cloves, peeled	

 Combine all ingredients in food processor or blender. Cover and process about 3 minutes or until smooth. Stop frequently to scrape sides of container.

Use immediately or refrigerate up to 4 or 5 days.

Serves 8 to 10.
Serving size: 2 tablespoons (30 ml)
Makes 1¼ cups (310 ml).

One Serving

Calories: 173	Sodium: 128 mg
Calories from Fat: 152	Total Carbohydrates: 1 g
Total Fat: 17 g	Dietary Fiber: 0 g
Saturated Fat: 3 g	Sugars: 0 g
Cholesterol: 7 mg	Protein: 4 g

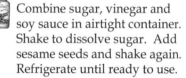

Pistou

*Pistou [pee-STOO] is the French
version of Italy's pesto sauce.*

2 tablespoons olive oil	30 ml
2 cloves garlic, minced	
1 (6 ounce) can tomato paste	170 g
/4 cup parsley, snipped	20 g
1 tablespoon dry basil	
leaves, crushed	15 ml
/4 cup parmesan cheese,	
freshly grated	25 g

 Combine olive oil and garlic in
10-inch (25 cm) skillet. Cook
and stir garlic over medium heat
for about 2 to 3 minutes. Stir in
remaining ingredients and
½ cup (125 ml) water and bring
to a boil.

 Serve warm or refrigerate until
ready to use.

Serves 6.
Serving size: ¼ cup (60 ml)
Makes 1½ cups (375 ml).

TIP: *Use with Slow-Cooker Pea Soup with
Pistou (page 117).*

One Serving

Calories: 68	Sodium: 92 mg
Calories from	Total Carbohy-
Fat: 39	drates: 6 g
Total Fat: 4 g	Dietary Fiber: 1 g
Saturated Fat: 1 g	Sugars: 4 g
Cholesterol: 4 mg	Protein: 3 g

Soy-Sesame Sauce

2 teaspoons sugar or sugar	
substitute	10 ml
2 tablespoons rice wine vinegar	
or white wine vinegar	30 ml
3 tablespoons reduced-sodium	
soy sauce	45 ml
¼ cup toasted sesame seeds	35 g

Combine sugar, vinegar and
soy sauce in airtight container.
Shake to dissolve sugar. Add
sesame seeds and shake again.
Refrigerate until ready to use.

Serves 3.
Serving size: 2 tablespoons (30 ml)
Makes ⅓ cup (75 ml).

One Serving
Nutrition facts are based on sugar substitute.

Calories: 81	Sodium: 604 mg
Calories from	Total Carbohy-
Fat: 43	drates: 7 g
Total Fat: 5 g	Dietary Fiber: 2 g
Saturated Fat: 1 g	Sugars: 3 g
Cholesterol: 0 mg	Protein: 3 g

All-Purpose Stir-Fry Sauce

2 tablespoons reduced-sodium soy sauce	30 ml
1 teaspoon sesame oil	5 ml
¼ teaspoon crushed red pepper	1 ml

Combine ingredients in airtight container. Shake.

Serves 3.
Serving size: 2½ teaspoons (12 ml)
Makes 2 tablespoons plus 1 teaspoon (35 ml).

TIP: Use with Sugar Snap Peas and Rice (page 185), Tofu Fried Rice (page 222), Bok Choy Stir-Fry (page 224), Mushroom-Bok Choy Stir-Fry (page 225), Napa Cabbage Stir-Fry (page 227) and Teriyaki-Vegetable Wraps (page 149).

One Serving

Calories: 38	Sodium: 383 mg
Calories from Fat: 28	Total Carbohy-drates: 0 g
Total Fat: 3 g	Dietary Fiber: 0 g
Saturated Fat: 0 g	Sugars: 0 g
Cholesterol: 0 mg	Protein: 0 g

Roma Tomato Sauce

1 tablespoon olive oil	15 ml
1 clove garlic, minced	
1 pound roma tomatoes, coarsely chopped	455 g
2 medium yellow bell peppers, seeded, finely chopped	
1 teaspoon dried basil leaves, crushed	5 ml

Heat oil in non-stick 12-inch (32 cm) over medium-high heat. Add garlic and cook about 1 minute. Add tomatoes, bell peppers, basil, 1 teaspoon (5 ml) salt and ¼ teaspoon (1 ml) pepper. Bring to a boil. Reduce heat to a simmer and cook uncovered stirring frequently for about 20 minutes or until tomatoes and peppers are tender.

Serves 8.
Serving size: ½ cup (125 ml)
Makes 4 cups (1 L).

TIP: Use with Cannellini Bean Cakes (page 179), Eggplant-Mushroom Lasagna (page 193), Linguine Primavera (page 190), Lasagna-Ricotta Rolls (page 195), Penne with Creamy Tomato Sauce (page 199) and Three-Cheese Baked Rigatoni (page 192).

One Serving

Calories: 25	Sodium: 5 mg
Calories from Fat: 10	Total Carbohy-drates: 3 g
Total Fat: 1 g	Dietary Fiber: 1 g
Saturated Fat: 0 g	Sugars: 0 g
Cholesterol: 0 mg	Protein: 0 g

Sweets

Contents

Carrot-Gingerbread Cake

This is moist, rich-tasting gingerbread your family will love!

1 (14 ounce) box gingerbread cake mix	400 g
½ cup egg substitute	125 g
¼ cup lightly packed shredded carrots	85 g
1 tablespoon finely grated orange peel	15 ml
¼ cup powdered sugar	30 g

Preheat oven to 350° (175° C).

Combine gingerbread mix, 1¼ cups (300 ml) water, eggs, carrots and orange peel in bowl. Stir vigorously for about 2 minutes.

Spoon into sprayed 9 x 9-inch (23 x 23 cm) baking pan and bake for 30 to 35 minutes or until toothpick inserted in center comes out clean. Cool.

Use sifter or wire strainer to sprinkle powdered sugar evenly on cooled cake.

Serves 8.

Serving size: 3-inch (8 cm) square.

TIP: *Dried orange peel is available in spice section of supermarkets, making this recipe even easier.*

One Serving (without powdered sugar)

Calories: 257	Cholesterol: 0 mg	Dietary Fiber: 1 g
Calories from Fat: 69	Sodium: 372 mg	Sugars: 28 g
Total Fat: 8 g	Total Carbohydrates: 43 g	Protein: 4 g
Saturated Fat: 2 g		

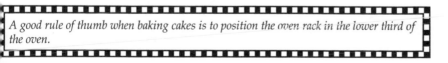

A good rule of thumb when baking cakes is to position the oven rack in the lower third of the oven.

Lemon-Yogurt Cake

This lemony soft crumb bundt cake is perfect for crushed fruit or ice cream toppings.

2¼ cups self-rising flour	280 g
½ teaspoon baking soda	2 ml
5 tablespoons butter, softened	85 g
1 cup sugar	200 g
1 egg and 2 egg whites	
1½ teaspoons lemon extract	7 ml
1 (8 ounce) carton nonfat plain yogurt	230 g

🍓 Preheat oven to 350° (175° C).

🍓 Spray and lightly flour 6-cup (1.5 L) bundt pan.

🍓 Mix flour and baking soda in large bowl.

🍓 Beat butter in mixing bowl on high speed until creamy. Gradually add sugar and beat for 2 to 3 minutes. Beat in eggs and lemon extract on medium speed.

🍓 Add and beat in flour mixture and yogurt alternately on low speed, beginning and ending with flour. Beat until smooth and scrape sides as needed.

🍓 Pour into bundt pan. Bake for 35 to 40 minutes or until top browns and toothpick inserted in center comes out clean.

🍓 Remove and cool on wire rack for 20 minutes before inverting onto serving plate.

Serves 10.
Serving size: 1 wedge

TIP: Add ½ cup (100 g) additional sugar for a sweeter cake.

One Serving

Total Calories: 243	Cholesterol: 15 mg	Dietary Fiber: 1 g
Calories from Fat: 55	Sodium: 428 mg	Sugars: 22 g
Total Fat: 6 g	Total Carbohydrate: 43 g	Protein: 4 g
Saturated Fat: 4 g		

Orange Bundt Cake

(18 ounce) yellow cake mix	510 g
tablespoons finely grated orange peel	15 g
cup orange juice	250 ml
¼ cup canola oil	60 ml
¼ cup sugar	50 g
cup egg substitute	245 g

Preheat oven to 350° (175° C). Spray and lightly flour 10-cup (25 cm) bundt pan.

Combine all ingredients in mixing bowl. Beat on low speed for 1 minute. Scrape down sides of bowl. Beat for 2 minutes on medium speed. Pour batter into bundt pan.

Bake for 45 to 50 minutes or until toothpick inserted in center comes out clean.

Transfer to wire rack and cool for 20 minutes. Invert onto serving plate.

Serves 12.
Serving size: 1 wedge

TIP: Make holiday festive by adding ½ to ¾ cup (60 - 90 g) chopped sweetened cranberries or dried sweetened cherries. For a different treat, add chopped dried mango slices.

One Serving

Total Calories: 272	Cholesterol: 1 mg	Dietary Fiber: 1 g
Calories from Fat: 93	Sodium: 324 mg	Sugars: 23 g
Total Fat: 10 g	Total Carbohydrates: 41 g	Protein: 5 g
Saturated Fat: 1 g		

Pear Upside-Down Cake

This is a very attractive cake with the pear slices and brown sugar baked into the cake.
Canned pineapple slices and maraschino cherries are traditionally used in this cake.

1 (15 ounce) can pear slices in extra-light syrup	425 g
2 tablespoons plus ¼ cup butter, softened, divided	30 g/60 g
1 cup packed light brown sugar, divided	220 g
1 teaspoon vanilla or almond extract, divided	5 ml
⅔ cup fat-free skim milk	150 ml
¼ cup egg substitute	60 g
1¼ cups self-rising flour	160 g

Preheat oven to 350° (175° C). Drain pears and set aside syrup. Cut pears into thin slices.

Melt 2 tablespoons (30 g) butter in non-stick 9-inch (23 cm) cake pan in hot oven. Remove and stir in ⅓ cup (70 g) brown sugar, 1 tablespoon (15 ml) syrup from pears and ½ teaspoon (2 ml) vanilla or almond extract. Arrange pear slices attractively in cake pan over butter mixture with no slices overlapping.

Beat ¼ cup (60 g) butter on medium-high speed until fluffy. Add remaining brown sugar and beat 1 to 2 minutes on medium speed. Add skim milk, egg substitute and remaining vanilla and beat 1 minute on low speed. Add flour and beat for about 2 minutes on low speed. Gently pour batter over pear slices and cover entire surface.

Bake for 30 to 35 minutes or until toothpick inserted in center comes out clean. Cool on wire rack for about 10 minutes. Loosen cake from pan and invert onto serving plate.

Serves 8.
Serving size: 1 wedge

One Serving

Calories: 317	Cholesterol: 31 mg	Dietary Fiber: 2 g
Calories from Fat: 108	Sodium: 286 mg	Sugars: 12 g
Total Fat: 12 g	Total Carbohydrates: 50 g	Protein: 4 g
Saturated Fat: 7 g		

Chocolate-Potato Cake

My mother frequently made chocolate potato cake with leftover mashed potatoes. We thought it was the best chocolate cake. This updated version of her cake has a dark dense chocolatey flavor and a velvety texture.

3 cup mashed potato flakes	40 g
(18 ounce) box devil's food cake mix	510 g
cup egg substitute	245 g
½ cup canola oil	125 ml

Preheat oven to 350° (175° C).

Spray and lightly flour 10-cup (25 cm) bundt pan.

Add 1 cup (250 ml) water to 1-quart (1 L) saucepan and bring to a boil. Remove from heat and stir in mashed potato flakes until it mixes well. Add 1 cup (250 ml) cold water and whisk until smooth.

Combine cake mix, egg substitute, oil and potato mixture in mixing bowl. Beat until mixture is moist. Then beat at medium speed for 2 minutes. Pour into bundt pan.

Bake for about 50 minutes or until toothpick inserted in center comes out clean.

Cool in pan for 20 minutes. Invert onto serving plate.

Serves 12.
Serving size: 1 wedge

TIP: To make chocolate glaze, heat ½ cup (140 g) prepared chocolate frosting in 1-quart (1 L) saucepan over low heat until mixture melts, stirring constantly. Drizzle over cooled cake.

One Serving

Total Calories: 296	Cholesterol: 0 mg	Dietary Fiber: 1 g
Calories from Fat: 149	Sodium: 401 mg	Sugars: 17 g
Total Fat: 17 g	Total Carbohydrates: 35g	Protein: 5 g
Saturated Fat: 2 g		

Quick-Mix Pumpkin Cake

This cake is like a pie for pumpkin lovers to savor!

1 (29 ounce) can pumpkin	805 g
1 (12 ounce) can fat-free evaporated milk	355 ml
¾ cup egg substitute	185 g
1 cup packed brown sugar	220 g
4 teaspoons pumpkin pie spice	20 ml
1 (18 ounce) box yellow cake mix	510 g
¾ cup butter, melted	170 g

🍓 Preheat oven to 350° (175° C).

🍓 Combine pumpkin, evaporated milk, egg substitute, brown sugar, ½ teaspoon (2 ml) salt and pumpkin pie spice in large bowl. Mix well.

🍓 Pour batter into 9 x 13-inch (23 x 33 cm) baking dish. Sprinkle cake mix over batter and drizzle with butter.

🍓 Bake for 55 to 60 minutes or until toothpick inserted in center comes out clean.

Serves 18.
Serving size: 1 (3 inch/8 cm) square

TIP: If you like nuts, sprinkle 1 cup (130 g) toasted coarsely chopped walnuts or pecans over top before baking.

One Serving

Calories: 271	Cholesterol: 21 mg	Dietary Fiber: 0 g
Calories from Fat: 103	Sodium: 240 mg	Sugars: 20 g
Total Fat: 11 g	Total Carbohydrates: 39 g	Protein: 4 g
Saturated Fat: 5 g		

Zucchini Cupcakes

These are not too sweet — just right for a quick, healthy lunch box or snack treat.

1½ cups self-rising flour	190 g
1 teaspoon baking soda	5 ml
1½ teaspoons pumpkin pie spice	7 ml
3 egg whites or ¾ cup egg substitute	185 g
¾ cup packed brown sugar	165 g
½ cup canola oil	125 ml
2 cups grated zucchini	250 g

Preheat oven to 350° (175° C).

Combine flour, baking soda and pumpkin pie spice in small bowl.

Beat eggs, brown sugar and oil in mixing bowl for about 3 minutes. Add zucchini and stir until they blend well. Add flour mixture and stir until ingredients combine thoroughly.

Fill sprayed non-stick muffin cups three-fourths full and bake for 20 to 25 minutes. Cool on wire rack 5 minutes.

Serves 12.
Serving size: 1 cupcake

TIP: You can replace zucchini with 2 cups (220 g) shredded carrot and ½ cup (125 ml) water, if you like.

One Serving
Nutrition facts are based on egg substitute.

Calories: 195	Cholesterol: 0 mg	Dietary Fiber: 1 g
Calories from Fat: 82	Sodium: 220 mg	Sugars: 14 g
Total Fat: 9 g	Total Carbohydrates: 26 g	Protein: 3 g
Saturated Fat: 1 g		

Down-Home Peach Cobbler

This old-fashioned cobbler will bring raves every time you make it!

5 tablespoons butter, divided	70 g
1½ cups sugar, divided	300 g
1½ tablespoons cornstarch	22 ml
2 (15 ounce) cans sliced peaches in extra-light syrup	2 (425 g)
1 teaspoon vanilla or almond extract	5 ml
¾ cup self-rising flour	95 g
¾ cup light plain soymilk or fat-free skim milk	175 ml

Preheat oven to 350° (175° C).

Add 3 tablespoons (45 g) butter to 9 x 9-inch (23 x 23 cm) baking dish and heat in oven while preparing cobbler.

Combine ¾ cup (150 g) sugar and cornstarch in 2-quart (2 L) saucepan. Add sliced peaches and syrup and remaining butter. Stir and cook over medium heat until peach mixture boils. Continue cooking and stirring until liquid is clear. Add vanilla or almond extract.

Whisk remaining sugar and flour in medium bowl. Add soymilk and whisk until it mixes well.

Pour batter over melted butter in hot baking dish. Spoon peach mixture on top. During baking, batter will rise to cover peaches. Bake for 30 to 35 minutes or until golden brown on top.

Serves 8.
Serving size: ½ cup (125 ml)

TIP: Serve warm with a scoop of frozen vanilla yogurt.

One Serving

Calories: 318	Cholesterol: 32 mg	Dietary Fiber: 1 g
Calories from Fat: 71	Sodium: 207 mg	Sugars: 39 g
Total Fat: 8 g	Total Carbohydrates: 61 g	Protein: 2 g
Saturated Fat: 5 g		

Double Berry-Peach Crumble

4 cups fresh peaches or
   1 (16 ounce) package frozen
   unsweetened peaches,
   thawed, drained   600 g/455 g
1 cup fresh blackberries
   or frozen blackberries,
   thawed, drained   150 g
1 cup fresh raspberries or
   frozen raspberries,
   thawed, drained   125 g
½ cup sugar   100 g
3 tablespoons unbleached
   white flour   25 g
Whole Wheat-Oat Topping
   (page 266)

🍓 Preheat oven to 375° (190° C).

🍓 Add peaches, berries, sugar
and flour in large bowl and toss
gently. Pour fruit into sprayed
2-quart (2 L) baking dish. Cover
with Whole Wheat-Oat Topping.
Bake about 45 minutes or until
peaches are tender. Serve warm
or cool.

Serves 8 to 10.
Serving size: ½ cup (125 ml)

*TIP: Serve with dollop of reduced-fat
   whipped topping.*

One Serving (excluding topping)

Calories: 94	Sodium: 0 mg
Calories from	Total Carbohy-
Fat: 2	drates: 23 g
Total Fat: 0 g	Dietary Fiber: 3 g
Saturated Fat: 0 g	Sugars: 16 g
Cholesterol: 0 mg	Protein: 1 g

Blueberry-Cinnamon Crunch

4 cups fresh blueberries or
   2 (16 ounce) packages
   frozen blueberries,
   slightly thawed   600 g/910 g
2 tablespoons sugar or sugar
   substitute   25 g
2 cups Whole Wheat-Oat
   Topping (page 266)   500 ml

🍓 Preheat oven to 375° (190° C).

🍓 Stir blueberries and sugar
in 9 x 9-inch (23 x 23 cm)
baking dish.

🍓 Sprinkle Whole Wheat-Oat
Topping evenly on fruit. Bake
for 30 to 35 minutes or until top
browns.

Serves 6.
Serving size: ½ cup (125 ml)

*TIP: If you like nuts, add ¼ cup (30 g)
   chopped pecans or walnuts to topping.*

One Serving
Nutrition facts are based on sugar substitute.

Calories: 301	Sodium: 7 mg
Calories from	Total Carbohy-
Fat: 120	drates: 45 g
Total Fat: 13 g	Fiber: 4 g
Saturated Fat: 7 g	Sugars: 20 g
Cholesterol: 31 mg	Protein: 4 g

Strawberry-Pecan Crumble

2 (16 ounce) bags frozen whole unsweetened strawberries, thawed 2 (455 g)
1 (18 ounce) box plain yellow cake mix, divided 510 g
1 cup chopped pecans 115 g
1 cup (2 sticks) butter, cut in small chunks, divided 230 g

Preheat oven to 350° (175° C).

Pour strawberries into 9 x 13-inch (23 x 33 cm) baking pan.

Combine cake mix and pecans in mixing bowl. Cover strawberries with half cake mixture. Scatter ½ cup (115 g) butter chunks over cake mixture. Cover with remaining cake mixture and top with remaining butter.

Bake on middle rack for 60 to 65 minutes or until brown and crisp.

Serves 12 to 15.
Serving size: 3 x 3-inch (8 x 8 cm) square

One Serving

Calories: 304	Cholesterol: 17 mg	Dietary Fiber: 2 g
Calories from Fat: 140	Sodium: 231 mg	Sugars: 27 g
Total Fat: 16 g	Total Carbohydrates: 41 g	Protein: 3 g
Saturated Fat: 5 g		

Store fresh berries in an airtight container with paper towels in the bottom. Wash right before use.

Cookie Crust Fruit Pizza

What a way to get your daily fruit servings! Party perfect!

(16 ounce) package refrigerated sugar cookie dough	455 g
(8 ounce) package reduced-fat cream cheese	230 g
cup sugar, divided	200 g
teaspoons vanilla	10 ml
cups seasonal fruit, sliced or cut into bite-size pieces	600 g
tablespoons cornstarch	25 g
cup orange or pineapple juice	250 ml

Press cookie dough into circle on 12-inch (32 cm) pizza pan. Bake according to package directions. Cool.

Combine cream cheese, ½ cup (100 g) sugar and vanilla in mixing bowl and beat until smooth. Spread evenly over cookie crust. Arrange fruit on top of cream cheese mixture.

Combine remaining sugar, cornstarch and juice in 1-quart (1 L) saucepan and cook over medium heat. Stir until sugar mixture boils and thickens. Cool and spread over fruit.

Serves 8.
Serving size: 2-inch (5 cm) wedge

TIP: *Use raspberries, blueberries, sliced strawberries, sliced kiwi fruit, sliced bananas, sliced peaches or drained pineapple tidbits. Use toasted macadamia nuts to add crunchiness and great flavor.*

One Serving

Calories: 443	Cholesterol: 25 mg	Dietary Fiber: 1 g
Calories from Fat: 131	Sodium: 297 mg	Sugars: 44 g
Total Fat: 15 g	Total Carbohydrates: 75 g	Protein: 5 g
Saturated Fat: 5 g		

Mom's Apple Pie

2 pounds Granny Smith apples	910 g
1 cup sugar	200 g
2 tablespoons unbleached white flour	15 g
½ - 1 teaspoon ground cinnamon	2 - 5 ml
Dash ground nutmeg	
2 (9 inch) refrigerated piecrusts	2 (23 cm)
1 tablespoon butter	15 ml

 Preheat oven to 375° (190° C).

 Core, peel and thinly slice apples and add to large bowl. Mix sugar, flour, cinnamon and nutmeg in small bowl; add to apples and toss.

 Press 1 piecrust into 9-inch (23 cm) pie pan. Spoon apple mixture into piecrust and dot with butter. Add top crust, seal and flute. With sharp knife, cut 4 (2 inch/5 cm) slits in top crust.

 Bake for 40 to 50 minutes. Cover crust edges with strips of foil to prevent excessive browning.

Serves 8.
Serving size: 1 wedge

One Serving

Calories: 333	Sodium: 204 mg
Calories from Fat: 106	Total Carbohydrates: 56 g
Total Fat: 12 g	Dietary Fiber: 2 g
Saturated Fat: 4 g	Sugars: 36 g
Cholesterol: 4 mg	Protein: 2 g

Apple-Streusel Pie

6 cups peeled, thinly sliced Granny Smith apples	1.1 kg
1 cup sugar	200 g
2 tablespoons unbleached white flour	15 g
½ - 1 teaspoon ground cinnamon	2 ml
Dash ground nutmeg	
1 (9 inch) deep-dish frozen piecrust	23 cm
Nut Streusel Topping (page 265)	

 Preheat oven to 375° (190° C).

 Add apples to large bowl. In separate bowl, combine sugar, flour, cinnamon and nutmeg, add to apples and toss.

 Fill piecrust with apple mixture. Cover with Nut Streusel Topping. Bake for 45 to 50 minutes. Cover crust edges with strips of foil to prevent excessive browning.

Serves 8.
Serving size: One slice

One Serving: (excluding topping)

Calories: 233	Sodium: 102 mg
Calories from Fat: 47	Total Carbohydrates: 47 g
Total Fat: 5 g	Dietary Fiber: 1 g
Saturated Fat: 2 g	Sugars: 34 g
Cholesterol: 0 mg	Protein: 1 g

Fresh Apricot Pie

The tart sweetness and fresh flavor of this pie wake up the taste buds!

4 cups pitted, sliced fresh apricots	660 g
1 tablespoon lemon juice	15 ml
1½ cups sugar	300 g
¼ cup unbleached white flour	30 g
⅛ teaspoon ground nutmeg	.5 ml
2 (9 inch) refrigerated piecrusts	2 (23 cm)
1 tablespoon butter	15 ml

Preheat oven to 375° (190° C).

Add apricots to large bowl and sprinkle with lemon juice.

In separate bowl, combine sugar, flour and nutmeg. Add to apricots and toss gently to coat.

Press 1 piecrust into pie pan. Spoon apricot mixture into piecrust. Dot with butter and add top crust. With sharp knife, cut four 2-inch (5 cm) slits in top crust. Seal and flute or press edges with fork and trim.

Bake for 40 to 50 minutes. Cover crust edges with strips of foil to prevent excessive browning.

Serves 8.
Serving size: 1 wedge

One Serving

Calories: 375	Cholesterol: 4 mg	Dietary Fiber: 2 g
Calories from Fat: 109	Sodium: 205 mg	Sugars: 46 g
Total Fat: 12 g	Total Carbohydrates: 66 g	Protein: 3 g
Saturated Fat: 4 g		

Luscious Lemon Pie

If you like refreshing lemon flavor, this smooth, creamy pie will delight you.

⅓ cup (⅔ stick) butter	80 g
¾ cup sugar	150 g
1¼ cups finely crushed graham crackers	130 g
1 cup Lemon Curd (page 265) or bottled lemon curd	250 ml
1 cup reduced-fat vanilla yogurt	230 g
1 (8 ounce) carton frozen reduced-fat whipped topping, thawed	230 g

 Melt butter in saucepan over medium heat and stir in sugar. Add crushed graham crackers and mix well. Spread evenly in 9-inch (23 cm) pie pan and press on bottom and sides.

 For unbaked crust, refrigerate about 1 hour or until firm. For baked crust, preheat oven to 375° (190° C) and bake for 4 to 5 minutes or until edges lightly brown. Cool.

 Whisk Lemon Curd and yogurt until they mix well. Spoon into unbaked or baked crust, cover with plastic wrap and refrigerate 1 hour. Spoon on whipped topping and refrigerate at least 30 minutes.

Serves 8.
Serving size: 1 wedge

TIP: If bottled lemon curd is unavailable, try using canned lemon pie filling.

One Serving

Calories: 374	Cholesterol: 17 mg	Dietary Fiber: 1 g
Calories from Fat: 106	Sodium: 296 mg	Sugars: 43 g
Total Fat: 12 g	Total Carbohydrates: 64 g	Protein: 6 g
Saturated Fat: 5 g		

Raisin-Walnut Pie

A sweet, tart filling makes this a delicious dessert with a walnut crunch.

¼ - ½ cup packed brown sugar	50 - 100 g
2 tablespoons cornstarch	20 g
1½ cups golden raisins or Craisins®	225 g/150 g
1 teaspoon finely grated orange peel	5 ml
1 teaspoon finely grated lemon peel	5 ml
½ cup orange juice	125 ml
2 tablespoons lemon juice	30 ml
½ cup chopped walnuts, toasted	65 g
2 (9 inch) refrigerated piecrusts	2 (23 cm)

Preheat oven to 375° (190° C).

Combine brown sugar and cornstarch in 2-quart (2 L) saucepan. Whisk in 1⅓ cups (325 ml) water, cook and stir over medium heat until mixture boils and is clear. Stir in raisins, finely grated peels and juices. Cook and stir about 3 minutes. Remove from heat and stir in walnuts.

Press 1 piecrust into 9-inch (23 cm) pie pan and fill with raisin mixture. Add top crust, seal and flute. Cut 4 (2 inch/5 cm) slits in top piecrust with sharp knife.

Bake for 40 to 50 minutes. Cover crust edges with strips of foil to prevent excessive browning.

Serves 8.
Serving size: 1 wedge

TIP: Golden raisins are dried with artificial heat and are a plumper light-colored raisin. Toasting brings out the flavors of nuts and seeds. Place nuts or seeds on baking sheet and bake at 225° (110° C) for 10 minutes. Be careful not to burn them.

One Serving

Calories: 339	Cholesterol: 0 mg	Dietary Fiber: 2 g
Calories from Fat: 136	Sodium: 210 mg	Sugars: 24 g
Total Fat: 15 g	Total Carbohydrates: 50 g	Protein: 4 g
Saturated Fat: 4 g		

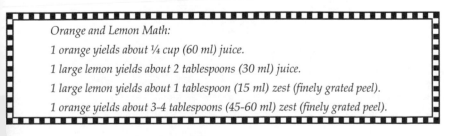

Orange and Lemon Math:

1 orange yields about ¼ cup (60 ml) juice.

1 large lemon yields about 2 tablespoons (30 ml) juice.

1 large lemon yields about 1 tablespoon (15 ml) zest (finely grated peel).

1 orange yields about 3-4 tablespoons (45-60 ml) zest (finely grated peel).

Hearty Blueberry-Rice Pudding

3 cups cooked brown rice	585 g
3 cups fresh blueberries or frozen blueberries, thawed, drained	450 g
½ cup packed brown sugar, divided	110 g
¼ cup whole wheat flour	35 g
¼ cup chopped walnuts	35 g
1 teaspoon ground cinnamon	5 ml
¼ cup (½ stick) butter, cut in small chunks	60 g

 Preheat oven to 375° (190° C).

 Combine rice, blueberries and 3 tablespoons (40 g) brown sugar in mixing bowl. Spoon into sprayed 2-quart (2 L) shallow baking dish.

 Combine remaining brown sugar, flour, walnuts and cinnamon in bowl. Add butter to brown sugar mixture and use pastry blender or mix with your fingers until small moist clumps form. Sprinkle on top of blueberry mixture.

 Bake for 15 to 20 minutes or until top browns lightly. Serve warm.

Serves 8.
Serving size: ½ cup (125 ml)

One Serving

Calories: 253	Sodium: 11 mg
Calories from Fat: 83	Total Carbohy-drates: 41 g
Total Fat: 9 g	Dietary Fiber: 3 g
Saturated Fat: 4 g	Sugars: 19 g
Cholesterol: 16 mg	Protein: 4 g

Cinnamon-Brown Rice Pudding

This pudding delivers the nutty flavor and great chewy texture of brown rice.

2 cups cooked brown rice	390 g
1½ cups soymilk	360 ml
½ cup honey or pure maple syrup	170 g/125 ml
1 tablespoon butter	15 ml
1 teaspoon ground cinnamon	5 ml

 Combine brown rice, soymilk and honey in 2-quart (2 L) saucepan. Bring to a boil, reduce heat and simmer about 20 minutes, stirring frequently. Remove from heat and stir in butter and cinnamon. Refrigerate and serve.

Serves 4.
Serving size: ¾ cup (175 ml)

TIP: Top with dollop of reduced-fat sour cream.

One Serving

Calories: 310	Sodium: 58 mg
Calories from Fat: 52	Total Carbohy-drates: 62 g
Total Fat: 6 g	Dietary Fiber: 3 g
Saturated Fat: 2 g	Sugars: 36 g
Cholesterol: 8 mg	Protein: 7 g

Sweet Potato Pudding

4 beaten eggs or 1 cup egg substitute	245 g
2 cups cooked, mashed sweet potatoes	660 g
½ cup light or dark molasses	125 ml
1 teaspoon ground cinnamon	5 ml
½ teaspoon ground ginger	2 ml
1 cup fat-free skim milk	250 ml

Preheat oven to 350° (175° C).

Combine all ingredients in large bowl. Stir until they thoroughly mix. Pour into sprayed 2-quart (2 L) baking dish. Bake for 1 hour or until toothpick inserted in center comes out clean. Chill before serving.

Serves 4 to 6.
Serving size: ½ cup (125 ml)

One Serving
Nutrition facts are based on egg substitute.

Calories: 214	Sodium: 135 mg
Calories from Fat: 14	Total Carbohydrates: 43 g
Total Fat: 2 g	Dietary Fiber: 3 g
Saturated Fat: 0 g	Sugars: 24 g
Cholesterol: 1 mg	Protein: 8 g

Cherry-Almond Parfaits

2 cups reduced-calorie cherry pie filling, divided	530 g
½ teaspoon almond flavoring	2 ml
¼ cup Grape-Nuts® cereal, divided	30 g
4 cups reduced-fat vanilla yogurt, divided	910 g
¼ cup toasted chopped almonds, divided	45 g

Combine pie filling and almond flavoring in small bowl.

To make 1 parfait, spoon ¼ cup (65 g) pie filling mixture in bottom of glass. Sprinkle with one-fourth Grape-Nuts® cereal. Spoon on 1 cup (230 g) yogurt and then an additional ¼ cup (65 g) pie filling mixture. Sprinkle one-fourth almonds on top.

Repeat to make 3 additional parfaits.

Serves 4.
Serving size: 1½ cups (375 ml) plus cereal and nuts
Makes 6½ cups (1.5 L).

TIP: If desired, add 1 tablespoon (15 ml) sugar or sugar substitute to cherry pie filling mixture.

One Serving

Calories: 490	Sodium: 267 mg
Calories from Fat: 167	Total Carbohydrates: 65 g
Total Fat: 19 g	Dietary Fiber: 6 g
Saturated Fat: 3 g	Sugars: 49 g
Cholesterol: 12 mg	Protein: 21 g

Strawberry-Cantaloupe Sundaes

Combine flavors of luscious strawberries and sweet cantaloupe for a low-cal dessert.

2 cups (1 inch) cantaloupe balls or pieces	355 g/2.5 cm
1 cup reduced-fat lime-flavor yogurt	230 g
1 cup strawberry halves	150 g
2 tablespoons sugar or sugar substitute	25 g

 Evenly divide cantaloupe balls into 4 individual dessert bowls. Spoon one-fourth yogurt over cantaloupe for each sundae.

 Sprinkle strawberries with sugar and mix lightly. Top each sundae with one-fourth sweetened strawberries.

Serves 4.
Serving size: 1 cup (250 ml)
Makes 4 cups (1 L).

One Serving
Nutrition facts are based on sugar substitute.

Calories: 81	Sodium: 58 mg
Calories from Fat: 12	Total Carbohydrates: 15 g
Total Fat: 1 g	Dietary Fiber: 2 g
Saturated Fat: 1 g	Sugars: 13 g
Cholesterol: 4 mg	Protein: 4 g

Macadamia Macaroons

2 egg whites or ⅓ cup liquid egg white	75 g
½ teaspoon vanilla	2 ml
⅔ cup sugar	135 g
1 (3.5 ounce) can flaked coconut	100 g
¼ cup coarsely chopped macadamia nuts	35 g

 Preheat oven to 325° (160° C).

 Beat egg whites and vanilla on high speed until soft peaks form. Add sugar gradually and beat until stiff peaks form. Fold in coconut and nuts.

 Mound mixture by rounded teaspoons 2 inches (5 cm) apart on parchment-covered cookie sheet.

 Bake for about 20 minutes or until edges are light brown. Transfer to wire rack and cool.

Makes 30 cookies.
Serving size: 2 cookies

One Serving

Calories: 96	Sodium: 10 mg
Calories from Fat: 53	Total Carbohydrates: 11 g
Total Fat: 6 g	Dietary Fiber: 1 g
Saturated Fat: 4 g	Sugars: 9 g
Cholesterol: 0 mg	Protein: 1 g

Macadamia Nut Bananas

¼ cup honey	85 g
¼ cup lime juice	60 ml
2 - 3 firm ripe bananas	
½ cup chopped macadamia nuts	65 g

Combine honey and lime juice in shallow bowl. Peel and halve bananas.

Dip each banana half in honey mixture. Arrange on plate and sprinkle with chopped nuts.

Serves 4 to 6.
Serving size: ½ banana

TIP: Replace macadamia nuts with walnuts, almonds or pecans.

One Serving

Calories: 237	Sodium: 2 mg
Calories from Fat: 117	Total Carbohydrates: 33 g
Total Fat: 13 g	Dietary Fiber: 3 g
Saturated Fat: 2 g	Sugars: 25 g
Cholesterol: 0 mg	Protein: 2 g

Spiced Skillet Bananas

4 firm ripe bananas	
2 tablespoons butter	30 g
3 tablespoons brown sugar	35 g
¼ teaspoon ground cinnamon	1 ml
⅛ teaspoon ground nutmeg	.5 ml
Reduced-fat vanilla frozen yogurt or ice cream	

Peel and cut bananas in half lengthwise. Cut each length into 4 pieces.

Melt butter in 10-inch (25 cm) skillet and arrange bananas in skillet with cut sides down. Cook over low heat for 5 minutes, turn bananas with spatula and cook additional 5 minutes or until tender.

Mix brown sugar, cinnamon and nutmeg and sprinkle evenly over bananas. Serve with frozen yogurt or ice cream.

Serves 4 to 6.
Serving size: ½ banana (4 pieces)

One Serving

Calories: 110	Sodium: 2 mg
Calories from Fat: 38	Total Carbohydrates: 20 g
Total Fat: 4 g	Dietary Fiber: 2 g
Saturated Fat: 2 g	Sugars: 11 g
Cholesterol: 10 mg	Protein: 1 g

Nectarine Dessert Sauce

What a glistening, golden sauce to serve over ice cream or cake!

½ cup sugar	100 g
1 tablespoon cornstarch	15 ml
4 medium ripe nectarines	
½ teaspoon almond extract or vanilla	2 ml

Whisk sugar and cornstarch in 2-quart (2 L) saucepan. Whisking constantly, add ½ cup (125 ml) water. Bring mixture to a boil over medium heat and cook until mixture is clear.

Cut each nectarine into quarters. Make ½-inch (1.2 cm) slices and cut away from seed. Continue around nectarine until all slices are removed. Add slices to sugar mixture.

After all nectarine slices are in sauce, bring to a slow boil and cook 2 to 3 minutes. Stir occasionally. Stir in almond extract and pinch of salt. Cool.

Makes about 2 cups (500 ml).
Serving size: ¼ cup (60 ml)

TIP: Try using other fruits, such as apricots or peaches. Spice up the sauce by using small amounts of nutmeg, mace, cinnamon or your favorite flavorings. Use with Cottage Cheese Pancakes (page 36).

One Serving

Calories: 87	Cholesterol: 0 mg	Dietary Fiber: 1 g
Calories from Fat: 2	Sodium: 0 mg	Sugars: 18 g
Total Fat: 0 g	Total Carbohydrates: 22 g	Protein: 1 g
Saturated Fat: 0 g		

Lemon Curd

Rich but worth the calories!

¼ cup butter	60 g
¼ cup lemon juice	60 ml
1 teaspoon finely grated lemon peel	5 ml
¾ cup sugar	150 g
¾ cup egg substitute	185 g

 Melt butter in 2-quart (2 L) saucepan over medium heat. Add juice, peel and sugar and stir until sugar dissolves. Add egg substitute, cook and stir until thick. Cool and refrigerate.

Serves 8.
Serving size: ¼ cup (60 ml)

TIP: Use with Luscious Lemon Pie (page 258).

One Serving

Calories: 120	Sodium: 42 mg
Calories from Fat: 34	Total Carbohydrates: 20 g
Total Fat: 4 g	Dietary Fiber: 0 g
Saturated Fat: 2 g	Sugars: 19 g
Cholesterol: 8 mg	Protein: 3 g

Nut Streusel Topping

Use a food processor to shorten this preparation time and to create an even consistency.

1½ tablespoons light brown sugar	22 ml
1 tablespoon sugar	15 ml
⅓ cup walnut or pecan halves	40 g
½ teaspoon ground cinnamon	2 ml
⅓ cup whole wheat flour	45 g
3 tablespoons butter	45 g
½ teaspoon vanilla	2 ml

 Add brown sugar, sugar, nuts and cinnamon to food processor. Cover and pulse 10 or 12 times. Add whole wheat flour, butter, vanilla and a punch of salt. Pulse several times until mixture is coarse and crumbly.

Serves 4.
Serving size: ¼ cup (60 ml)
Makes 1 cup (250 ml).

TIP: This recipe makes enough topping to cover a 9-inch (23 cm) pie. Use with Apple Streusel Pie (page 256).

One Serving

Calories: 202	Sodium: 3 mg
Calories from Fat: 140	Total Carbohydrates: 16 g
Total Fat: 16 g	Dietary Fiber: 2 g
Saturated Fat: 6 g	Sugars: 8 g
Cholesterol: 23 mg	Protein: 3 g

Whole Wheat-Oat Topping

¼ cup packed light brown sugar	55 g
⅔ cup unbleached white flour	80 g
½ cup old-fashioned oats	40 g
½ teaspoon ground nutmeg	2 ml
6 tablespoons canola oil or butter, cut in small chunks	90 ml/75 g

Add brown sugar in medium bowl and remove any hard lumps. Add flour, oats, nutmeg and ¼ teaspoon (1 ml) salt and stir.

Place brown sugar mixture and oil in food processor. Cover and pulse just until topping mixes well.

Makes about 2 cups (500 ml) (enough topping for 2-quart/2 L baking dish).
Serving size: 1 tablespoon (15 ml)

TIP: For use with Blueberry Crunch (page 253) and Double Berry-Peach Crumble (page 253).

One Serving

Calories: 91	Cholesterol: 12 mg	Dietary Fiber: 1 g
Calories from Fat: 44	Sodium: 2 mg	Sugars: 3 g
Total Fat: 5 g	Total Carbohydrates: 11 g	Protein: 1 g
Saturated Fat: 3 g		

Glossary

Baking Products

Refer to the Sweets section to locate cakes, pies, fruit desserts and other sweets. Fruits and/or vegetables in various forms are used – fresh, frozen, canned and dried.

Unbleached white flour, whole wheat flour and self-rising flour are used in recipes requiring flour. Of course, baking is more convenient when frozen pastry and cake mixes are used. Reduced-fat cake mixes and reduced-fat frostings are now available.

Beans and Peas

Beans and peas, also known as legumes, are a major food source for vegetarians. Find them dried, canned and frozen. A great variety of beans and peas are used in the recipes, including familiar pinto, black and kidney beans. Others such as cannellini and fava may be less familiar to you. Also look for packaged mixes that include spices and flavorings.

Breads

Whole wheat and whole grain breads are recommended to provide nutrients and fiber. Specialty whole grain artisan breads now fill the bakery shelves. Look for whole wheat and multigrain tortillas, pitas and pizza doughs. Of course, whole wheat homemade breads are made easier with mixes and good equipment.

Broth

Vegetable broth is used throughout the recipes. You'll find delicious recipes for homemade vegetable broths (see Soups) if you have time. Read can labels to make the best choice of canned vegetable broths or organic vegetable broths. Because of high-sodium content, dried vegetable broth products are not used.

Cheese

To help meet calcium needs, women and teenage girls should frequently include cheeses in their food intake. A large variety of cheeses are used in recipes, including blue cheeses (feta, gorgonzola, blue), hard cheeses (parmesan, romano) and soft cheeses (ricotta, cream cheese). Look for reduced-fat and fat-free products.

Chiles

Green chilies are included in many delicious recipes. Canned chopped and whole green chilies should be available in supermarkets everywhere. New Mexican or Anaheim are the long, dark green chiles usually found fresh in produce sections.

Jalapeno and serrano chiles spice up salsas and appetizers. Remember to handle these hot chiles carefully. Wear rubber gloves and use sharp knives when preparing hot chiles. Some recipes use chipotle chiles (smoked jalapenos), usually found canned in adobo sauce.

Dairy Products

The rule of thumb in choosing milk products is to use reduced-fat. In some recipes, fat-free milk products may not produce the desired results. Light plain soy milk, fat-free skim milk or reduced-fat (1%) generally can be used interchangeably in recipes.

Reduced-fat yogurt is a bonus dairy product for vegetarians, eaten alone or in recipes. When sour cream is called for, choose reduced-fat or fat-free. You'll find several recipes calling for fat-free half-and-half cream, which provides richness but not fats. Nonfat dry milk powder is an economical and convenient choice for milk. If choosing canned milk products, look for fat-free or reduced-fat.

Eggs

You will find some terrific egg dishes in this collection. Whole large eggs or equivalent amounts of egg substitutes are specified. Cholesterol-free liquid egg substitutes and liquid egg whites make it easy to reduce cholesterol in cooking. Egg substitute math: ¼ cup (60 g) liquid egg substitute = one large egg; 1 cup (245 g) egg substitute = 4 large eggs; 1 pint (490 g) egg substitute = 8 large eggs.

Please note: Whenever a choice of eggs or egg substitute is indicated, nutrition facts are based on egg substitute.

Fats and Oils

Unsalted butter is generally used in small amounts, for rich flavor and for baking consistency. However, 80% fat margarine can be substituted. Health effects of butter versus hydrogenated margarine are debated. Or you may wish to use reduced-fat margarine products, which have different cooking qualities because of added water.

Canola and olive oils are the vegetable oils of choice. Other vegetable oils generally have the same cooking qualities. Extra-virgin olive oil is popular for cooking, whereas lighter olive oils have a lighter flavor.

You will definitely need non-stick cooking spray to cook with little or no fat. Non-stick cooking spray comes in many forms – olive oil, canola oil and others. These sprays are typically interchangeable. High quality non-stick surfaces of cookware require little or no fat and produce excellent results.

Fruit

Fresh, dried and canned fruits are used throughout. Choose fresh fruits carefully and store properly. Make use of the fruit and vegetable cleaning sprays that safely remove pesticides, waxes, chemicals and soils. Even berries need to be washed, but right before you use them. When purchasing frozen fruits, choose unsweetened or lightly sweetened.

A variety of canned and dried fruits is available. When choosing canned fruit, read labels to find those canned in fruit juice, water or very light syrup. Avoid heavy syrups. Dried fruits include mixed dried fruit, dried sweetened cranberries, dried cherries, dried mango slices, dark and light raisins and apricots.

Garlic

A garlic clove is one of the smaller segments of a garlic bulb. The strongly scented, pungent flavor of minced, cooked garlic enhances many of the recipes. You will find it specified as *minced or pressed* garlic.

To quickly peel garlic, smash with a heavy large blade knife on a stable cutting board. The outer dry layers can be easily removed, and then the clove can be minced finely with a sharp knife. A garlic press (my preference) is a hand tool that presses peeled garlic cloves through small holes. Cut large cloves in half. Remove pulp left in press when several garlic cloves are needed.

One medium garlic clove yields ½ teaspoon minced. For one fresh clove, substitute ⅛ teaspoon garlic powder or ½ teaspoon bottled minced garlic.

Herbs and Spices

Many of the more common spices are used, such as cinnamon and nutmeg. Other dried spice powders are Creole seasoning, pumpkin pie spice, curry, cumin, chili powder, ginger, taco seasoning mix (reduced-sodium) and chili seasoning mix. Check the expiration dates on spices and keep them in the freezer for longest shelf life.

Although dried herbs are used in the recipes, fresh herbs should be used whenever possible. Spice blends are also used, such as Italian herbs and other dried herb blends.

One tablespoon chopped fresh herbs is equivalent to 1 teaspoon dried herbs. Be sure to crush the dried herbs with your hands or use a mortar and pestle to release flavor before use. Again, check expiration dates and store dried herbs in the freezer.

Mayonnaise

Many recipes include reduced-fat mayonnaise. You may choose to use regular mayonnaise, fat-free mayonnaise or soy mayonnaise with equal success.

Nuts and Seeds

As a group, nuts are cholesterol-free and naturally contain just a trace of sodium, unless salt is added. Although relatively high in calories, nuts provide protein, "good" fats and even vitamin E (almonds). In this cookbook, nuts are usually found as garnishes and are a delicious addition to vegetarian dishes.

Sesame seeds are the most common seed used in recipes. Tahini, or sesame seed paste, is used in the garbanzo dip and hummus. You'll also find poppy seeds, celery seeds, dill seeds and mustard seeds in recipes.

Organic

Organic typically describes food grown and processed without using chemicals of any kind including fertilizers, insecticides, additives and artificial color or flavoring. More and more organic foods are now available in supermarkets. Many vegetarians choose organic foods and products as part of their desired natural lifestyle.

Pasta

Pasta, *paste* in Italian, is popular throughout the world and is a great boon for vegetarians. Look for the Pasta Main Dishes and also check out Pasta Salads. Whole wheat, multigrain or whole grain, and vegetable pastas are on supermarket shelves. You may wish to try the recipes that include orzo, couscous and tortellini.

Of course, spaghetti, egg noodles and elbow macaroni top the popularity list. Dried pasta comes in hundreds of shapes, sizes, thicknesses and

colors. Fresh, refrigerated and frozen pastas are good choices. A general rule is to use light sauces for delicate pastas like angel hair, chunky sauces with pastas that have holes or ridges and heavier sauces for sturdy pastas like lasagna noodles.

How much pasta to cook? Allow about 1 cup cooked pasta for an average person. Eight ounces uncooked small-medium pasta (elbow macaroni, rotini) yields 4 cups cooked. Eight ounces (1½ inch diameter bunch) uncooked long pastas such as spaghetti and linguine also yields 4 cups cooked. Eight ounces uncooked egg noodles yields 2½ cups cooked.

Rice and Grains

Brown rice is used almost exclusively as the type of rice. Brown rice is an unpolished rice grain with the bran layer intact. It is nutty in flavor and pleasantly chewy. Although it requires a longer cooking time than white rice, a number of precooked versions are available. The microwaveable packets of precooked brown rice are very convenient.

Also, check out the recipes for quinoa, bulghur wheat, barley, grits and polenta. Shop for easy to fix brown rice pilaf mixes, brown rice jambalaya mixes and tabbouleh (bulghur wheat) mixes.

Salt and Pepper

In these recipes, the kind of pepper is unspecified. You may prefer freshly ground black pepper or coarse or fine grind black pepper. To avoid black specks, choose white pepper. Cayenne (ground red pepper) is very strong and should be used sparingly. Dried crushed red pepper flakes spice up many recipes. Store pepper in the freezer to retain freshness.

Choose regular iodized salt or equivalent salt substitutes for the recipes calling for salt. Keep sodium intake low by using regular salt sparingly in recipes and putting away the salt shaker at mealtimes.

Seasoning Blend

Frozen seasoning blend includes chopped onions, celery, bell pepper and parsley and typically comes in 16-ounce packages. Seasoning blend is used in a large number of recipes, typically prepared in a non-stick skillet using non-stick cooking spray.

The frozen blend does not need to be thawed before use and should be cooked and frequently stirred over medium to medium-high heat until

most of the water has evaporated and the vegetables are tender. It is a great timesaver!

However, you can make your own fresh seasoning blend with 1 cup (160 g) chopped onion, ½ cup (50 g) chopped celery and ½ cup (75 g) chopped bell pepper.

Soy Products

All kinds of soy products are now available in supermarkets and many have been successfully used in the recipes. Look for soy products in the Soy Main Dishes section. Some of the products are veggie protein hot dogs, veggie soy cheddar- or mozzarella-flavored shreds (cheese-like), veggie protein chorizo, veggie protein crumbles (like ground beef), veggie soy bacon and pepperoni slices, frozen meatless cheeseburgers, and meatless "chicken" patties.

Tofu, also known as soy bean curd, is a custard-like product extracted from soybeans. The firmness of the tofu depends on how much whey has been extracted. Tofu is bland and takes on the flavor of the food with which it is cooked. It is smooth and creamy yet firm enough to slice. Tofu comes in regular, reduced-fat and nonfat varieties and in soft, firm and extra firm styles. Look for tofu recipes in the Soy Main Dishes section.

Sugar

Brown sugar (usually light) and honey are the predominant sweeteners used. If you prefer, granulated sugar should substitute where desired. However, sugar substitutes have different cooking qualities and may not produce desired results in some recipes. Be sure to use the correct equivalent measurement when using a sugar substitute.

Please note: Nutrition facts are based on the use of sugar substitute.

Vinegar

Vinegars are used mainly in salad dressing recipes. The most popular vinegars are fruity apple cider vinegar and sharp-tasting white distilled vinegar. Delicious wine vinegars can be either red or white. Some recipes call for balsamic vinegar, which can be dark or light and should be used sparingly because it may overpower some foods.

Index

V

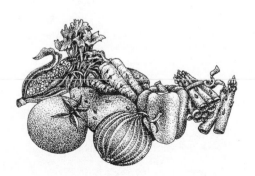

Cookbooks Published by Cookbook Resources, LLC

Bringing Family and Friends to the Table

The Best of Cooking with 3 Ingredients

The Ultimate Cooking
with 4 Ingredients

Easy Cooking with 5 Ingredients

Diabetic Cooking with 4 Ingredients

Healthy Cooking with 4 Ingredients

Gourmet Cooking with 5 Ingredients

4-Ingredient Recipes
for 30-Minute Meals

Essential 3-4-5 Ingredient Cookbook

The Best 1001 Short, Easy Recipes

1001 Fast Easy Recipes

Busy Woman's Quick & Easy Recipes

Busy Woman's Slow Cooker Recipes

Easy Slow Cooker Cookbook

Easy One-Dish Meals

Easy Potluck Recipes

Easy Casseroles

Easy Desserts

Sunday Night Suppers

Easy Church Suppers

365 Easy Meals

365 Easy Chicken Recipes

365 Easy Soups and Stews

Quick Fixes with Cake Mixes

Kitchen Keepsakes/More
Kitchen Keepsakes

Gifts for the Cookie Jar

All New Gifts for the Cookie Jar

Muffins In A Jar

Brownies In A Jar

Gifts In A Pickle Jar

The Big Bake Sale Cookbook

Classic Tex-Mex and Texas Cooking

Classic Southwest Cooking

Southern Family Favorites

Miss Sadie's Southern Cooking

The Great Canadian Cookbook

Texas Longhorn Cookbook

Cookbook 25 Years

The Best of Lone Star Legacy Cookbook

A Little Taste of Texas

A Little Taste of Texas II

Trophy Hunters' Wild Game Cookbook

Italian Family Cookbook

Old-Fashioned Cookies

Grandmother's Cookies

Quilters' Cooking Companion

Mother's Recipes

Recipe Keeper

Cookie Dough Secrets

Casseroles to the Rescue

Texas Longhorn Cookbook

Holiday Recipes

Mealtimes and Memories

Southwest Sizzler

Southwest Olé

Class Treats

Leaving Home

www.cookbookresources.com

Your Ultimate Source for Easy Cookbooks

To Order: **365 Easy Vegetarian Recipes**

Please send ___ copies @ $19.95 (U.S.) each $ _____

Texas residents add sales tax @ $1.60 each $ _____

Plus postage/handling @ $6.00 (1st copy) $ _____

$1.00 (each additional copy) $ _____

Check or Credit Card (Canada-credit card only) Total $ _____

Charge to: ☐ MasterCard   ☐ VISA   Expiration Date ⌞_⌟⌞_⌟ (mm/yy)

Account No. ⌞_⌟⌞_⌟⌞_⌟⌞_⌟

Signature _____

Name (please print) _____

Address _____

City _____ State/Prov. _____ Zip/Postal Code _____

Telephone (Day) _____ (Evening) _____

Mail to: Cookbook Resources   Call Toll Free: (866) 229-2665
        541 Doubletree Drive
        Highland Village, Texas 75077   Fax: (972) 317-6404

Or – order online at www.cookbookresources.com

- - - - - - - - - - - - - - - - - -

To Order: **365 Easy Vegetarian Recipes**

Please send ___ copies @ $19.95 (U.S.) each $ _____

Texas residents add sales tax @ $1.60 each $ _____

Plus postage/handling @ $6.00 (1st copy) $ _____

$1.00 (each additional copy) $ _____

Check or Credit Card (Canada-credit card only) Total $ _____

Charge to: ☐ MasterCard   ☐ VISA   Expiration Date ⌞_⌟⌞_⌟ (mm/yy)

Account No. ⌞_⌟⌞_⌟⌞_⌟⌞_⌟

Signature _____

Name (please print) _____

Address _____

City _____ State/Prov. _____ Zip/Postal Code _____

Telephone (Day) _____ (Evening) _____

Mail to: Cookbook Resources   Call Toll Free: (866) 229-2665
        541 Doubletree Drive
        Highland Village, Texas 75077   Fax: (972) 317-6404

Or – order online at www.cookbookresources.com